A history of Catholicism from the Council of Trent in the middle of the sixteenth century to the suppression of the Society of Jesus in the eighteenth century, this accessible study of Catholicism offers the first synthesis of the vast scholarship on Catholic renewal in Europe and on Catholic missions in the non-European world. Professor Hsia discusses the doctrinal and ecclesiastical renewal after Trent and the progress of Catholic reconquest in various lands. He also analyzes the social composition of the Tridentine clergy and the papal curia and explores the making of early modern sainthood and the enclosure of religious women. With a chapter encompassing art and architecture, Hsia attempts to understand Catholic renewal as a vast historical development that shaped European civilization between the sixteenth and eighteenth centuries and at the same time explores its expansion and encounter with non-Christian civilizations in America, Africa, and Asia.

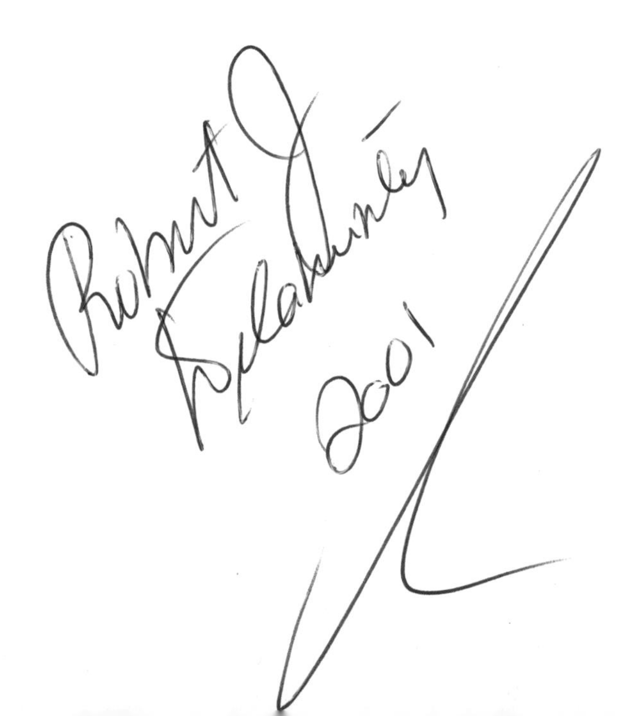

NEW APPROACHES TO EUROPEAN HISTORY

The world of Catholic renewal 1540–1770

NEW APPROACHES TO EUROPEAN HISTORY

Series editors
WILLIAM BEIK *Emory University*
T. C. W. BLANNING *Sidney Sussex College, Cambridge*
R. W. SCRIBNER *Harvard University*

New Approaches to European History is an important new textbook initiative, intended to provide concise but authoritative surveys of major themes and problems in European history since the Renaissance. Written at a level and length accessible to advanced school students and undergraduates, each book in the series will address topics or themes that students of European history encounter daily: the series will embrace both some of the more "traditional" subjects of study, and those cultural and social issues to which increasing numbers of school and college courses are devoted. A particular effort will be made to consider the wider international implications of the subject under scrutiny.

To aid the student reader scholarly apparatus and annotation will be light, but each work will have full supplementary bibliographies and notes for further reading: where appropriate chronologies, maps, diagrams, and other illustrative material will also be provided.

The first titles in the series are

1 MERRY E. WIESNER Women and gender in early modern Europe
2 JONATHAN SPERBER The European revolutions 1848–1851
3 CHARLES INGRAO The Habsburg monarchy 1618–1815
4 ROBERT JÜTTE Poverty and deviance in early modern Europe
5 JAMES B. COLLINS The state in early modern France
6 CHARLES G. NAUERT, JR. Humanism and the culture of Renaissance Europe
7 DORINDA OUTRAM The Enlightenment
8 MACK P. HOLT The French Wars of Religion 1562–1629
9 JONATHAN DEWALD The European nobility 1400–1800
10 ROBERT S. DUPLESSIS Transitions to capitalism in early modern Europe
11 EDWARD MUIR Ritual in early modern Europe
12 R. PO-CHIA HSIA The world of Catholic renewal 1540–1770

The world of Catholic renewal 1540–1770

R. Po-chia Hsia
New York University

PUBLISHED BY THE PRESS SYNDICATE OF THE UNIVERSITY OF CAMBRIDGE
The Pitt Building, Trumpington Street, Cambridge CB2 1RP, United Kingdom

CAMBRIDGE UNIVERSITY PRESS
The Edinburgh Building, Cambridge CB2 2RU, United Kingdom
40 West 20th Street, New York, NY 10011-4211, USA
10 Stamford Road, Oakleigh, Melbourne 3166, Australia

First published 1998

Printed in the United Kingdom at the University Press, Cambridge

Typeset in 10/12pt Plantin [SE]

A catalogue record for this book is available from the British Library

Library of Congress cataloguing in publication data

Hsia, R. Po-chia, 1953–
The world of Catholic renewal, 1540–1770 / R. Po-chia Hsia.
p. cm. – (New approaches to European history ; 12)
Includes bibliographical references and index.
ISBN 0 521 44041 6
1. Catholic Church – History – 16th century. 2. Catholic Church – History – 17th century. 3. Catholic Church – History – 18th century. 4. Counter-Reformation. 5. Church renewal – Catholic Church – History. I. Title. II. Series.
BX1304.H75 1998
282′.09′03–dc21 97–14444 CIP

ISBN 0 521 44041 6 hardback
ISBN 0 521 44596 5 paperback

Contents

Illustrations and tables

Acknowledgments

Robert Scribner first suggested the idea of writing two parallel texts – he on the Reformation and I myself on the Catholic world. It was a collaboration born out of our concern not to leave society out of the history of religion, but to investigate practices as well as theological norms. I acknowledge with pleasure his intellectual comradeship over the years.

Many people have contributed with ideas and suggestions; some generously shared with me their ongoing research. I am indebted to all: Renée Baernstein, Wietse de Boer, Sara Nalle, Carlos Eire, Gerald Chaix, Cecilia Nubola, Franz Bosbach, David Gentilcore, John Headley, Marc Forster, Alfons Thijs, David Lederer, James Palmitessa, Werner Freitag, Nicholas Canny, Claudine Spitaels, and Wolfgang Behringer. Members of the Folger Institute seminar (spring 1994) which I directed on this subject offered stimulating ideas and shared their own research. My graduate seminar (spring 1996) – Duane Corpis, Nicoletta Pellegrino, Joel Budd, and Leticia Adel Clavecilla – suggested ideas for last-minute revisions.

During my research and writing, I have benefited from the support and generosity of the following institutions; to them and their staff my gratitude: Woodrow Wilson Center for International Scholars, National Center for the Humanities, Duke University, University of North Carolina at Chapel Hill, Centre for Religion and Society at the University of Amsterdam, and my own institution, New York University.

The greatest debt is to Sophie de Schaepdrijver, who has contributed numerous ideas to improve this book and has shared fully in its making. To her this book is dedicated.

An abridged version of this book will appear in German published by Fischer Verlag.

Chronology

1540	Papal recognition of the Society of Jesus
1541	Religious Colloquy at Regensburg between Protestants and Catholics in the Holy Roman Empire
1545	General Church Council opened in Trent
1547	Charles V victorious over Lutheran German princes at Battle of Mühlberg Church Council translated to Bologna
1548	Termination of first period of Church Council
1551–52	Second period of Church Council reconvened at Trent
1552	Francis Xavier died in Macao
1555	Religious Peace of Augsburg established Lutheranism as official confession alongside Catholicism in the empire
1559	First Jesuit mission in Japan
1562–63	Third and concluding period of the Church Council at Trent
1564	Proclamation of Tridentine decrees in the dominions of Philip II of Spain
1565	Archbishop Carlo Borromeo began reforms in Milan Permanent Spanish settlement in the Philippines
1570	The Inquisition established in Mexico and Peru
1572	French Calvinists massacred on the feast of St. Bartholomew
1577	First in a wave of executions of Catholic missionaries in Elizabethan England
1580	First Jesuit mission established in China
1581	First anti-Catholic legislation in the United Provinces
1584	Japanese Catholic emissary to Europe
1588	Reorganization of papal government resulted in the creation of congregations of cardinals for secular and spiritual affairs
1598	Edict of Nantes established toleration of Protestants in France
1610	Carlo Borromeo canonized
1614	Japanese government began systematic suppression of Christianity

1615	Tridentine decrees recognized by the clerical estate in France
1622	Canonizations of Ignatius of Loyola, Francis Xavier, Teresa of Avila, and Filippo Neri, new saints of the Catholic renewal
1624–29	Anti-Protestant repression in Habsburg-conquered Bohemia
1626	Consecration of the new Basilica of St. Peter in Rome
1641	Anti-English and anti-Protestant uprising in Ireland suppressed by Cromwell
1643	First volumes of the *Acta sanctorum* published
1653	Papal condemnation of propositions from *Augustinus* by Cornelius Jansen
1685	Revocation of the Edict of Nantes in France
1692	Christianity recognized by Emperor Kangxi in China
1710	Prohibition of "Chinese Rites" by papal envoy
1731	Expulsion of 17,000 Protestants from the principality of Salzburg
1732	Seminary for Chinese priests established in Naples
1759	Expulsion of Jesuits from all Portuguese dominions
1761	Suppression of the Society of Jesus in France
1767	Expulsion of Jesuits from all Spanish dominions
1773	Suppression of the Society of Jesus by papal decree

Introduction

In a letter written in 1678, the Belgian Jesuit Ferdinand Verbiest, provincial of the China mission and future director of the Astronomy Bureau under the Ch'ing emperor Kangxi, appealed to his fellow Jesuits in Europe: so many souls to be won, yet so few workers in the harvest. Painting a glorious picture of conversion, Verbiest described the arduous sea voyage from Europe to China, during which many missionaries met martyrdom in shipwreck. Those who reached China, Verbiest sighed, would look back to the ocean after a long labor of evangelization, longing for the glorious shipwreck that was not their fate.

This rhetoric of heroism and self-dramatization, reminiscent of the language of the early Reformation, hints at the underlying unity between the histories of the Reformation and Catholicism in early modern Europe. Both sides claimed martyrs, compiled liturgies, and rewrote Church histories: the mirroring of images in a divided Christianity suggests developments far more profound, far more complex than a simple contradistinction between the terms "Reformation" and "Counter-Reformation" would imply. This book represents an attempt to understand the Catholic side of that experience: it cannot pretend to offer a comprehensive history of early modern Catholicism (that task is beyond the capacity of any single individual); it tries instead to offer an interpretation of the historical events experienced in the Catholic lands of Europe and the wider world; and it navigates a path in the seemingly endless ocean of scholarship (like Verbiest, I sometimes wished I had been shipwrecked en route).

In choosing the title for this book, I have consciously steered clear of the reefs of controversial historical concepts. The term "Counter-Reformation," as Albert Elkan pointed out in his 1914 essay,[1] originally appeared during the 1770s in the handbooks for the history of the Holy Roman Empire published by the Göttingen jurist Johann Stephan Pütter.

[1] "Entstehung und Entwicklung des Begriffs 'Gegenreformation,'" *Historische Zeitschrift* 112 (1914), 473–93.

Used as a concept in legal history, "Counter-Reformation" denotes the reversion of confessional allegiance in the Holy Roman Empire between 1555 and 1648, when Catholic emperors and princes captured and recatholicized territories hitherto under the banner of Protestant reform. Describing a period embedded between the 1555 Religious Peace of Augsburg that established the principle of territorial churches (epitomized by the formula *cuius regio eius religio*) and the 1648 Peace of Westphalia that stabilized confessional boundaries, the term "Counter-Reformation" was not intended to apply beyond the confines of the Holy Roman Empire. It was ironic that the concept "Counter-Reformation" appeared in the 1770s during the suppression of the Society of Jesus to describe a legal system in the Holy Roman Empire that would itself disappear in 1803. Gaining acceptance in the 1830s, the terms "Counter-Reformation" and "Counter-Reformations" achieved distinction with the history of the popes by the great Protestant historian Leopold von Ranke. Impressed by the resurgence of Catholicism during the second half of the sixteenth century, especially in Italy, Ranke imparted a dynamic and creative dimension to Catholicism. Deeply influenced by the Romantic movement, Ranke's interpretation of the early modern papacy no doubt echoed the remarkable recovery of the Church after its debacle during the French Revolution and Napoleonic domination.

The spirit of the Restoration, marked by a reconstituted Society of Jesus and resurrected papacy, yielded to a new rancor in the 1870s and 1880s, just when the term gained currency in German university teaching and scholarship, provoked by the *Kulturkampf* in the newly united German Empire. Objecting to the passive and reactionary connotations of the term, Catholic scholars have contested the term "Counter-Reformation," substituting instead "Catholic reform," "Catholic Reformation," or "Catholic Restoration." That debate has continued, on and off, beyond 1945. It is not necessary to follow every twist and turn in the subsequent historiography, which is succinctly spelled out in the brilliant essay by Henry Outram Evennett (written in 1951 and published in 1968)[2] and in the much fuller dissection by Erwin Iserloh and Hubert Jedin.[3]

An echo of that debate is still heard in the English-language historiography. Catholic historians, quite naturally, emphasized the positive and creative aspects of sixteenth-century Catholicism. The 1963 study by Pierre Janelle, stressing both the continuity between medieval and sixteenth-century mysticism and the "modernity" of the Jesuits, calls the phenomenon "Catholic Reformation."[4] Entrenched in the historical

[2] *The Spirit of the Counter-Reformation* (Cambridge, 1968).
[3] *Reformation, katholische Reform, und Gegenreformation* (Freiburg, 1967).
[4] *The Catholic Reformation* (Milwaukee, 1963).

imagination, however, the term "Counter-Reformation" resists exorcism. Even a profoundly sympathetic study of Catholicism by Henry Outram Evennett employs the term, albeit with reservation: "I feel convinced that in the case with which we are dealing, the concept of the Counter-Reformation as essentially 'reactionary' and backward-looking has tended to obscure, and certainly to obstruct, any attempt to synthesize the many ways in which it was, in effect, the evolutionary adaptation of the Catholic religion and of the Catholic Church to new forces both in the spiritual and in the material order." Evennett was working against the image of Spanish (and Habsburg) arms propping up the authority of the Catholic Church and suppressing liberty of conscience, the "Black Legend" elaborated in Protestant historiography since the sixteenth century. Instead of diplomacy and armed conflict, Evennett focused on spirituality: of Filippo Neri, Ignatius of Loyola, and generally of the spirit animating the work of charity and piety in the Italian cities of the early sixteenth century. Here, then, was a gentle, moderate Catholic spirit in contrast to the unbending and harsh image of the Spanish Inquisition.

By the 1970s, there was considerable interest in rewriting the history of early modern Catholicism; one such attempt equated good history with the establishment of confessional balance in historiography. In his introduction to Marvin R. O'Connell's *The Counter-Reformation 1559–1610* (1974), William L. Langer, the editor of the series, declares precisely this intention: "Most histories of the Counter-Reformation have been written by Protestants and even the most scholarly can hardly be called free of prejudice. For this reason it was decided . . . to entrust the stormy period from 1559 to 1610 to a competent Catholic scholar, who would be able to write understandingly of the determined efforts of the Catholic Church to reform itself." Langer did not specify the qualities of "a competent Catholic scholar"; and the book, written with verve and color, follows a narrow chronological framework established by the series itself. Chronology notwithstanding, the diversity and multiplicity of historical currents linked to Catholic resurgence clearly cannot be captured within a narrow periodization. Both ends of the timeframe 1559 to 1610 were being stretched: while John C. Olin pushed back the origins of reform within the Catholic Church to the Spain of Isabella and Ferdinand and the Florence of Savonarola,[5] German and French historians were extending their investigation forward to the eighteenth century. Perhaps the single most important impetus, in this spate of new scholarship on the history of Catholicism, was the publication in 1975 of the final volume in

[5] *The Catholic Reformation: Savonarola to Ignatius Loyola* (New York, 1969); see also his *Catholic Reform: From Cardinal Ximenes to the Council of Trent 1495–1563* (New York, 1990).

Hubert Jedin's monumental *Geschichte des Konzils von Trient*, the first volume of which had appeared in 1950.

In Germany, where Jedin's *oeuvre* made the most impact, the new approach in Catholic historical scholarship was not so much to contest the term "Gegenreformation" as to elevate the concept to a par with "Reformation." A landmark essay by Wolfgang Reinhard in 1977 rejects the antithesis of "progressive Reformation" and "reactionary Counter-Reformation."[6] Criticizing both the terms "Counter-Reformation" and "Catholic Reform" as inadequate concepts in understanding the totality of historical development, and not just ecclesiastical history, Reinhard argues in favor of the term "Confessional Age" (*konfessionelles Zeitalter*) whereby Lutheranism, Calvinism, and Catholicism can be analyzed as parallel developments in a still larger historical unfolding of structures. The most original contribution in this provocative essay is Reinhard's description of the modernity of the Counter-Reformation: its disciplinary and Christianizing measures, its reforms of Church administration, its dissolution of archaic primary ties (i.e., kinship), its push toward individualization, its emphasis on internalization of values and activism (Jesuits), its push toward state poor relief, its modification of European ethnocentrism (in missions), and its ties to a new pedagogic system, new political themes, and new economic ethics. Although schematic in his formulations (and some of the theses are untenable), Reinhard has challenged the Protestant monopoly on "modernity," established on the authority of Max Weber. A similar focus on parallel structures and developments between the confessions is also manifest in *Das Zeitalter der Gegenreformation von 1555 bis 1648* (1979) by Ernst Walter Zeeden. Devoting most of his attention to describing and analyzing the history of Calvinism and the Jesuits, Zeeden amplifies the structural balance between Tridentine Catholicism and Calvinism by elaborating a theory of confessionalization, in which he stresses the interpenetration of political power and religious spirituality on both sides.

While the antithesis between Reformation and Counter-Reformation was slowly being resolved in the dialectic of German university debates, English and French historians have considerably expanded the terms of the discussion. In his 1971 book, *Le catholicisme entre Luther et Voltaire*, Jean Delumeau dismisses the significance of the Counter-Reformation as such: "The Counter-Reformation existed . . . but it was not essential to the transformation of the Catholic Church from the sixteenth century."[7]

[6] "'Gegenreformation als Modernisierung?' Prolegomena zu einer Theorie des konfessionellen Zeitalters," *Archiv für Reformationsgeschichte* 68 (1977), 226–52.

[7] "La Contre-Réforme a existé . . . mais elle n'a pas été l'essentiel de la transformation de l'Eglise catholique à partir du XVIe siècle."

Instead, Delumeau establishes a sharp contrast between medieval and early modern Europe: medieval Christianity ("the legend of a Christian Middle Ages") was, in this interpretation, magical and pagan; Tridentine Catholicism represented a massive attempt at Christianization, characterized by the training of a new clergy, the catechizing of the common folk, evangelizing in the non-European world, and the combating of popular superstitions.

This process, still imperfectly completed by the eighteenth century, gave way to the assault of the Enlightenment, with declining rates of sacramental conformity and flagging religious fervor, a phenomenon described by some scholars as "dechristianization." Questioning the appropriateness of this term, Delumeau asks how one can speak of dechristianization when the masses were not even properly Christianized. Christianity, as it was preached by the Church between the thirteenth and eighteenth centuries, according to Delumeau, presented a vengeful, angry God, inspiring fear and anxiety, not the Christianity he himself had come to understand. In the twenty years since the publication of that book, Delumeau has expounded at great length on his original thesis. In *La peur en Occident* and *Le Péché et la peur*, he describes, in massive detail, the pervasive anxiety and fear, transformed into feelings of guilt and sin by the relentless effort of the Church, the "culpabilization" of society, as it were.[8] To assuage that fear, a vast paraphernalia – both sacramental and para-sacramental – was offered by the Church: benedictions, processions, saints, guardian angels, requiem masses, and Marian devotion.[9] Resisting both Protestant eradication and Tridentine reform, this popular religion, suffused with deep anxiety, was alleviated only by the gradual improvement of material life during the eighteenth century. Under this vast vision of *histoire de sentiment*, Delumeau subordinates both Protestant Reformation and Catholic Counter-Reformation to the even longer duration of Christianization, and the finer points of historical details seem lost in the overarching fresco that elude the eye of the beholder.

Among Delumeau's critics (and admirers), the English historian John Bossy has carefully analyzed the fundamental transformation from late medieval to early modern Christianity. Taking issue with Delumeau's vision of a pagan Middle Ages, Bossy, in a series of essays on confession, mass, and parish administration, contrasts a pre-Tridentine Christianity

[8] *La peur en Occident, XIVe–XVIIIe siècles. Une cité assiegée* (Paris, 1978), and *Le Péché et la peur. La culpabilisation en Occident (XIIIe–XVIIIe siècles)* (Paris, 1983).

[9] Two books by Delumeau elaborate on this argument: *Rassurer et protéger. Le sentiment de sécurité dans l'Occident d'autrefois* (Paris, 1989), and *L'aveu et le pardon. Les difficultés de la confession, XIIIe–XVIIIe siècles* (Paris, 1990), analyze the inadequacy of confession as an instrument for reassurance.

based on the natural allegiances of late medieval society – kinship, friendship, and locality – to one organized theologically and administratively from above by the official Church.[10]

A rough consensus has thus emerged, at least in the English-language historiography. Michael Mullett puts it succinctly when he argues that all reforms, Protestant and Catholic, had their origins in late medieval Christianity, and that any understanding of early modern Catholicism must take into consideration the period after 1650.[11] Yet, as the title of Mullett's short essay reveals, a certain unease still obtains in the choice of terminology. Nicholas Davidson calls his survey *The Counter-Reformation*, although admitting that neither that term nor "Catholic Reformation" is entirely satisfactory;[12] Keith Randell simply gives up choosing between contending concepts in his short textbook;[13] and the most recent introduction by Martin D. W. Jones retains the term "Counter-Reformation" even as the selection of documents include a large variety of topics previously excluded from similar texts.[14]

One of the prominent themes ignored in the traditional historiography of early modern Catholicism, and still neglected in the current crop of texts, is the history of non-European Catholicism. To be true, the history of missions constitutes a venerable subject in ecclesiastical history, but until recently the practitioners of the field have described the encounter between Christianity and non-European civilizations from the perspective of European missionaries, an understandable bias given the overwhelming preponderance of sources in European languages. Things have changed. There is now a greater recognition that any history of Christianization in Europe, or what constitutes the subject matter of popular religion, would be enriched by investigations into the encounter between European and non-European civilizations during the expansion of Catholic Europe. The Tridentine Church recognized as much. Jesuit missionaries spoke of "the Indies" in the remote rural corners of Catholic Europe, whose populations were equally in need of evangelization and ecclesiastical discipline; Italian intellectuals of the Enlightenment dis-

10 Bossy's argument for the centrality of parish devotion after Trent is set out in "The Counter-Reformation and the People of Catholic Europe," *Past and Present* 47 (1970), 51–70. For his contrasting models of a kin-based late medieval Christianity and one organized hierarchically from the top, see Bossy, "The Social History of Confession," *Transactions of the Royal Historical Society*, 5th series, 25 (1975), 21–38; Bossy, "The Mass as a Social Institution 1200–1700," *Past and Present* 100 (1983), 29–61; and Bossy, *Christianity in the West 1400–1700* (Oxford, 1985).

11 *The Counter-Reformation and the Catholic Reformation in Early Modern Europe* (London, 1984).

12 *The Counter-Reformation* (Oxford, 1987).

13 *The Catholic and Counter Reformations* (London, 1990).

14 *The Counter Reformation: Religion and Society in Early Modern Europe* (Cambridge, 1995).

cussed the necessity of the seminary for Chinese priests, the Collegio dei Cinesi, established in 1732 in Naples, whose foundation would benefit the Chinese peasants much more than the "more barbaric" Neapolitan peasants; and as early as 1585 a German translation of Jesuit reports from Japan praised the spread of the Catholic faith "to the other side of the world," a wondrous act of God to punish the Germans for falling away from his true Church and to compensate for the lost souls of central Europe with new ones won from the land of heathens. The Counter-Reformation, even in its strict definition, acquires a world-historical dimension; hence the centuries of Catholic renewal formed the first period of global history.

These then are some of the ideas underlying my interpretation. By entitling this book "The world of Catholic renewal," I mean to incorporate the concepts "Catholic Reform" and "Counter-Reformation" under the larger rubric of world history. Four themes inform my analysis of Catholic renewal: the reorganization of doctrine and Church from above; the interaction between politics and religion in Europe; the social and cultural manifestations of Catholic renewal; and the encounter between Catholic Europe and the non-Christian world.

Under the first theme I describe the measures undertaken by the Catholic Church to reassert sacerdotal authority in the face of Protestant and lay challenges. I begin this story with the Council of Trent, weaving into this narrative moments of earlier Catholic reform. Five subsequent chapters explore various parts of the reinvigorated Ecclesiastical Body: chapter 6 offers an analysis of the early modern papacy focusing on the changing character of the Papal States and the social history of the papacy; chapter 2 introduces the leading Tridentine religious orders that played a crucial role in the Catholic renewal; chapter 7 examines two processes central to Tridentine reform – reinforcing episcopal authority and disciplining the clergy; chapter 8 offers a social history of sanctity in early modern Catholicism by presenting a profile of the men and women canonized and beatified by the resurgent Roman Catholic Church; chapter 9 sharpens the focus on women's experience in the Tridentine Church by looking at the lives of nuns and beatas. I have organized these chapters in a conventional manner not only to give sufficient credit to ecclesiastical history, but also to emphasize that Catholic renewal, at least in its early phase, represented an ecclesiastical effort to strengthen sacerdotal authority, a move contested, as we shall see, by other religious visions on the part of secular authorities and the laity.

The second theme informs a cluster of three chapters (3–5). By dividing Catholic Europe into the "martyred Church," "militant Church," and "triumphant Church," I hope to underscore the role played by geography, national sentiment, and international politics in shaping the experience of Catholic renewal. National differences marked the very inception of Tridentine reform: whereas the decrees of the Council were readily adopted in Spain, Belgium, Italy, and Poland, their implementation in France and Germany lingered into the eighteenth century. Evennett has described a sixteenth-century Catholicism centered in Spain and Italy giving precedence to French spirituality in the seventeenth century. Although he may have underestimated the Mediterranean contribution in the seventeenth century, Evennett is certainly right in remarking on national differences in spiritual styles and ecclesiastical politics. I have attempted in these chapters to sketch the complicated interplay between politics and religion without losing the thematic structure in a morass of narrative details.

We depart from Europe in chapters 11 and 12. The encounter between Catholic Europe and non-Christian civilizations is organized geographically and analytically. Conquest, settlement, forced evangelization: this was the pattern established in the Americas that duplicated to a considerable extent the experience of Iberian Catholicism at home – the collaboration and tension between secular and ecclesiastical authorities, the mystical and missionary fervor of the Iberian Church, and the repression of heresy and "superstitions." Our understanding has been enriched in particular by recent scholarship on colonial Latin America; more subtle theories of cultural encounters and adaptations have replaced an earlier paradigm of evangelization and spiritual conquest. China, Japan, and the Philippines represent another model of Catholic expansion. In these lands far from the heartland of Catholic Europe the friars and the Jesuits advanced the cause of Catholicism without the threat of swords and arquebuses. Unlike the experience of Latin America, whose history of Christianization was based overwhelmingly on European sources, historians of China and Japan can tap on a fairly large body of sources in indigenous languages that document the other side of the encounter. Whether evangelization resulted in rejection, as in the case of Japan, or in accommodation (some scholars prefer the term "inculturation"), as in China, the insights gained in this analysis allow historians to examine the European experience in a new light. The paucity of European priests, the thinness of ecclesiastical institutions, the incompleteness of indoctrination, the incomprehension of local customs: these were all issues that confronted the missions; pondering this problematic allows historians to establish in turn a comparative framework to question the relationship between Church and people, official and popular religions in Catholic Europe.

The final theme addresses "the Counter-Reformation and the people of Catholic Europe," to quote from the title of Bossy's landmark essay. Chapter 10 deals with the impact of Catholic renewal on art; it examines patronage, production, and the consumption of art, ranging from the sculpture and paintings of the Baroque papal court to the massively printed devotional images for the devout. Chapter 13 reflects on the influence of Tridentine reform on the religious sentiments and practices of the population: it addresses the question of success, defined in terms of sacramental conformity, parish devotion, popular cults, and the eradication of "superstitions," criteria established by the ecclesiastical hierarchy; and finally, it offers a tentative interpretation of the experience of Catholicism in early modern Europe, in light of theories of "Christianization" and "social discipline."

My interpretation is necessarily selective. No historian in a lifetime can hope to master the sources and languages required to write a comprehensive history of Catholicism in early modern world history that transcends the traditional boundary of Church history. Specialists will recognize my indebtedness to the large and growing scholarship in many fields of historical research. I have tried to give an introductory orientation to the scholarship in an extended bibliographical essay. If this synthesis generates debates and research, it will more than have served its purpose.

1 The Council of Trent

The Council of Trent opened on the thirteenth of December, 1545. A host of ecclesiastical dignitaries assembled in the Church of the Most Holy Trinity. They then marched in solemn procession to the Gothic cathedral in the center of town. First came the secular and regular clergy of the city – the priests in black cassocks and white surplices; the friars in black, grey, and white. Next came the exalted canons of the cathedral chapter, all members of the nobility. After them marched the prelates of the Council and the envoys of King Ferdinand I of the Romans, followed by the nobility and a great crowd of citizens. Three archbishops, twenty-one bishops, and the generals of five mendicant orders – the Conventual and Observant Franciscans, the Augustinians, the Carmelites, and the Servites – represented the official delegates. While waiting to file into the vaulted cathedral for solemn high mass, the opening act of the long-awaited Church Council, the three papal legates, in their cardinal purple, could look up at the snow-capped hills and remember the vineyards in spring when they had first arrived in this forlorn frontier city.

They had waited almost a year. The opening of the Council was repeatedly postponed from March to May, as delegates and bishops slowly drifted into Trent. By July, most of the delegates were Italians, although French and Spanish delegates arrived in late summer. But there were still no Germans, the nation that had started this schism in the first place. The delegates at the opening session represented a tiny section of the universal Church. Most were Italians, with the exception of two Spanish bishops, one English, one French, and one German bishop. Little did they know that, when the work of the Council was finally done – after eighteen years, two long interludes, and twenty-five sessions – they themselves would be long dead.

It was a distinguished trio that presided. Giovanni Maria del Monte (1487–1555), son of a well-known Roman jurist, studied law at Perugia and Siena and became chamberlain to Pope Julius II. In 1511 he succeeded his uncle as archbishop of Siponto, became bishop of Pavia in 1520, and served in the papal government as governor of Rome and vice-legate of Bologna under Clement VII and Paul III. Elevated to cardinal in October 1543, del Monte was elected pope in February 1550 and took the name of Julius III. The second legate, Marcello Cervini (1501–55), born near Siena, was the son of an official in the Sacred Penitentiary (the tribunal of the holy see which handled cases of conscience). A devoted humanist and bibliophile, he became a client of Paul III, who appointed him protonotary apostolic and tutor to his grandson Cardinal Alessandro Farnese. Appointed to the bishoprics of Nicastro, Reggio Emilia, and Gubbio, which he administered through a vicar, and elevated to cardinal in 1539, Cervini was a trusted advisor of the cardinal-nephew and served in important diplomatic missions. He was elected pope in April 1555, but his reign as Marcellus II lasted only three weeks. The third legate, Ercole Gonzaga, hailed from one of the leading princely families, the Gonzagas of Mantua with numerous family ties to leading princely dynasties in Italy and Germany. This prince of the Church brought with him a huge retinue of 160 servants, far surpassing the others.

As princes in the papal establishment, the legates presided over a Council that faced the greatest challenge to the Roman Church and the papacy. Sparked by the criticisms of a German Augustinian monk, the reform movement led by Martin Luther had swept most of Germany. In 1545, just one year before Luther's death, only Bavaria remained a stronghold of Catholicism in central Europe; even the archbishoprics seemed in danger of falling to Protestant reform. Joined in the League of Smalkald, Protestant princes and imperial cities swore to defend their new faith in defiance of emperor and pope. The Protestants abhorred the Roman Babylon: there, ambition not faith reigned; laws not conscience guided action; letters and arts, not the Word of God, were in fashion; and in this world of privilege and power, one advanced through patronage and family, with little regard, it seemed, for ecclesiastical laws or personal piety. Many Catholics shared these views. Here and there, conscientious churchmen preached repentance, studied the Scriptures, and called for the reform of "the head and members" of the Church even well before the Reformation. We find these isolated voices throughout Europe: Geiler von Keyersberg in Strasburg, Johannes Gropper in Cologne, Lefevre d'Etaples and Bishop Briçonnet in France, Cardinal Reginald Pole in England, Cardinals Gasparo Contarini and Gabriele Paleotti in Italy. The German schism shocked some into action. Under the influence of Luther's writings, a small circle gathered in Italy urging spiritual renewal and austerity. But acceding to reforms implied acknowledging Protestant criticisms, the thrust of which denied the very legitimacy of the papacy. Yet without a general Church Council heresy would spread: England had abjured allegiance to Rome, proclaiming a national Church; and reform movements were attracting supporters in France, Poland, and even in the Habsburg realms.

Reforms and heresy: these represented the twin problems facing the Council. As they were entrusted with negotiating a balance between conflicting demands, the legates' task became entangled in the larger politics that shaped the Council. The outcome of this period of the Council (1545–48) was determined by the empire and the papacy. In lieu of a national council of the German Church, Emperor Charles V needed a general Church Council to settle the religious schism in Germany. For Charles, politics and religion went hand in hand. Locked in a struggle for hegemony with Francis I of France, Charles faced invasions by Ottoman Turks and Algerian corsairs. As defender of Christendom and universal empire, he needed men and money from the princes and cities of Germany. He paid the price of peace with religious concessions to German Protestants. As a good Catholic, Charles tried to bring concord. He enjoined moderate theologians from both camps to talk, but the religious compromise reached in 1541 at Regensburg was rejected by Protestants and Catholics alike. His only chance lay in an universal Church Council that would reform the corruption in Christendom and thus bring German Protestants back into the fold. To this end he insisted the Council be convoked within the empire.

The pope had a very different agenda. For Paul III and the Roman curia, it was too late to heal the schism. Catholic Europe looked to Rome for guidance in combating heresy. If Germany was lost, southern Europe still remained faithful. A Church Council could meet only under the authority of the pope. Beginning with the pontificate of Martin V (1417–31), the papacy had been gradually restoring its power and prestige. It had defeated the challenge of the conciliarists (those who argued for the supremacy of the Church Council over papal authority), reached accords with monarchs over ecclesiastical jurisdiction, and strengthened the administration and finances within the Papal States. The Lutheran heresy was simply the last in a long series of challenges to the successors of St. Peter. Paul III instructed his delegates to define doctrine in order to mark heretics from the faithful; they must ward off any challenges to papal authority which came under the guise of reform. The Council should thus take place in Italy, under the guidance and supervision of Rome.

Trent was a compromise. Situated at the foothills of the Alps, at the very linguistic divide between Latin and Germanic Europe, this small cathedral town lies on the most important route linking Germany and Italy. With a predominantly Italian population, Trent nevertheless belonged to the Holy Roman Empire. Like their German counterparts, the bishops of Trent also ruled as secular princes, and during the fifteenth and sixteenth centuries they were recruited mostly from the German-speaking nobility in service to the Habsburgs. Cardinal Cristoforo Madruzzo, bishop of Trent at the time of the Council, was the spokesman for the imperialist party. Charles himself resided in Innsbruck during much of the sessions, receiving reports and sending instructions to Trent, only one day's ride away to the south. At the other end of the spectrum, Paul III and his cardinal-nephew exerted close supervision over the Council through the delegates, who acted as spokesmen for the papal party.

After the general congregation of December 18, the delegates discussed procedure and agenda during the subsequent sessions. There were immediate difficulties. The majority voted in favor of giving precedence to discussing reform; the papal legates prevailed on a compromise procedure of parallel discussion of dogma and reform, which was rejected by Paul III. Nevertheless, the churchmen set down to work. In the next six months, meeting in many committee sessions and six general sessions, they affirmed the authority of the Vulgate Bible (even though some delegates favored vernacular translations), discussed scriptural studies and preaching, defined original sin, and skirmished on the question of whether holders of Church benefices must reside in their see. The most important discussion was on the doctrine of justification.

Justification by faith alone (*sola fides*) had become the battle-cry of the Lutheran reformation. Based on the writings of St. Paul and St. Augustine, this understanding of salvation, deeply individual and spiritual, threatened to undermine both Catholic sacraments and clerical authority. Nonetheless, it exerted a powerful attraction at the Council and several prominent delegates – notably the general of the Augustinians Seripando, Archbishop Carranza of Toledo, and Cardinals Reginald Pole and Giovanni Morone – showed enough sympathy to land them in suspicion of heresy later.

While the theologians argued over justification in Trent, the German Protestants at the Second Religious Colloquy in Regensburg rejected the general Church Council held under the authority of the pope. Convinced that Protestants would yield neither to colloquies, diets, nor Church Council, Charles decided to settle the religious schism by arms. In June 1546 he declared the Smalkald League in rebellion and mobilized troops for a campaign. Papal troops passed near Trent on their way north, adding further to the alarming reports from the theater of war circulating among the Council fathers. Many called for a postponement; others argued for moving the site of the Council. Under intense pressure from Charles V, the fathers resumed debate on justification in the hot summer months.

In August, the theologians headed by Seripando reported back to the general congregation. The draft on the decree on justification argued for the idea of a twofold justice, intended as a bridge to Luther's idea of *sola fides*. Most Council fathers argued against the draft and opted for a strongly anti-Lutheran definition that stressed the sanctity of charitable work. A heated argument ensued because the imperialist faction was reluctant to define dogma so as to leave room for later compromise with Protestants. On January 13, 1547, after numerous revisions, the Council fathers voted in favor of the decree on justification in what was to date the longest and most difficult session.

In the realm of reform, the fathers continued the debate on the bishops' obligation of residence. The aim of the reform was to raise the level of pastoral ministry, but this issue touched on the very center of papal power. The debate hinged on the fact that non-residence was sanctioned by the papal curia: bishops regularly obtained dispensation from Rome, often because they were serving at the curia; and cardinals commonly held several benefices and bestowed them on their clients. Any reform in this important issue touched on the prerogative of Rome; after all, the edifice of patronage at the papal curia rested on the foundations of plurality of benefice and non-residence. There was an additional difficulty for the papacy: the suggestion that episcopal residency was divinely ordained implied that the origins of episcopal office were divine, and threatened to put the Council's authority (as the meeting of all bishops) over that of the pope.

Although Session VII reached an impasse on reform, the discussion on doctrines evoked little controversy. In the session of January 17, 1547, the fathers affirmed the seven sacraments of the Church and condemned a list of Protestant teachings on this matter.

After a year of meeting, the mood darkened among the Council fathers. The gradual falling out between pope and emperor heightened the discord between the imperialist and papal factions at Trent. Rome feared imperial hegemony: his troops already victorious in South Germany, on April 27, 1547, Charles V won a decisive battle at Mühlberg over Saxon and Hessian troops; he was in a position to dictate terms not only to the German Protestants, but perhaps also to the Church as well. To escape imperial hegemony, the Council could reconvene outside the empire in papal territory. The decision for "translation" was opposed by the imperialist party (Spanish and Neapolitan bishops). Charles wanted the Council to remain at Trent, so that he could force the Protestants to attend after their defeat; a translation to the papal territory would make it unacceptable. The majority (mostly Italians), however, supported the translation. In addition to their support for the papacy, many had long complained of the cold and discomfort in Trent. The outbreak of typhus and the death of a Council father in March strengthened their determination to decamp. Within a few weeks, most of the fathers had left Trent for Bologna.

Thus concluded the first phase of the Council of Trent. On the opening day no more than twenty-nine bishops and cardinals attended. But the legates persisted and at the end, a total of five cardinals, twelve archbishops, and seventy-four bishops had attended, although this figure was never attained at any single session. To the bishops must be added the six generals of the mendicant orders, the three abbots of the Cassinese Congregation, and proctors of the archbishop of Trier and the bishop of Augsburg. All Catholic countries were represented, with the exceptions of Switzerland, Poland, and Hungary. And not a single ruling German bishop came in person to Trent. In addition to the 100 bishops, another 100 theologians also attended this first period of Trent. Armed with far-reaching powers from Rome, the papal legates were the helmsmen at the Council. The existence of an opposition testified to considerable freedom of speech. But the Lutheran faction which some fathers dreaded did not actually exist.

The result of the wearisome discussions of a whole year were four dogmatic and four reform decrees. The decree of Session IV on Scripture and tradition defined the canon of the Bible: while affirming the authority of the Vulgate, it balanced scriptural teaching against the weight of accumulated ecclesiastical tradition, which it reasserted with firmness in the face of Protestant challenge. The two decrees on original sin and justification promulgated in Sessions V and VI respectively defined the differences between Catholicism and Protestantism; the decree on the sacraments in general and on baptism and confirmation in particular, as worked out in Session VII, defined the Catholic conception of a sacrament as well as the septenary number. While none of the four dogmatic decrees met with any strong objections, the four reform decrees were the object of violent wrangling both before and after their promulgation. In this, the legates found themselves between two fires: on the one hand, the conservative conception of reform which prevailed at the curia and among the Italian bishops; and on the other, the radical demand of the Spaniards, the French, and one group of Italians that a new spirit be breathed into the pastoral ministry on both the diocesan and the parochial level, regardless of the long-standing practices and interests of the curia.

The first session at Bologna began on April 21, 1547. It met only until

June 1548. Among the doctrines debated at the Bologna "Interim" were the eucharist, contrition, confession, extreme unction, and consecration. The theologians also discussed indulgence and purgatory. On Church reform, the Council fathers debated the accumulation of benefices, the poor quality of confessors, and many abuses of the clergy. They also held extensive discussions of clandestine marriages, contracted among young people outside ecclesiastical authority.

Displeased with the translation of the Council, Charles V pressured the new pope, Julius III, the erstwhile legate del Monte who had faced the anger of the emperor on more than one occasion, to return the Council to Trent. At the height of his power, Charles persuaded the three German archbishops as well as the Protestants to participate. The second period of the Council of Trent (1551–52) represented the definitive break between Catholicism and Protestantism. In Session XIII (October 11, 1551), the Council fathers carried on their discussion of eucharistic theology and issued a canon affirming the doctrine of transsubstantiation – the transformation of the bread and wine in mass into the body and blood of Christ. As this was one of the major doctrinal differences between Protestants and Catholics, its proclamation even before the arrival of the Protestants signaled the impossibility of compromise. The German Protestants arrived in Trent in January 1552. They were cordially received, but for all practical purposes their presence accomplished nothing.

Charles V found his plans thwarted not only at Trent. In Germany, a new rebellion broke out. Betrayed by an alliance of German princes led by his former ally, Moritz of Saxony, the emperor, militarily unprepared, saw his fortunes reversed. He asked for a suspension of the Council to which Pope Julius III agreed. By this time, the Council fathers were worn down by exhaustion. The new papal legate Cardinal Marcello Crescenzio died at the end of the Council in 1552, a broken man, torn between the clashing demands of emperor and pope. During this second period, Charles increased pressure on the pope; Francisco de Toledo, the imperial ambassador, was perhaps the leading presence. Julius III acceded to the emperor's will, much against the protest of France. At these two sessions (XIII and XIV), there was a majority of Spanish and German bishops who pushed for Church reform, whereas the Italian and papal party found itself in the minority. In spite of the decrees and canons promulgated, many delegates left the Council at the end of April 1552 with the sense that little if anything had been accomplished in the way of reforms. The presence of theologians from Germany and the Low Countries meant that the delegates as a group now had a much better knowledge of Protestant theology than earlier. Although the outbreak of war in the empire prevented the attendance of Protestant theologians, the distance between the two sides was much too great for any compromise. In 1552, the division between Catholic and Protestant became irrevocable. Three years later at the Diet of Augsburg, Ferdinand acknowledged his defeat in Germany and legally recognized the Lutheran confession in the empire.

The year 1552 also marked a new turn in the papacy. Julius III appointed a deputation of cardinals to discuss the reform of the curia. Its members included such dedicated reformers as Carafa, Cervini, Pole, Toledo, and Morone; the topics touched on the reform of the conclave, the Consistories of cardinals, the Signature and the Penitentiary, the duty of residence of cardinals, and the reform of religious orders. The papal bull *Varietas temporum* incorporated their recommendations and outlined in 150 chapters a comprehensive plan of reforms. Its publication was repeatedly delayed and it was filed away after Pope Julius III died on March 23, 1555. The spirit of reform, however, had triumphed: in a short conclave Cardinal Cervini, the papal legate at Trent, was elected Pope Marcellus II. His determination to act on reform was cut short by his death a mere three weeks later. But the reform party elected as his successor Gian Pietro Carafa, who took the name Paul IV (1555–59).

Aged seventy-nine at the time of his election, scion of a Neapolitan baronial family, Carafa was fired by his dedication to reform and by his hatred for the Spanish subjugation of his fatherland. Austere and ascetic, Carafa dedicated himself to reform early on; in 1524, together with Gaetano di Thiene (Cajetan), he founded the Theatines, an order dedicated to poverty and restoring the apostolic way of life, and became their first superior. His zeal for reform was marred by a harsh sense of righteousness, exemplified by his severity as head of the reactivated Roman Inquisition. After his election, he failed to fulfill the expectations of the reform party. Autocratic and passionate, Paul IV made war on the Habsburgs, trusting in the political advice of his corrupt nephew Carlo Carafa to ally with France until the papacy was defeated and overrun by imperial forces in 1557. In his zeal to combat Protestantism, he unleashed a regime of repression: he ordered the imprisonment of Cardinal Giovanni Morone in the Castel San Angelo on the groundless suspicion of Lutheran heresy; he deprived Cardinal Reginald Pole of his legateship to England and instituted an heresy investigation just before the death of the esteemed churchman; he established a strict censorship in 1557 through the Index of Forbidden Books, which proscribed both Protestant and humanist works; and he confined Jews in ghettos and forced them to wear distinctive badges. His intolerance cast a long shadow over the promise of reform. On his death on August 18, 1559, popular hatred exploded against the Carafa family. The crowd stormed the prison of the Inquisition and freed prisoners; and they toppled the pope's statute at the Capitol to signify their fury over his tyranny.

In one of the longest conclaves of the papacy (September 5–December 25, 1559), the Milanese Gian Angelo Medici was elected as a compromise candidate and took the name of Pius IV (1559–65). In contrast to his despotic predecessor, Pius IV was moderate and affable. He relaxed the rigor of the Roman Inquisition and the Index. And one of his first acts was to release the much-respected Cardinal Morone from the Castelangelo. Alarmed by the rapid progress of the teachings of John Calvin in France, Pius decided to reconvene the general Church Council.

In 1560 the European situation looked very different. The rivalry between emperor and pope had been replaced by a more complex political landscape. Four powers would play a crucial role in the third concluding period of the Council: France, Spain, the Holy Roman Empire, and the papacy. The formidable Charles V was gone from the scene, succeeded by his son Philip II, king of Spain, and by his brother Ferdinand, the emperor. The Habsburgs and Valois concluded peace in 1559 at the Treaty of Cateau-Cambrésis, restoring peace to Christendom. Confined largely to Germany, Lutheranism had achieved legal recognition, but a new Protestant movement, inspired by the teachings of the Frenchman John Calvin, was rapidly gathering support throughout Europe, particularly in France. Both Pius IV and Philip II feared that the French monarchy, faced with a divided realm, would call on a national Church to resolve differences. To preempt the convening of a Gallican national council, Pius IV proclaimed a bull on December 2, 1560, to reconvene the Council of Trent.

On the eve of the third period of the Council of Trent, Filippo Gherio, bishop of Ischia and confidant of Cardinal Morone, the papal legate and president of the Council, confided in the duke of Savoy: "It is the opinion of His Holiness that, if one cannot heal the sickness in France and Germany, one would have to take care that the still healthy in Italy and Spain are not infected." For the papacy and its chief political support, the king of Spain, the Council represented a continuation of the two previous sessions. For the French monarchy and Church, who had not officially participated before, the Council would ideally have been a new one, whose decrees would supersede the canons and decrees of the previous sessions, which France did not feel itself bound by. The French chancellor, Michel de L'Hôpital, who favored a political solution to his country's religious divisions, did not see how a French national council could be avoided. The German Protestant princes, gathered in Naumburg,

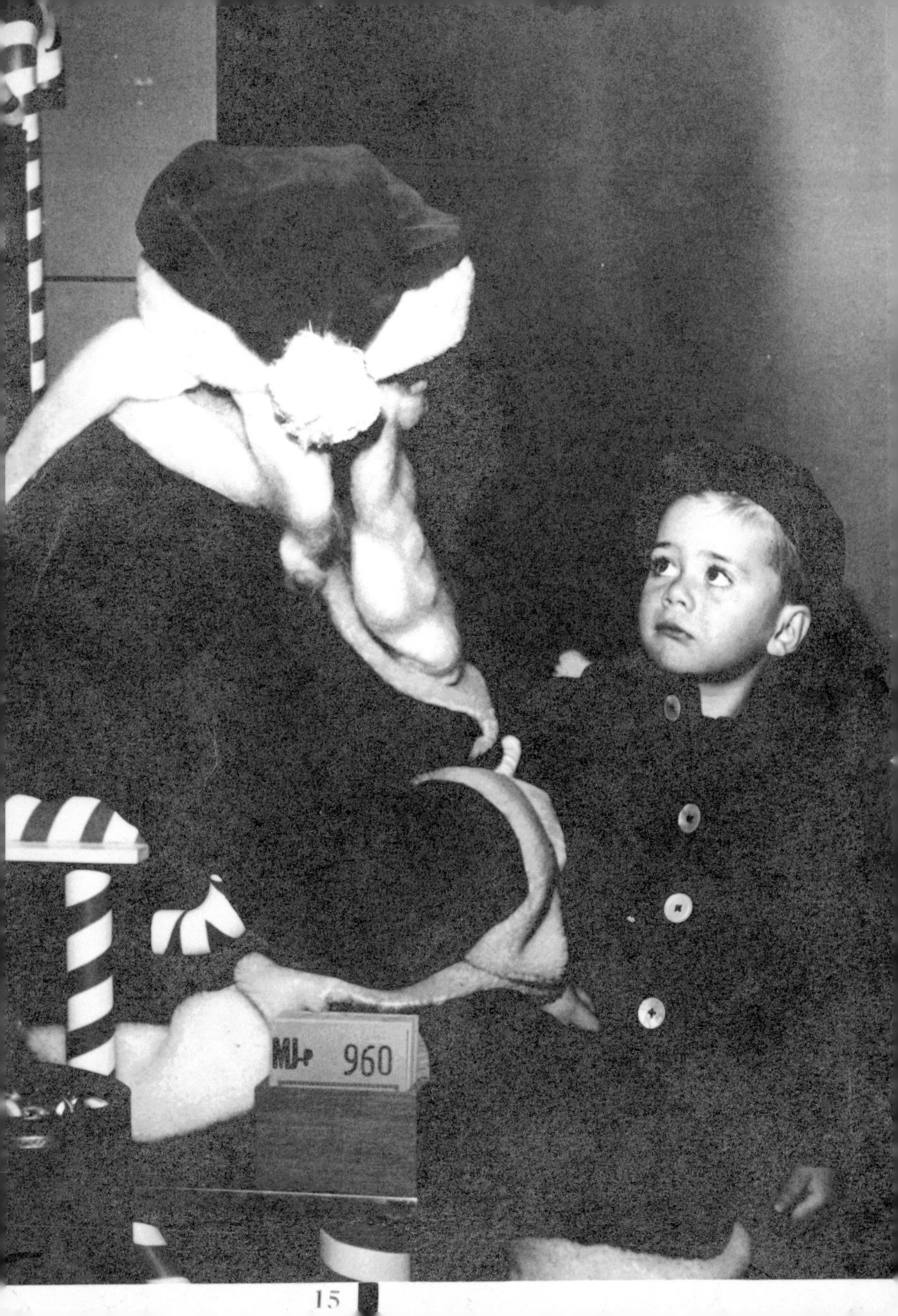
MJ-P 960

rejected the invitation in January 1561. In Spain, opinion feared that France and the empire might reject the published decrees of the previous Councils and undermine the work of reform. Indeed, on July 31, 1561, a French national council was convoked in Poissy. Thanks to Cardinal Tournon, the French bishops did not accede to the monarchy's wishes that national reforms be carried out to accommodate the Calvinists. Much to Rome's relief, the French bishops affirmed papal authority; in the autumn of 1561, a delegation of twenty-six French bishops left their country for Trent.

In Rome, Pope Pius IV named a large legation: Cardinals Ercole Gonzaga, Girolamo Seripando, Giacomo Puteo, Ludovico Simonetta, Mark Sittich von Hohenems, and Stanislas Hosius. Most had participated in the previous Councils; and Hosius represented a new voice for Catholicism from Poland. Philip II sent a large delegation of Spanish bishops. England and Scotland refused to participate; and the German bishops were lukewarm for fear that their presence would provoke the Protestants and disturb the religious settlement of 1555 in the empire. The largest contingent consisted of Italian bishops, who numbered seventy by the end of November 1561.

The papal legates harbored different interests. Cardinal Simonetta, the pope's confidant, whose main purpose was to defend the interests of the papacy, had a private secret code to correspond with the cardinal-nephew. Seripando, who had attended all sessions of the Council, still entertained the vague hope of reconciliation with the Protestants. The precisely opposite position was held by Hosius, the bishop of Ermland, convinced that Protestants were out to destroy the Catholic Church. On January 18, 1562, the Council opened with 110 fathers in attendance, a favorable augury to Seripando, who remembered the poor showing in 1545.

A number of secular political powers were represented; the presence of the Portuguese, Swiss, Florentine, Bavarian, and imperial ambassadors added to the prestige of the Council. Never before had the Council witnessed the attendance of 145 fathers as at Session XVIII.

The splendid beginning of the Council soon turned into a crisis. On April 20, two parties clashed so bitterly over the duty of episcopal residency that the Council was unable to proceed with any real work. At issue was whether the duty of bishops to reside in their sees originated in canon law or divine law. Although the decree of Session VI had already stipulated the duty of residency, reform remained a dead letter. Too many entrenched interests were at stake. A literal enforcement of this duty would require most ecclesiastical dignitaries in the papal curia to leave Rome: advancement in the papal curia depended on the accumulation of benefices and the dispensation of residence, a significant power of patronage enjoyed by the papacy. Under the leadership of Simonetta and backed by Rome, a curial party at Trent (largely Italian bishops) rejected any principled discussion of episcopal residency. Their opponents, the episcopal party, consisted of practically all the non-Italian bishops plus a minority of Italian, mainly Venetian, bishops. Led by Archbishop Guerrero of Granada, the reform party enjoyed the sympathy of two papal legates, Seripando and Gonzaga, and saw the obstructionism in Rome as the greatest stumbling block to Church reform. Suspected in the papal curia of plotting against Rome, Seripando and Gonzaga were reprimanded; Gonzaga submitted his resignation, but Pius IV refused to accept it. Although the crisis over the residency question remained (Gonzaga promised the reform party it would be discussed together with the question of the consecration of the clergy), some measure of papal confidence in its legates at Trent was restored.

In the summer heat of Trent sixty-one theologians lectured on communion in both kinds (in both bread and wine), in response to a memorandum presented by the imperial ambassador on granting the chalice to the laity, a central feature of Protestant worship. Some theologians were willing to grant dispensation for Protestants who returned to the Church, but the papal theologian, the Jesuit Salmerón, attacked the practice. The question of the chalice for the laity came up again in the autumn when the Council fathers discussed the nature of the Catholic mass. Both the imperial and Bavarian ambassadors pleaded for dispensation since this issue had become important in retaining Catholic loyalty in Germany. The Hungarian bishop of Fünfkirchen also pleaded for regional dispensation on the model of Bohemia (the Bohemian Utraquists were granted dispensation in the fifteenth century after the Hussite uprising). But the great majority of fathers argued against concessions. On September 17, 1562, at Session XXII, the fathers confirmed the sacrificial character of the mass and lay communion in one form only, drawing a sharp distinction with Protestant worship.

In late autumn the conflict between the episcopal and curial parties flared up once more over consecration. Spanish theologians argued that bishops had been divinely ordained to consecrate and stand over priests, implying that their jurisdiction came directly from God; only their specific diocese was appointed by the pope. The curial party objected that this formulation of the divine right of bishops detracted from papal authority: the pope was not only the first among equals among bishops but the only vicar of Christ. Professing their loyalty to the papacy, the episcopal party stated that their wish was not to undermine papal power but merely to bolster their authority over the diocesan clergy. A compromise formula in the wording of the decree was thus found.

As tempers cooled, the French appeared. On November 13, under the leadership of Cardinal Guise of Lorraine, the delegation of twelve bishops, three abbots, and fifteen theologians arrived. The question of divine right of bishops again heated up. Simonetta and the curialists feared that any concessions on the wording of divine right would make the Council superior in authority to the pope. The two parties exchanged charges. Amidst this renewed crisis, the papal nephew Federico Borromeo died, deeply affecting his brother Carlo, the papal secretary, who began to turn away from curial politics toward asceticism.

Over winter the Council ground to a halt. On a few occasions, the opponents exchanged *ad hominem* attacks: a partisan of the Roman curia accused the Spanish and Portuguese bishops of living with concubines and children; a Spanish bishop in turn decried the blasphemy and children's tricks on the part of the curialists. Cardinal Guise tried to mediate by bringing together opponents to discuss a compromise, but he was repeatedly frustrated. Many fathers distrusted Rome's will to reform itself; in January 1563 Pius IV elevated two princes to the cardinalate: the eighteen-year-old Federigo Gonzaga, nephew of Ercole and a younger son of Duke Fernando dei Medici, of Florence, who was only fourteen. A widespread discontent pervaded the Council. The imperial ambassador reported to Ferdinand that no reforms could be expected from Trent. In a letter to the pope, dated March 3, 1563, the emperor expressed his deep concern that there were in fact two Councils, one at Trent and one at the Roman curia where cardinals sabotaged any reform proposals.

The same day that Ferdinand addressed his letter, the Council's president Ercole Gonzaga died in Trent at the age of fifty-seven. Another papal legate Seripando followed him on March 17 at the age of seventy. Both men were physically exhausted by the long and bitter controversy over episcopal residency during the winter months. The tension at the congregation spilled over to the streets: on March 12 servants of the Spanish and Italian bishops clashed, leading to deaths and injuries. Pius named two new legates, Cardinals Morone and Navagero.

Cardinal Morone, the new president of the Council, enjoyed the trust of his fellow Milanese, Pius IV, as well as that of Ferdinand, thanks to Morone's diplomatic service in Germany and his long experience and knowledge of the Reformation. In several visits to Innsbruck during April and May, Morone succeeded in convincing Ferdinand of the pope's true intentions of reform. The danger for the papacy, as Morone explained, lay in the fact that all three major Catholic powers – Spain, France, and the empire – wanted their orators to be able to propose items for discussion. Secular intervention would then open the door for national initiatives, leading ultimately to the revival of conciliarism and anti-papalism.

Hence, Morone defended the right of the papal legates alone to propose items for the agenda. The reform of the members, not the head, of the Church, was to be the task of the Council; the papal curia would reform itself.

Under Morone's leadership the Council came back to life. After numerous committee meetings over episcopal residency and repeated revisions over its wording, the congregation voted in favor of the decree. With significant concessions to the Spanish and French bishops (non-residency was declared a mortal sin), the wording of the decree avoided the words "divine right," sidestepping altogether the power relationship between papacy and episcopacy; it confirmed the superiority of bishops over the diocesan clergy and provided for the establishment of seminaries for their training. Just how close the Council came to failure was reflected in the quarrel over diplomatic precedence between the French and Spanish ambassadors, which went on during the theological negotiations of June and July. The arrival of the Spanish ambassador, the count of Luña, provoked a crisis when the papal legates accorded him second ranking after the imperial ambassador, ahead of the French ambassador. Their national pride insulted, the French ambassador and bishops threatened to withdraw from Trent, and only Spanish concessions saved the day.

As the Council entered its final phase, more churchmen than ever crowded into Trent. In the July session no fewer than 236 Council fathers participated, of whom over two-thirds were Italians. They did not, however, form an united block; they were divided among a larger curialist party under the leadership of Simonetta, somewhat weakened under Morone's presidency, and a smaller group of humanist reformers, deprived of leadership after Seripando's death. After the Italians, the Iberian episcopacy constituted the next largest group, with a respectable number of prominent theologians among them. The French bishops stood behind the leadership of Cardinal Guise; the presence of theologians from the Sorbonne further strengthened their influence at the Council. From the British Isles came only three Irish bishops and a single Englishman; the new Catholic bishops named by Mary Tudor in 1559 were either imprisoned or had fled to Belgium for their refusal to recognize the new queen Elizabeth as head of the English Church. Not a single German bishop was personally in attendance.

The next item of business was the sacrament of marriage. In March 1563 a congregation of theologians held preliminary discussions on divorce and clandestine marriages; their report came on the agenda of the general congregation on July 24. Previously, canon law recognized a marriage as legitimate when contracted by two parties at the age of reason. In practice, the promise of marriage between young adults became the prelude to sexual intercourse, but the intimate nature of the verbal contract gave occasion to numerous disputes when the men reneged on the promise of marriage. Seduction, pregnancy, abandonment, illegitimacy, and lawsuits: these were the problems created by the abuse of clandestine marital vows. The Portuguese ambassador reported to the Council that in the diocese of Lisbon alone, 94 out of 100 confessors were confronted with cases of the abuse of clandestine marriages. Cardinal Guise added that, in a single year, twenty lawsuits of broken promises were heard by the Parlement of Paris. A majority of Council fathers opted for reforming clandestine marriage, although a vocal minority defended the canonicity of the practice. In a vote in September, 133 fathers voted for the decree "Tametsi [Although]," 59 against, with 3 abstentions. After four revisions and protracted debates, the fathers finally voted on November 10 to accept the decree: 126 votes for, 47 against, 7 abstentions. The decree "Tametsi" read that, although clandestine marriages or unions contracted without parental consent had been valid, the Council decided that in the future all engagements and marriages without at least three witnesses were invalid, as were those contracted by men under twenty and women under eighteen without parental consent, except when the Church determined that permission was unjustly denied. The decree further prohibited remarriage as a result of marital infidelity, thus marking another significant difference from Protestantism.

Parallel with the discussion on clandestine marriages, the Council dealt with the difficult question of clerical reform in two final sessions (XXIV and XXV) from September to December 1563. The Council fathers accepted reform decrees that touched on all aspects of clerical life: the strengthening of the authority of bishops over chapters and colleges; restrictions on appeals to Rome; regular episcopal visitations of dioceses; removal of unchaste priests from parishes; reform of all religious orders, including the enforcement of strict closure for female convents. The Council succeeded in pushing through the reform decrees in spite of opposition, thanks to the support of Pius IV and his cardinal-nephew Carlo Borromeo. If some cardinals still believed in the perpetuation of the Renaissance papacy and their own privileges – notably cardinals Alessandro Farnese, his brother Ranuccio, and Ippolito d'Este, all creatures of previous popes – they faced a new papal secretary, austere and committed to reform. If the cardinals and their clients at the Council still obstructed reforms, they encountered a much more powerful alliance of emperor, king, and pope. A prelate such as the archbishop of Braga struck a pious figure in comparison to the worldly cardinals: though, with an annual income of 18,000 ducats from his see, larger than that of any of his colleagues at Trent, the archbishop had a moderate entourage of nine servants, unlike the dozens in the entourages of the more prominent dignitaries. He spoke out in favor of reform, even when it meant a diminution of his own income. On a visit to Rome, this embodiment of the ideal Tridentine bishop, Braga, deeply impressed Carlo Borromeo, who would one day himself become the model reform bishop.

On November 27, report of the pope's illness reached Trent. Seizing the moment, Morone urged the conclusion of the Council. On December 3, the text of the reform decrees were read aloud at Session XXV. The session continued the next day with the reading of five other decrees. After a short discussion, the Council fathers voted to accept them. As president, Morone stood up and declared the end of the Council; papal approval of the accepted canons and decrees would be sought in due course; and he thanked the fathers and bade them "depart in peace." Cardinal Guise followed Morone. He acclaimed the contributions to the Council by the previous popes Paul III and Julius III, and by the secular rulers Charles V and Ferdinand I. To the gathered fathers, he called out: "Let us confess to the faith of the holy ecumenical synod of Trent and always observe its decrees!" The fathers answered: "We will always confess and observe its decrees!" Cardinal Guise continued: "Thus all of us believe in it and give our signature in complete agreement. This is the faith of St. Peter. This is the faith of the Church fathers. This is the orthodox faith." Again the congregation answered in approbation. Finally, Cardinal Guise proclaimed: "In accepting these decrees may we become worthy through the mercy and grace of our first and great high priest Jesus Christ, our God, through the intercession of our immaculate mistress, the holy mother of God and of all saints." The Council fathers shouted in reply: "So be it, Amen! Amen! Anathema to all false teachings, Anathema!" Morone began the first notes of the Te Deum, followed by all. After giving his blessing, he bid the fathers "to go in peace." The decrees and canons of the Council were signed by 4 legates, 2 other cardinals, 3 patriarchs, 25 archbishops, 168 bishops, 7 abbots, and 7 generals of religious orders. The Council of Trent had come to an end.

As stated in the papal bull *Laetare Jerusalem* (Rejoice Jerusalem), which convoked the Church Council, Trent had a threefold aim: to eradicate religious schism; to reform and bring peace among Christians; and to reclaim the holy sites in Palestine for Christians. For the papacy, the first aim was paramount; and hence, the first two periods of the Council (1545–48, 1551–52) focused on Germany, while the third (1562–63) concentrated on France. Trent confirmed the divisions of Christendom:

rejected by Protestants, the Council witnessed the presence of the German Church only in 1551–52, when the three archbishop-electors (Cologne, Mainz, and Trier) and a dozen German bishops attended the congregations. The Lutheran Church superintendent of Brunswick, Martin Chemnitz, spoke for his co-religionists when he decried the Council as "unfree and popish" in his polemic work, *An Examination of the Council of Trent* (4 parts, 1564–74).

Indeed, the Council did meet under the authority of the pope, and it focused on the reform of the members of the Church, leaving the reform of its head to the Roman curia itself. While Pius IV promulgated the decrees and canons of the Council in June 1564, the reform of the curia proceeded slowly and unevenly due to strong entrenched interests, as we shall see in the following chapters. Nevertheless, the spirit of reform finally prevailed in Rome: four of the seven remaining popes of the sixteenth century were participants at the Council (Gregory XIII, 1572–85; and the three successive popes Urban VII, Gregory XIV, and Innocent IX, 1590–91). The various national delegates carried back with them the determination of reform, where the process of Catholic renewal made most uneven progress during the next century.

2 The new religious orders

One of the most vigorous defenders of papal authority at the Council of Trent was the Spaniard Alfonso Salmerón (1517–85), theologian at the papal court and member of a new religious order, the Society of Jesus. A young student at the Sorbonne in 1533, the seventeen-year-old Salmerón, who did not speak French, quickly joined the company of an older countryman. The compatriot, Iñigo of Loyola, a Basque nobleman, aged forty-two, had given up a military career after sustaining a serious leg injury in battle in 1521.

During his long convalescence Iñigo underwent a profound crisis. Inspired by his readings on the saints and Jesus, Iñigo renounced his former life as a cavalier, with its code of honor and fantasies of chivalric glory. His conversion to religious asceticism was further strengthened by a vision of the Virgin Mary; and Iñigo abandoned his noble clothes at the Marian shrine of Monserrat for the rough habit of a pilgrim. Though determined to travel on foot to Barcelona, then by ship to Italy and the Holy Land, Iñigo stayed on as a hermit in Manresa, his body ravaged by fever and his soul plunged into despair by prolonged meditation. Saved by a powerful vision, he recovered and traveled on to Jerusalem. Upon his return to Spain in 1523, Iñigo pondered his future and decided to study for the priesthood. Enrolled as a student at Alcala, Iñigo preached among the poor women of the town until he was arrested by the Inquisition. His charismatic personality, nourished by his mystical experiences, attracted a devout following, which reminded the inquisitors of the *alumbrados*, a small group of Spanish mystics recently condemned for heresy. When his name was cleared, Iñigo transferred to the University of Salamanca and in 1528 pursued his theological studies in France.

In Paris, Iñigo, or Ignatius as he would start calling himself, attracted around him a small group of foreign students dedicated to his charismatic vision of an ascetic apostolic life: there was Francis Xavier, a Basque nobleman like Ignatius, Pierre Favre, whose father was a humble shepherd in Savoy, the Spaniards Diego Laínez, who had *converso* or Jewish ancestors, Alfonso Salmerón, Nicolas de Bobadilla, and the Portuguese

Simão Rodrigues. They were soon joined by three Frenchmen – Claude Jay, Paschase Broët, and Jean Codure. Ignatius was the spiritual leader. Drawing on his own mystical experiences, he guided his companions on a rigorous program of meditation and self-examination, which was later published as *The Spiritual Exercises*. From Paris, the group set out for Rome in 1537 to obtain papal blessing for a pilgrimage to the Holy Land. The fame of the ascetic Basque nobleman had spread from Spain to Italy; and the group was well received in Rome, thanks to the patronage of the Spanish clerics and ambassador. Ordained priests in June 1537, Ignatius and his followers were received by Pope Paul III, who told them that their Jerusalem was in Rome. Having dedicated themselves to absolute obedience to the pope, Ignatius and his followers founded a new religious order, the Society of Jesus, in order to imitate the work of the early apostles in preaching the faith. In 1540 the new religious order counted ten members. Sixteen years later, at the death of Ignatius, the Jesuits would number 1,000. They soon became the most important force in Catholic renewal.

For the Catholic world, the sixteenth century witnessed a renewed fervor in the founding of religious orders. While the Society of Jesus became the most significant order in early modern Catholicism, it was by no means the only one. Feeding on the energy of religious renewal that preceded the Protestant Reformation, the Catholic reform planted new seeds of growth in the fertile soils of Spain and Italy. Other new male religious orders sprang up: the Capuchins began as a renegade movement of reform within the Observant Franciscans and grew into an order second in importance only to the Jesuits; the Theatines, co-founded by the future Pope Paul IV, embodied a spirit of asceticism so lacking in the established orders; the Barnabites, Somaschi, and other smaller communities flourished primarily in Italy; the Lazarists, a preaching order, were founded by St. Vincent de Paul (1580–1660) in Paris; and finally, a cluster of new female religious orders – the Angelics, Ursulines, Visitadines, English Sisters – won grudging acceptance by the male ecclesiastical hierarchy, and took their places alongside the reformed convents of Carmelites, Benedictines, and Franciscan Tertiaries.

The Congregation of Clerks Regular, the Theatines, was founded in Rome in 1524 with Carafa (later Paul IV) as the first superior. Their title came from Carafa, who had been bishop of Chieti (*Theate* in Latin). Dedicated to the ministry and liturgical reform, the Theatines grew rapidly in Italy and reached their greatest strength during the first half of the seventeenth century, with forty-six communities in 1644. They attracted both noblemen and artisans, and enjoyed limited reception in

Catholic Europe outside Italy. Like the Theatines, the Barnabites were also founded as an ascetic and reforming order. The Clerks Regular of St. Paul took their name from the church of St. Barnabas in Milan, where it was founded in 1530 by Antonio Zaccaria. The Clerks Regular of Somascha was founded in 1528 by the layman Girolamo Emiliani in Venice to care for orphans; approved by Paul III in 1540, the order at first included both laity and clergy; it was briefly merged with the Theatines (1540–55). All these new orders shared certain characteristics, in spite of differences in styles: they originated and flourished in the cities of northern and central Italy, a region ravaged by warfare between the Habsburgs and the Valois for the first half of the sixteenth century; they addressed the ills of the urban society around them, ministering to the poor, orphans, and destitute women; they enjoyed noble and patrician patronage, for by their work they repaired the torn social fabric of corporate society, redistributing its material and spiritual capital between rich and poor; and finally, by their personal asceticism they represented a counter-example to the laxity and worldliness of established orders.

Indeed, with the Protestant Reformation the traditional religious orders faced a momentous crisis. Many had embarked on a course of reform in the fifteenth century, returning to a stricter observance of the Rules of St. Benedictine, St. Dominic, and St. Francis. This movement of monastic reform divided many, as the Observants, as they came to be called, embodied rigor and discipline over the Conventuals. The Reformation dealt a severe blow: the Augustinians, Luther's order, lost nearly all of their houses in England and Germany, and recovered largely due to the leadership of Girolamo Seripando; the Benedictines lost some 800 out of 3,000 monasteries; and the Conventual Franciscans lost friaries and personnel throughout the sixteenth century. Yet recovery was quick after the Council of Trent. The seventeenth century witnessed a reinvigoration of the established religious orders: Benedictine reform radiated out from nuclei of exemplary monasteries – St. Vanne and St. Maur in France, Valladolid in Spain – and culminated in the foundation of a Benedictine university in Salzburg in 1617; the Dominicans, staunch defenders of Rome against the early Reformation, had maintained their strength during the sixteenth century, providing 130 bishops and theologians at the Council of Trent, and, by staffing the Inquisition and promulgating the Index, defended Catholic orthodoxy; the Franciscans, split into reform and conventual branches in 1517, witnessed a proliferation of reform houses, represented by the Discalced Franciscans in Spain, the Recollects in France, and the Reformed in Italy. While these reform movements stayed within the larger Observant family, the Capuchins broke free and became a driving force in the Catholic renewal, second in significance only to the Jesuits.

The Capuchins began as a renegade movement within the Italian Observant community. In 1525, Fra Matteo da Bascio left the monastery of Montefalcone, dissatisfied with the lax observance of the Rule of St. Francis. Within a few years, he was joined by other friars, who also yearned for a still stricter observance of poverty in imitation of their founding father St. Francis. Abandoning the solid friaries in town and comforting meals in the refectory, these men sought refuge in the wilderness and begged for their daily bread. When they appeared in towns to preach repentance, they were greeted as *scapuccini* (hermits) and the name stuck to this group of wandering hermits. Against strong opposition from the Observants, the Capuchins obtained papal recognition in 1528, due to the support of Caterina Cibo, the duchess of Camerino, who protected the renegade friars. Indeed, the first Capuchins from the wilderness of the Marches of Ancona flourished under the protection of powerful urban noble families: the duchess of Camerino was a niece of Pope Clement VII; Vittoria Colonna, another patron and a leading voice in Catholic reform, hailed from one of the most powerful aristocratic Roman clans; other protectors included the duke of Nocera, viceroy of Naples, and other noble families such as the Orsinis who constituted the core of the papal curia.

From the wilderness of Ancona and Calabria, the birthplaces of the Capuchins, the order spread rapidly throughout Italy, counting some 700 friars during the 1530s, attracting many Observants disappointed with the lack of reform within their order. Their dress and actions exemplified their asceticism: with habits of rough fabric and distinctive hoods, barefoot or sandaled, the Capuchins begged for food and lived in makeshift hermitages. Embodying the renewal of Franciscan spirituality, the Capuchins endeared themselves to the common people by their works of charity, caring for the sick, feeding the poor, and preaching the simple message of the Gospels. The order survived the defection of its general, Fra Bernardino Ochino, who fled to Geneva in 1542 when summoned by Pope Paul IV to Rome on suspicion of Protestant sympathies. Recovering from this disastrous shock, the Capuchins continued to grow under the patronage of both lay and ecclesiastical elites, among the latter Cardinal Carafa (Paul IV), Bishop Giberti of Verona, and Cardinal Francesco Gonzaga. In 1574 Pope Gregory XIII granted permission for the Capuchins to expand beyond Italy; in 1587 they numbered almost 6,000.

The years 1580 to 1650 saw the height of their success. The activities of the Capuchins reflected the wide spectrum of class and talent embodied in the order; whereas in France and central Europe they embodied spiritual fighters in the Counter-Reformation, in Italy they distinguished themselves in works of charity. Their engagement in an age of plagues won the Capuchins widespread support: in 1576–77 they aided Archbishop Carlo Borromeo in caring for the thousands afflicted by the plague in Milan, and took over the hospitals for lepers where the ill were consigned when the rich and powerful fled the city; in 1629, when a more calamitous epidemic swept Italy, they mobilized for charity, nursing the sick and comforting the dying, while succumbing themselves in droves – forty-seven out of two hundred friars in the province of Brescia, fifty-one out of ninety-two enlisted friars in Tuscany, twelve in Milan, twelve in Parma, and eighteen in Piacenza; during the 1636 plague in Burgundy more than eighty Capuchins died caring for the sick. The Capuchins also succored the poor and hungry: in Italian towns, they helped establish the *bottega di Cristo* (shop of Christ) to sell subsidized foodstuffs, communal granaries for times of famine, and *monti di pietà* for interest-free loans. To pry loose donations from the rich, they scourged the conscience of the powerful in sermons. To instill piety in the simple folk, they embarked on extended preaching tours to rural areas, addressing the unlettered in Italian, illustrating the lessons of the Gospels in plain language. These preaching tours reached a climax during the seventeenth century, when whole towns and villages were called to march in penitential procession. During the preaching tours, confraternities were organized, sins were confessed, the forty-hour eucharistic devotion promoted; in these moments of religious revival, Capuchin preachers temporarily healed the many social schisms, reconciling parents and children, rich and poor, and feuding factions. Their success lay in transforming the emotions of a Catholic society of orders while leaving essentially intact its structures of power.

For this reason, perhaps, the Capuchins gained the favor of popes, emperors, kings, and princes, and attracted, in turn, many noble recruits: they served as chaplains in the papal fleet at Lepanto (1571) and in the imperial armies in the 1590s during the Turkish wars; their churches in Lorraine served as ducal burial places; their ranks included the count of Bouchage, Henri de Joyeuse, close companion to Henri III of France, Alfonso III, duke of Modena, and the brothers William and John, Lord Forbes, peers of Scotland; they played leading roles in the theater of European diplomacy during the Thirty Years War, sometimes at cross purposes, when Joseph le clerc du Tremblay (Cardinal Richelieu's confessor), Valeriano Magni, Lorenzo da Brindisi, and Giacinto da Casale ran the thread of negotiations between Habsburg, Bourbon, and Wittelsbach interests. Together with the Jesuits, they hammered away at the gains of Protestantism in northern Europe, converting the duchy of

Chablais at the frontier with Geneva and sustaining Catholics in Ireland and Scotland. Grey friars and black robe: the Capuchins and Jesuits became emblematic religious orders of the Catholic renewal.

Unlike traditional religious orders, the Jesuits did not share a communal liturgical life; instead of divine offices, chants, and prayers within a communal convent, their priority was to preach and minister, in streets, hospitals, prisons, and in foreign lands. Theirs was a mobile company, dedicated to the spread of the Catholic faith in imitation of the early apostles. Their departure from tradition and their very name earned the Jesuits both fervent supporters and implacable enemies within the Church. Some saw them as tools of papal supremacy; others suspected their work among prostitutes; still others resented their intrusion into pastoral work. Also unlike the established religious orders, the Society of Jesus was highly centralized. Ignatius, by virtue of his personality, exercised strong control as the first elected general of the order. The constitutions of the Jesuits, hammered out during his lifetime, provided for a centralized yet highly flexible structure: the diverse nature of their work and the geographic dispersion of their missions necessitated measures to give coherence to a rapidly expanding order. By means of letters and annual reports, the general in Rome directed, as it were, a vast array of troops who battled for Christ in far-flung regions (Ignatius wrote more than 8,000 letters during his generalship!). Moreover, individual Jesuits underwent periodic retreats, guided by the *Spiritual Exercises* of Ignatius; their *esprit de corps* was further fortified by memory of the founding father, who acquired mythic status shortly after his death in ritual remembrance through his writings, his tomb, and pious biographies.

Of their many contributions to Catholic renewal, two roles stood out for the Jesuits: as missionaries and teachers. In 1540 Francis Xavier embarked on a Portuguese ship to India and became the first in a long line of Jesuit missionaries to the non-European world. He was followed by others during the next two centuries of Catholic renewal. Jesuits from all European countries went on missions: in Japan they converted thousands, sponsored the first Asian embassy to Europe in 1584, and suffered many martyrdoms during the seventeenth century; in China they brought European culture to the imperial courts and created, together with their literati converts, a synthesis of Christian faith and Confucian ethics; in Spanish and Portuguese America, they ministered to the native populations, often protecting them against predatory colonists; in North America, India, and wherever they journeyed, they became ethnographers, learning the indigenous languages, observing and describing the customs and politics of the land. Closer to home, Jesuit missionaries went on preaching tours in the countryside in Italy and France, explaining the faith, combating folk beliefs, and reconciling feuding factions; they established Catholic missions in Protestant territories, succoring the Catholic populations in the Netherlands, North Germany, and Ireland; they embarked on journeys into hostile realms, sometimes in the wake of Catholic arms as in Bohemia, at other times at grave personal risk as in England. In the two centuries after the Council of Trent, they expanded the Catholic world to non-Christian lands while rolling back the frontiers of Protestant Europe.

The glamor and spectacle of missions and martyrdom notwithstanding, the major achievement of the Jesuits lay elsewhere, in educating the clerical and lay elites of Catholic Europe. During the first decade of their existence, individual Jesuits were invited to lecture at universities. The need to train the flood of new recruits and their spreading fame soon led to the establishment of colleges. At Gandía, Messina, Palermo, and Cologne, the first Jesuit colleges were founded. In 1551, the Roman College was established with the inscription "School of Grammar, Humanities, and Christian Doctrine, free." It became the main training institution for future Jesuits. From then on, the leadership of the Society threw their energy into education. Requests and offers poured in from all over Europe. Endowed by princes, prelates, city governments, merchants, and rich laypeople, some thirty-five colleges were in operation by 1556, the year of Ignatius's death. The numbers exploded thereafter: 144 colleges in 1579, 444 colleges plus 100 seminaries and schools in 1626, 669 colleges plus 176 seminaries and schools in 1749. On the eve of its suppression in 1773, the Society had established more than 800 colleges in the Catholic world, spreading from Macao in South China to Lima in Peru, engaging the substantial part of the Society's personnel and educating both Catholics and Protestants.

For the Jesuits themselves, the colleges provided a steady stream of recruits: the 1,000 members of 1556 became 3,500 in 1565, 15,500 in 1626, 20,000 in 1710, and 22,600 in 1749. Other students at Jesuit educational institutions were destined for the secular clergy, such as those trained in the English, Irish, and German Colleges in Rome, which were entrusted to the Jesuits. Still other students graduated to pursue secular vocations, becoming princes, officials, and lawyers, filling the ranks of the ruling elites in Catholic lands. In northern Europe, not a few Protestant youngsters attended these colleges, and some converted to Catholicism. On the whole, the Jesuit colleges recruited their students from the middling to upper classes of society. The curriculum provided for a classical education in Latin and Greek, plus a heavy dose of Catholic theology and ethics. It is easy to imagine the attraction of Jesuit schools: tuition was free, instruction rigorous, and prestige enormous. There, future prelates, princes, and professors hobnobbed, learning the "Jesuit way of proceeding" – memorizing their Latin, striving to excel, and undergoing the *Spiritual Exercises*. Famous alumni were legend: Emperor Ferdinand II, Duke Maximilian II of Bavaria, Cardinal Richelieu, Justus Lipsius, and René Descartes, just to name a few. For many bishops, Jesuit colleges served as substitutes for the diocesan seminaries stipulated by the reforms of Trent, which were often not established due to the lack of funding; Jesuit colleges became the yeast to leaven the bread of the secular clergy. For princes, the Jesuits schooled sons of the nobility and the bourgeoisie for service, training loyal and pious servants to the Catholic states. For city governments, Jesuit colleges provided Latin education at a bargain; in exchange for donations, the instructors came self-supported and provided free tuition for local boys, who entered the doors of the colleges into the vast network of patronage in the wider Catholic world.

The colleges also shaped the activities of the Jesuits. To train students in Latin rhetoric, professors wrote plays in Latin, drawing themes from the classical repertoire, from early Church history, and even from contemporary events of conversion and confessional confrontation. Many hundreds of these plays were written; produced every school year, Jesuit theater represented Catholic renewal in vivid histrionic symbols. To the multitude of sponsors, parents, students, and citizens, the Jesuit spectacle represented a quintessential truth in the unfolding of Catholic faith, a symbolic revelation visible here and there in historical events of the real world.

In that external world of Catholic renewal, as royal confessors the Jesuits shaped the interior universe of its rulers: they had access to the consciences of all French kings, from Henri III to Louis XV, to all German emperors after Ferdinand II, with William Lamormaini as a crucial political advisor during the Thirty Years War, to all dukes of Bavaria after Maximilian II, to most rulers of Portugal and Poland, and to the Spanish Bourbon kings during the eighteenth century. Their enterprise represented the militant and masculinist face of Catholic renewal, a sharp contrast to the gender roles expected of religious women.

The Council of Trent signified a turning point for the history of religious women. In 1566 the papal bull *Circa pastoralis*, issued by Pius V, reinforced the 1563 reform decree of Session XXV, Cap. V: it called for the enclosure of all female religious communities, including Third Order and hitherto exempted convents of nuns. This simple and straightforward injunction belied the social complexities of female religiosity, and provoked determined resistance well into the next century. Behind the enclosure injunction was the desire to segregate the holy from the profane, an impulse central to the entire endeavor of the Catholic renewal. It animated the reform decrees that excoriated the secular lives of clerics; it inspired the canons that purified the sacramental practices of the Church from profane abuse. At the heart of this segregation of the holy and the profane was sexuality: the Catholic clergy's authority over the flock rested on its avowed sexual abstinence, the frequent violations of which became the cause of lay resentment and scandal; clerical celibacy thus distinguished the Catholic clergy from their Protestant counterparts, who hailed marriage as a godly institution if not a sacrament of the Church.

Two motives thus underlay the reform of female convents in post-Tridentine Catholicism: the ecclesiastical hierarchy aimed at the stricter enclosure of nuns to protect them (and their chastity) from the evils of the world; upper-class families sought to preserve their wealth in the stringent marriage market by placing surplus daughters in convents, where female chastity and family honor could be safeguarded. Neither one of these goals was new. The Tridentine reforms, however, brought into sharper focus the potential conflict between these two goals. The rule of enclosure, as we shall see, was strongly contested by elite families, who saw convents as extensions of their social milieu; they resented the inaccessible walls, the iron grids, the parlatory screens that restricted communication between the nuns and their kin. Growing up in Avila, the young Teresa remembered her novice years in the Carmelite convent of her own town, where friends and relatives visited frequently, exchanging news and gossip. The convent was a special social space for upper-class women: servants and laysisters attended to manual work; sisters enjoyed individual rooms furnished by their families; plays, music, and dances were performed; and a constant stream of visitors led occasionally to scandal and rumor. Turning away from this liminal existence between living in the world and living in the convent – devoid of the ultimate pleasures of both flesh and soul – Teresa plunged into a life racked by illness and mystical transports. She poured her energies into convent reform, founding Discalced Carmelite houses of strict enclosure and asceticism. Traveling all over Spain in the last decades of her life, Teresa became the embodiment of the ideal female religious, tirelessly (and visibly) rendering women invisible in enclosed and reformed convents.

Teresa's success lay in her ability to reconcile two potentially conflicting interests in convent life: the male clerical impulse for control and the elites' appetite for honor. The Catholic renewal of the sixteenth century fashioned a tighter male control of female religiosity: social hierarchies were strengthened both in the social division of the new female religious orders and within the ranks of the convent; and a Mediterranean model of female religiosity, with greater male supervision and impulse toward enclosure, displaced the late medieval model so well embodied by the beguinages – the autonomous and open communities of pious women of northern Europe – in an indeterminate zone between enclosed religiosity and secular family life. Unlike late medieval piety, the religious energies inspired by the Catholic reform flowed in gendered channels, as we will see in a brief examination of the new female religious orders of Catholic Europe.

The Angelics of San Paolo, founded in 1535 at Milan as an unenclosed order, exemplified in its transformation the larger history of female religiosity in Catholic Europe. As the sister order to the Barnabites, the early Angelics included women from a diversity of background: Ludovica Torelli, a twice-widowed countess, who provided the finances for the fledgling order; Paola Antonia Negri, mystic and spiritual mother; and a mixture of professed and lay women and young girls. United in their dedication to a common pious life, the Angelics mingled closely with the Barnabites, sharing at times a common family bond, with husbands and wives, brothers and sisters, joined in the movement of religious revival. In their initial enthusiasm, the Angelics and Barnabites discussed spiritual matters, examined conscience, and humiliated themselves in public penitential processions. Their intermingling, their public personae, and the spiritual authority of Mother Paola over male clerics got the new orders into trouble: in 1536 they were investigated by the Inquisition on suspicion of the heresy of the Beghards; and in 1551–52, the "Spiritual Mother" was removed and imprisoned, the Barnabites and Angelics were separated, and the latter were put under enclosure.

The Angelics were transformed: appointed by the archbishop of Milan, a male cleric replaced the authority of the original female leadership; the social and age diversity of the first generation gave way to a narrower band of professed nuns from elite families; and the Angelics forsook charity in the streets of Milan for cloistered piety behind their walls and grill. The danger they posed, it has been argued, lay in the scandal of public female power – a countess parading in penitential clothes in open streets, a divine mother dispensing advice to priests who threw themselves at her feet. Thus domesticated, the Angelics became a paradigm for post-Tridentine female religious orders: after enclosure, age at profession narrowed from the range of thirteen to forty-five to the range of seventeen to twenty-five; social divisions were introduced between the laysisters from lowly families who did the manual work and the noble nuns whose families paid a handsome dowry for their entry.

Founded in neighboring Brescia, the Ursulines escaped enclosure. In

1532 a Franciscan tertiary, Angela Merici (1470/75?–1540), moved into a room with her spiritual daughters; three years later there were twenty-eight women in her group who came together for mass and prayer. The Company of St. Ursula flourished in a commune where mixed lay–clerical confraternities dedicated themselves to hospitals, orphanages, and halfway houses for prostitutes. The first Ursulines consisted of women from artisanal or mercantile backgrounds, who became patrons to poor or orphaned girls; they resembled the beguines of northern Europe, holding modest properties in common, living in communities or with their families, taking a simple vow of chastity and donning a habit. Numbering among themselves both married women and virgins (guided by priests), the Ursulines grew to 150 in 1539; they lived according to simple rules written by Merici, who warned the virgins in her will against male confessors and religious.

Thanks to the more humble origins of the Ursulines, in 1544 they resisted successfully an attempt to transform the order into an enclosed convent. In 1556 the Ursulines became a female affiliate of the Fathers of the Company of Peace: although the original autonomous structure gave way to obedience to male religious authority, the Ursulines also gained greater ecclesiastical recognition and the company grew rapidly in size. The Ursulines' active charity – visiting hospitals, teaching catechism – saved them from further pressure at enclosure. They even won the support of Archbishop Carlo Borromeo, who sponsored a company of Ursulines in Milan in 1566 to teach catechism to girls. In Milan the Ursulines again recruited primarily from the artisans: the typical dowry brought by an Ursuline averaged 250 lire, whereas a dowry for entrance into convents ranged from 1,000 to 3,000 lire, depending on the social prestige of the institution. In this early phase of development in Italy, the Ursulines served as a social counterpart to the established convents with their clientele from elite families, providing instead a religious institution for women from modest social backgrounds, who lived in unenclosed communities or at home and engaged in teaching and charity. From Milan, the movement spread to Avignon, where the reform circle around the Fathers of the Christian Doctrine became its main supporters. From Avignon new foundations spread to France during the seventeenth century: in Bordeaux the Ursulines adopted Jesuit rules and became the mother house for a series of new communities in Belgium and Germany; in Paris the order assumed a distinctly aristocratic character under the patronage of two noble widows, Madame Acarie and Madame de Sainte-Beuve, who had been active in introducing the Discalced Carmelites (St. Teresa's order) into France. Founded in 1607, the Ursulines at the Faubourg St. Jacques acquired a noble aura, providing boarding and instruction for girls of the nobility; the majority of the 114 nuns between 1614 and 1662 came from the nobility and the elevated bourgeoisie.

The two tendencies – enclosure and Jesuit rules – reflected contradictory developments in the history of the Ursulines: their success among the social elites increased pressures for enclosure, but their dedication to an active apostolic life inspired them to imitate the Jesuits. Both these tendencies were at work in northern Europe. Anne de Xainctonge (1567–1621), daughter of a Dijonais councilor, dedicated herself to teaching catechism "in imitation of St. Ignatius" and founded an unenclosed Ursuline community in 1609 in Dole for the free education of girls; her sister Françoise had earlier founded an Ursuline house in 1605 at Dijon, which was later enclosed in 1619. Other female religious orders also imitated the Jesuits: encouraged by the example of "the holy father Ignatius" Alix le Clerc (1576–1622), daughter of a rich Lorraine merchant, established the Congregation of Notre Dame, a teaching order. She rejected enclosure, resisting the archbishop's effort in 1603 and turning down an offer from the Paris Ursulines to join their community. In 1618 Alix and her followers received papal approval for their unenclosed order; in 1640 the order counted forty-eight houses in Lorraine, Savoy, France, and Germany.

Female religious represented both danger and potential for the male ecclesiastical hierarchy. Three rules seemed necessary before founders of the new female religious orders won acceptance from the Church: support of male clerics, piety without pretensions to authority, and class standing. Among the female imitators of St. Ignatius, the Englishwoman Mary Ward (1585–1646) came closest to breaking these rules. Of Yorkshire gentry, in 1606 Mary Ward went to the college of the English Jesuits at St. Omer in the Spanish Netherlands as a Catholic refugee; in neighboring Gravelines, she founded a St. Clare's convent for English women. The idea to establish a new religious order came in a 1609 vision, but her desire "to take the same [path as] the Society" was roundly rejected by the Jesuits. Nevertheless, Ward and her followers established a teaching order in 1611 for English Catholic girls in exile on the Continent; they adopted the educational rules of the Jesuits and won papal approbation in 1616. New houses were founded in Liège (1616), Cologne (1620), Trier (1621), Rome (1622), Naples (1623), and Perugia (1624) for the "English sisters."

Ward went to Rome in 1621, with a letter of introduction from Archduchess Isabella of the Spanish Netherlands; she was received by Pope Gregory XV and Vitelleschi, general of the Jesuits, who refused Ward the use of their name. Her independence led to the suppression of the Italian houses in 1625; but Ward journeyed north to establish new communities in Munich, Vienna (both 1627), Pressburg, and Prague (both 1628). Despite protection from the Bavarian duke and the emperor, hostility toward her project continued within the Society of Jesus; Johannes Herennius, provincial of the Gallo-Belgian province (with jurisdiction over St. Omer) complained to the general in Rome about Ward's plan to teach Latin in "women Jesuit colleges"; they were dismissed as "galloping girls" and "wandering nuns." In 1630 the houses in Belgium and lower Germany were suppressed; in 1631 she was imprisoned for two months in Munich by order of the Inquisition; a papal bull of the same year forbade "women or virgins to assume the name of Jesuits." After her release, Ward abandoned the idea of an order of Jesuitesses and transformed the houses into secular teaching communities for girls. She returned to England in 1637 and died near York.

Other smaller female teaching orders thrived due to Jesuit support: the Catherine nuns founded by Regina Protmann (1552–1613) enjoyed the support of Cardinal Hosius and the Ermland Jesuits; the Company of St. Ursula in Cologne, founded by the widow Ida Schnabel in 1606, resembled the early Ursulines in Brescia and grew out of a Jesuit Marian sodality. Among the early Cologne Ursulines, several were important patrons of the Jesuits; between 1618 and 1629 they contributed to the building of five altars in the Jesuit Church. Jesuit support, however, came at a price: the new rules adopted in 1646 strengthened the authority of the Jesuit father confessor at the expense of the abbess, Ida Schnabel; removed from her position for disobedience, Schnabel and her supporters eventually submitted to the new regime.

For religious women of Catholic Europe, the twin impulses of the Catholic renewal – control and innovation – came to direct conflict. In the end submission to the Church mattered more than religious zeal, an injunction to be obeyed not only by Mary Ward but also by François de Sales and Jeanne de Chantal, declared saints of the Church. The Visitadines, established in 1610 at Annecy by a bishop of Geneva for a baroness, could not escape the fate of enclosure in 1618, despite the strenuous objection of Chantal and François de Sales's negotiations with Rome. Thereafter, the Visitadines or Visitation nuns enjoyed great success among the elites, with 149 houses (mostly in France and Lorraine) founded during the seventeenth century. Sponsored by the ducal house of Savoy, the mother houses at Annecy attracted the most prominent visitors – Elizabeth de Vendôme, duchess of Genevais-Nemours and her two daughters, future duchess of Savoy and queen of Portugal. All nuns at the mother house at Annecy between 1610 and 1792 came from elite families: of the 300 nuns, 166 came from the nobility, 134 from the upper bourgeoisie (50 percent in service to the state, mostly legal officials, and 20 percent merchant families) – the two exclusive social groups that constituted only 4–5 percent of the Savoyard population. The picture of opulence was completed by the presence of domestics and extensive land ownership, making the Visitadines a privileged religious order.

The danger of social exclusivity, which the Visitadines seemed to have escaped, was laxity and worldliness, leading, perhaps, to scandal. Such was the case with female monasteries in Naples during the seventeenth century. During the tenure of Archbishop Ascanio Filomarino (1641–66), the first visitations were carried out in the urban monasteries. The reports revealed a picture of convent life little affected by the injunctions of the Council of Trent: young girls without religious vocations were placed in convents by families unwilling or unable to pay their dowries; in St. Chiara, the nuns performed comedies in spite of archiepiscopal injunction; in Donna Regina, two noble nuns entertained their female and male relatives (including a "scandalous lady" dressed as a man) at supper with music and a play; still other convents had windows, belvederes, and campanili, where cloistered nuns could look out into the streets, violating the spirit if not the letter of enclosure. Archbishop Filomarino failed to enforce a stricter monastic discipline; there was too much entrenched social interest against reform. The obstacle to religious rigorism was succinctly described by the seventeenth-century Venetian nun Arcangela: the nobility and the Venetian Senate colluded in forcing girls into convents because an oversupply of marriage-age girls would be prejudicial to the "reason of state" as there would be an excess of new noble lineages and the rising dowry market would ruin many noble families. Given the marital regime of the ruling elites, cloistered life had to be made tolerable for the many upper-class women (some 20 percent according to one estimate) condemned to a life of enforced chastity and enclosure.

There are four themes one can draw from this cursory examination of the history of female religious orders in Catholic Europe. I shall call them paired saintliness, the women's question, engendered sanctity, and enclosure and transport.

Paired saintliness. As I have argued above, the cooperation of male and female was indispensable in the success of the new female religious orders. In fact, the examples we have seen reflected a parallel or paired effort at the construction of religiosity. The Barnabites and Angelics were paired until 1552, led by their respective founders Antonio Zaccaria and Ludovica Torelli; the Ursulines were similarly wed, so to speak, to various male clerical orders – the Fathers of the Company of Peace in Brescia, the

Fathers of the Christian Doctrine in Avignon, and later the Jesuits in France. In many cases, the founding mothers shared the limelight with founding fathers; such was the case with Jeanne Françoise de Chantal and François de Sales. In other examples, the sanctity of founding mothers was shaped and in turn fired the piety of male clerics, be they confessors or spiritual directors, as the relationship of Teresa of Avila superbly demonstrates. Central to this paired sanctity was the force of Catholic renewal: the spirit of reform arose directly from experiences in the secular world; and the continuity of family ties wove a thousand threads between the secular and religious realms. Two examples should suffice. The close ties between the Ursulines of Paris and the Jesuits rested on sibling ties: Marie Coton (1597–1654), abbess of the Ursulines of St. Jacques, was the sister of the Jesuit Pierre Coton; theirs was a noble family from Lyons. The Spanish beata María Agreda (1602–65), Discalced Franciscan, mystic, author of *The Mystical City of God*, and venerated by King Philip IV, came from a deeply religious family: her mother Caterina had convinced her father Francisco to renounce their marriage, whereupon mother and daughter entered the Discalced Franciscans while father and sons became Observants.

The women's question. Religious choices for women, it seemed, hinged more on family than it was the case for men. Life cycle and family standing structured female religiosity: among elite families, young girls boarded at prestigious schools until they reached puberty when vocation as much as family strategy dictated their future in the marriage market or cloistered life. For those who married, widowhood offered another chance at the religious life, a choice made more attractive by the greater resources available to widows from the elite. The convent also provided a haven for battered wives, if they were of sufficient social standing, who could petition the bishop for admission as laypersons. For girls and women from the lower social orders, the Ursulines offered a religious life within their financial means; they lived and worked at home, keeping company with other religious women without having to raise a dowry for the spiritual marriage required of upper-class women. Their pious work gave aid to the poor, whose ranks were disproportionately filled with women, thus joining Catholic charity and female piety, and closing the social circle at its weakest link. One should note, however, that the experimentation during the early years of Catholic reform, when women of different classes, stations, and ages joined in pious communities, gave way during the 1550s to a stricter regime of classification and control. Catholic Europe divided women into estates: virgins, spouses, unhappy wives (*malmarite*), public women, reformed prostitutes (*converte*), and widows. In this classificatory scheme, gender, as such, did not matter as much as female sexuality.

Engendered sanctity. Chastity had always been upheld in Christianity as the ideal for female religiosity, but during the Middle Ages the marital state was not an obstacle to sainthood. Enforcing clerical celibacy as one of its primary tasks, the Counter-Reformation Church placed chastity above all other attributes for female religiosity. Sermons, treatises, and books lauded early Christian women martyrs who defended their virginity: Agnes, Agatha, Cecilia, Thekla, Catherine of Alexandria, Ursula, and the 11,000 virgins of Cologne shone as exempla for the nuns of early modern Europe.

Enclosure and transport. To protect chastity, urban convents had to be enclosed and rural ones moved within city walls, in order "to protect the nuns from the evil men that roam," as Carlo Borromeo put it. Enclosure, as we have seen, met with considerable resistance; in this regard the Church hierarchy met with only moderate success. Asceticism and enclosure succeeded best when the will to reform came from within the convent, as the examples of the Discalced Carmelites and the Ursulines showed. Within these enclosed convents mysticism flourished: the tighter space of female monasticism encouraged a stricter discipline of the body – with fasting, scourging, and other means of self-mortification – while nourishing a vivid life of the soul; as walls and grills in convents shut off the outside world, in mystical visions the privileged few saw into infinity. Teresa's vision transcended the confines of time and space, allowing her to see people and actions far from her; and María Agreda saw herself transported from Spain to Mexico preaching to the Indians. The realm of the imagined promised to lie beyond the reach of male control, or so it seemed; but, as we will see in chapter 9, the supervision of the Catholic Church extended even to the innermost visions of women in early modern Europe.

3 The triumphant Church

In the Catholic body afflicted, with limbs withered by Protestant heresy, only the heart stood between demise and recovery. That heart, for early modern Catholicism, was beating strongly in the Iberian peninsula and in Italy, sending a flow of fresh blood to rejuvenate the diseased members of the Catholic body. In the western Mediterranean and in Atlantic Portugal, the triumphant Church kept Protestant infection at bay while spreading Catholic allegiance to Africa, Asia, and the Americas through explorations, conquests, and missions. The vast majority of Counter-Reformation saints came from this triumphant Catholicism, as did most of the new religious orders.

Yet a difference in style distinguished Catholic renewal in its Italian and Iberian varieties. Catholic missionaries in seventeenth-century China described an Italian "gentleness [*suavitas*]" in contrast to the uncompromising inflexibility of Spanish methods, a difference due no doubt to the Spanish experience of imperial conquest. Catholic renewal in Italy seemed to inspire greater devotion to charity. By pricking the conscience of the rich and powerful, religious fervor offered aid to the poor, orphans, and widows, thus renewing the economy of Catholic salvation and strengthening the order of society. Catholic renewal in the Iberian peninsula seemed to harden the boundaries of faith. The Inquisition in Spain and Portugal combated Protestant contagion from outside and enemies of the faith from within. Europe was mesmerized by the images of this Iberian Catholicism: the secret procedures of the Holy Office of the Inquisition, its ostentatious ceremonies of reconciliation and condemnations (the *autos de fe*), and the number of victims (vastly exaggerated). Historians have mined the largely intact archives of the Iberian Inquisitions to reconstruct its manifold operations. Repression, however, was only one feature in Iberian Catholicism; it existed alongside the many expressions of religious fervor that characterized the Catholic renewal. Moreover, the Inquisition was also vigilant against religious crimes in Italy, although its history is less well known due to the fragmentary survival of records (those of the Roman Inquisition remain inaccessible; the archives of other tribunals are extant only in part). The existence of the Inquisition also distinguished the Spanish–Portuguese empires and Italy from other Catholic countries, its unique mix of political and religious concerns became representative of a triumphant Catholicism.

Portugal

Bartolomeu dos Martires, archbishop of Braga, played a leading role in the last period of the Council of Trent, as we have seen. Portugal, not surprisingly, was also one of the first countries to accept the Tridentine decrees. A maritime and crusading nation, Portugal was ruled by a dynasty and a nobility that dominated the Church. After the death of King Sebastian in the disastrous 1578 crusade in Morocco, together with a good part of the Portuguese nobility, his brother Cardinal Henrique, who had served also as inquisitor-general since 1539, ascended to the throne with papal dispensation. This combination of ecclesiastical and royal authority was continued during the union of the Spanish and Portuguese crowns (1580–1640): Cardinal Albert, appointed viceroy in Portugal by Philip II, served as inquisitor-general for ten years (1586–96); Pedro de Castilho, bishop of Leiria, served two terms as viceroy and ten years as inquisitor-general (1605–15). The royal–noble character of the Portuguese Church was manifest in the episcopacy: among the 135 bishops appointed between 1550 and 1670, at least 115 were noble. New religious foundations also owed much to noble patronage. Tridentine revival spurred a new wave of foundations. Between 1550 and 1668, some 166 new religious houses were established; in 1630 Portugal had 450 monasteries, with 4,200 male and 3,200 female religious clerics. Similar to Spain and Belgium, the clergy in Portugal was unmistakably growing in numbers in an otherwise stagnant or declining demographic regime in early modern Europe.

Tridentine reform encountered the same inertia and entrenched privilege in Portugal as elsewhere in Catholic Europe, in spite of the early reception of its decrees; the latter was manifest, for example, in the establishment of seven diocesan seminaries by the end of the sixteenth century. Up to the 1640 revolt against Spain, by which the Portuguese recovered a native dynasty, close religious ties connected the two Iberian nations. The Capuchin reform came from Spain, as did the Dominican reform movement; and prominent Spanish churchmen worked and died in Portugal, such as the Dominican mystic Luis de Granada (d. 1588) and the Jesuit scholastic theologian Francisco Suárez, who lectured at the university in Coimbra. The 1640 Revolution, built upon resentment against preferment of Castilian interest, destroyed bilingualism and weakened ties with Spain. Catholicism in Portugal took on three distinctive characteristics: firstly, the strong imperial sense of the nation nourished a strong undercurrent of messianism and millenarianism from the middle of the sixteenth to the late seventeenth century; secondly, the repression of Jewish converts absorbed the overwhelming energy of the Inquisition and of Catholic renewal for the better part of two centuries; and lastly, the very embodiment of that renewal, the Portuguese Jesuits, were themselves repudiated and destroyed by the government in the 1750s.

Messianic movements in Christianity, inspired perhaps by the proximity of Judaism, sprang up at intervals in the history of Christianity. A shoemaker in Setúbal in 1538, a "New Christian" or convert named Luis Dias, called himself the Messiah and attracted a small following. This messianic sect, suppressed by the Inquisition, may perhaps point to the ambiguous relationship between heterodox ideas and Jewish converts in Portugal, but messianic–millenarian dreams fed on still another source: the destiny of Portugal as a nation that brought Christianity to the non-Christian world. The death of the crusader-king Sebastian in 1578 gave rise to the myth of a future messianic king who would bring Catholic faith and peace to all, if only through the sword. During the period of dynastic union, this royal messianism, called Sebastianism after the king, nourished anti-Spanish sentiments; and the 1640 restoration was interpreted by some, such as the famous Jesuit preacher António Vieira (1608–97) as heralding the Fifth Monarchy, the last historic kingdom predicted by the prophet Daniel in the Old Testament prior to the end of the world and the Last Judgment. Court preacher, diplomat, missionary, Vieira was the leading religious figure in Baroque Portugal. In two prophetic works, *História do futuro* and *Clavis prophetarum* (Key of prophets), Vieira speculated on the date and nature of the End. Interrogated by the Inquisition and disappointed by the failure of his prophecies, Vieira left Lisbon for Brazil, where he died a missionary. The missionary impulse, and the exotic fantasy of Portugal's vast overseas dominion, helped to sustain a mystical religious fervor at home. Another leading preacher of the Baroque, the Franciscan mystic António das Chagas (1631–82), had been a soldier in Brazil before his religious conversion in 1667.

Portugal, like Spain, was a land of mystics and missionaries; and both empires inspired visions of world conversions to Catholicism. Yet Portugal, also like Spain, was beset by internal foes of the faith. The Inquisition, established in 1547, set out to protect the nation from internal Judaizing foes and external Protestant enemies. Organized along lines similar to its Spanish counterpart, the Portuguese Inquisition was directed at the top by a general office (*Conselho Geral*) and divided into four regional tribunals: Lisbon (governing also Brazil and the Atlantic islands), Coimbra, Evora, and Goa (covering the entire Portuguese East). Between 1540 and 1732, the Inquisition passed sentence on 23,000 persons, of whom 1,454 were relaxed to the secular arm and burned (some in effigies). The vast majority of cases investigated (c. 40,000) by the Holy Office dealt with accusations of "Judaizing." Of the 10,347 cases investigated by the Holy Office in Coimbra, more than 84 percent (8,769) pertained to "Judaizing"; in Evora, the percentage of "Judaizing" cases was 89 (7,269 persons); in Lisbon, the proportion was 3,751 "Judaizers" out of 5,503 investigated or 68 percent of total cases. To put this in perspective: whereas New Christians (converts or *marranos*, as they were called) constituted no more than 5 percent of the two million population in 1542, they totaled 85 percent of the victims of the Inquisition. A minority of these New Christians were "secret Jews"; most were denounced for their ancestry or adherence to traditional family ways (diet, ceremonies, etc.). A small number belonged to the elites of Portuguese society, notably Antonio Homem (1564–1624), professor of canon law at Coimbra, and the two dozen prominent men of the Church, law, and medicine in his circle, whose interest in their ancestral religion was probably provoked by Old Christian intolerance. Again, similar to Spain, purity-of-blood statutes served as a mechanism for social exclusion. But in addition to the merchants and financiers, professions preferred by New Christians, many ordinary New Christians were also prosecuted by the Inquisition. Women constituted a higher proportion of its victims: they outnumbered men 53 percent to 47 percent among all sentenced by the Evora tribunal; the proportion among "Judaizing" victims was even higher.

In Portugal, the Inquisition and episcopal visitations became two complementary institutions to enforce social discipline and religious conformity. Whereas New Christians comprised 80 percent of Inquisition victims, Old Christians constituted more than 95 percent of those accused in diocesan visitations. Working in conjunction (unlike in Spain), the Holy Office and episcopal government clearly demarcated jurisdictional boundaries: the former specialized in prosecuting the major crimes against faith (Judaism, Islam, and Protestantism), while the latter censored the lesser crimes of morals. Among the offenses prosecuted by episcopal authority were blasphemies, sexual sins, and magic, offenses commonly prosecuted in Spain by the Inquisition. The two institutions often shared the same personnel. Many bishops of Coimbra in the seventeenth and eighteenth centuries also worked for the Inquisition: Bishop João de Melo (1684–1704) had been previously inquisitor in Evora; Bishop António de Vasconcelos e Sousa (1706–17) was appointed in

1671 to the Inquisition in Lisbon. This overlap in personnel also extended further down the administrative hierarchy. The complementarity of the two institutions was also reflected in their rhythms of repression: whereas the caseload of the Inquisition dropped substantially after 1690 (except for a short anti-Judaic wave in the 1730s), the diocesan visitations increased their vigilance and condemnations drastically after 1700. This shift of focus from faith to morals, from repressing Jews and Protestants to disciplining the Catholic masses, was characteristic of the Inquisition in both Spain and Portugal.

The third and final point, the fate of the Jesuits, is symbolic of the larger history of Catholicism in early modern Europe. Favored from the beginning by the monarchy, the Society of Jesus expanded rapidly in Portugal until it seemed to threaten central control in Rome. Once reorganized, the Portuguese province assumed an important role in the Catholic enterprise, for the pope had placed all missions to Asia under Portuguese *padroado* and Jesuits played the leading role in the religious missions of the Portuguese empire. Their success made many enemies for the Jesuits – the Inquisition and the Oratorians among them – but they faced the greatest foe in the marquis de Pombal (1699–1782), the minister who identified the Society as the chief obstacle to enlightened monarchy. Provoked by the fathers' protection of native missions in Paraguay (see chap. 11), in 1759 Pombal expelled some 1,700 Jesuits from Portuguese dominions and temporarily broke off diplomatic ties with the papacy. His actions, undertaken in the name of regalism and an enlightened anti-papal Catholicism, closed the book in the history of the Counter-Reformation in Portugal and represented the end of Catholic renewal.

Spain

In 1555, the prominent Spanish Dominican, Melchor Cano, an authority on theology and orthodox doctrine, expressed profound skepticism that the papacy could really reform itself. Spanish bishops, it may be recalled, led the reform party at the Council of Trent and bitterly opposed the partisans of the Roman curia, defenders more of privilege than of Catholic fervor in their eyes. As late as 1632, a committee on abuses in the Roman see was established in Madrid. The Spanish Church, it seemed, regarded itself as superior to the papacy, which was subjected, as all Italians were wont, to the decadence of the flesh.

A profoundly religious nation, whose Catholic identity was forged in the "Reconquest" against Islam and the Moors, Spain came to identify its destiny with that of Catholicism. Much of that character in the early modern period was formed in the crucial years of the 1550s. While all

Catholic lands battled Protestant heresy, Spain seemed to have been favored by God with its orthodox faith. The shock was all the greater in 1557–58, when two small Protestant "cells" were discovered among clerics and merchants in Valladolid (the royal capital) and in Seville (the largest port). Although quickly crushed, Philip II and the Spanish Church reacted with alarm. In 1558 new censorship laws were enacted; in 1559, Spanish students were forbidden to study in foreign universities; and the Inquisition was given directives to sharpen its hunt for Protestants. This "Protestant fear" culminated in the 1559 arrest of Bartolomé Carranza, the newly appointed archbishop of Toledo, the primate of the Spanish Church.

Carranza, a Dominican, had participated at the Council of Trent and while in the entourage of Cardinal Pole, the papal legate to England under Queen Mary, composed a catechism in Spanish that was printed in the Low Countries. His emphasis of "faith" (already noted by opponents during the sessions of the Council), his presence in the heresy-infected north, his association with the soon-to-be-disgraced Cardinal Pole, and the fact that the catechism was published in the vernacular all aroused suspicion at home. Elected to the see of Toledo, Carranza returned to Spain where he was promptly arrested by the Inquisition. Among those who denounced the catechism as heretical was his co-religionist, Melchor Cano. Stunned by the news of Carranza's arrest, the papacy tried to negotiate his release. The archbishop's fate was very much on the minds of the Church fathers who again convened in Trent in 1562; most considered his catechism to be orthodox. Philip II, however, refused repeatedly pleas for Carranza's release. The archbishop was eventually transferred to the jurisdiction of the Roman Inquisition and he died in 1576 shortly after all charges were dropped.

The fate of Archbishop Carranza reflected three major characteristics of Spanish Catholicism: firstly, the immense authority and elevated self-image of the Spanish monarchy, which considered itself the staunchest defender of the faith; secondly, the reach of the Inquisition, the power of which spared no rank or estate; and thirdly, the legitimacy of both institutions, which remained unchallenged by the majority of the population, who came to identify Hispanicity as the most perfect form of Catholicism.

In 1564, Philip II ordered the proclamation of the Tridentine decrees in his dominions. Spanish bishops who returned from Trent eager for reform could count on royal support. In 1565, Philip II called upon all bishops to hold provincial and diocesan councils to carry out reforms. A deeply pious man, Philip also ruled as a monarch to whom the papacy had conceded the most far-ranging rights; the Spanish king, in fact, had the right to nominate all bishops, prelates, and all heads of religious orders in Spain. In his role as king-pope, Philip was rarely deferential to the popes: he cajoled, he threatened, and he made war, but he also supported the papacy in defending the frontiers of Catholicism against Protestants and Muslims. Abroad, Philip funneled Spanish money and Spanish arms to fight for the Catholic faith: he failed to crush the Dutch rebels; he suffered a fiasco in sending the Armada against England (1588); but he checked Ottoman expansion at Lepanto (1571); and funded the cause of the Catholic League in civil-war-torn France. At home, he promoted the twin causes of central royal authority and Catholic reform: he suppressed a Moorish uprising in Granada (1568–78); he ordered all Castilian parishes to submit reports of devotional practices; he honored saints and holy men and women, especially of Castilian provenance; and he built for himself a palace that was also simultaneously monastery and mausoleum, keeping a community of Jeronimite monks to say perpetual mass for the salvation of his soul and the souls of the Habsburgs. At his death, the elaborate royal cult of death symbolized both the grandeur of a divinely ordained Catholic monarchy that drew legitimacy from Catholic faith, as well as the humiliation of all earthly powers before Death and God. Under his successors, the Spanish monarchy continued its close alliance with the Catholic cause: in 1609, his son Philip III expelled all Moriscos from Spain to further purify the Christian nation; his grandson, Philip IV, although lacking the asceticism of the "Prudent King," carried on a long correspondence with the mystic María Agreda and vigorously promoted the cult of the Immaculate Conception of the Virgin Mary in the wider Catholic world.

In promoting the twin causes of royal centralism and Catholic orthodoxy, Spanish kings possessed an institution of great effectiveness: the Inquisition. Established by the papacy to fight heresies in the Middle Ages, the Inquisition assumed an institutional longevity only in 1483, when the papacy conceded jurisdiction to the Catholic monarchs. Its original mission was to combat *converso* apostasy. For a century prior to the expulsion of Spanish Jews in 1492, waves of repression against Judaism had coerced and enticed many Jewish converts to Christianity. Often occupying positions of privilege and wealth, the *conversos* aroused widespread resentment; numerous accusations of apostasy or "Judaizing" were raised and the Inquisition was established to handle these charges. Coupled with the statutes of "pure blood" (*limpieza de sangre*) that established prerequisites of non-Jewish genealogies for ecclesiastical and public positions, the Inquisition created the mechanism by which a minority was nominally excluded from full participation in civic and religious life. Pure-blood statutes were strongly opposed by some Spanish institutions (notably the Jesuits and the Discalced Carmelites); in practice their full rigor was often circumvented by false genealogies and extensive mixed marriages between *conversos* and Old Christians. Nonetheless, Christians of Jewish ancestry – first Spanish *conversos* and later Portuguese New Christian immigrants – continued to be special targets of the Holy Office. Even after the furor of the first persecutions (1480s–1540), when *conversos* were the major targets, about 10 percent of all subsequent cases tried by the Inquisition concerned Judaizers. (The percentage was much higher in Castile, 17.5 percent, for example, than in Aragon, 3.8 percent.) Sentences were usually much harsher: in Galicia 12.5 percent of all Judaizing cases resulted in death sentences (as against 0.4 percent in Lutheranism cases). Anti-*converso* repression followed a distinct rhythm, as exemplified by records from Toledo: from 1481 to 1530, about 77 percent of all defendants were *conversos*; the percentage dropped sharply until 1621, when a campaign against Portuguese New Christians pushed the rate up to 50 percent between 1621 and 1700.

It has been observed that the Protestant Reformation gave the Spanish Inquisition a new lease on life in the 1540s, just when it was running out of suspects. The twenty-one tribunals of the Spanish Inquisition (including Mexico and Lima) processed and sentenced 50,000 cases between 1540 and 1700 (in addition to many investigations that were dropped). After the initial anti-*converso* campaign leveled off in the 1530s, the pace of prosecution accelerated from 1540, drawing in *alumbrados*, Protestants, and Moriscos as new targets. Sentencing reached a peak from 1580 to 1600, sustained by massive investigations of Morisco apostasy. After 1620, the rate of prosecutions dropped precipitously; and the focus of repression oscillated between periodic outbursts of vigilance against Judaizers and constant survey of Old Christians. This was the overall pattern. But significant regional variations pointed to the great diversity of Spain. Prosecutions against Judaizers, as we have seen, were more than four times as likely in Castile than in Aragon. Conversely, repression against Islam was concentrated in Aragon and Granada: the most active tribunals against Moriscos were Saragossa, Granada, and Valencia; Toledo, the second most active tribunal against Judaizers, came fourth. Anti-Lutheran repression was strongest in the frontier tribunals, as might be expected in a realm where heresy was identified with foreignness: the most active tribunals were Barcelona, Saragossa, and Seville. In Aragon, xenophobia fueled religious orthodoxy, targeting French immigrants as natural suspects of "Lutheranism" (a generic term for all Protestants). Between 1578 and 1635, the most active period for the Holy Office in Barcelona, some 37 percent of all cases dealt with foreigners, mostly anti-Lutheran prosecutions against French immigrants. In coastal areas (Seville, Galicia), the Inquisition exercised special vigilance against foreign sailors and merchants. Nearly all Protestants prosecuted in Galicia between 1560 and 1700 were foreign; the four largest categories were English (45 percent), French (23 percent), German (13.7 percent), and Dutch (10 percent). In Barcelona, not a single major heresy case was discovered among Catalans during the height of anti-Lutheran repression, testifying again to the strong identification between Protestant heresy and foreignness.

While Judaizers, Moriscos, Protestants, and *alumbrados* constituted the most dangerous enemies of Spanish Catholicism between 1540 and 1700, the majority of cases processed by the Holy Office (59 percent) concerned minor offenses against the faith by Old Christians. These could be further classified into two broad categories: sexual crimes (bigamy, simple fornication, solicitation by clerics during confession, homosexuality, bestiality) and crimes against doctrine and Church (blasphemy, crimes against the Holy Office, and superstitions). The death sentence was rare in these cases, except for a handful of witch trials by regional tribunals that the *Suprema* (the Supreme Council of the Inquisition) roundly condemned. Inquisitors understood these transgressions as the result of ignorance and the weakness of human nature, and imposed correspondingly moderate sentences. In some regions, such as Galicia, prosecutions against blasphemy and bigamy intensified in the decades after Trent, revealing the wide gap between clerical expectations and actual behavior in the religious and moral life of the rural populace. Very often these prosecutions took on a didactic character: in many cases sinners denounced themselves in expectation of a mild sentence; in other instances, the guilty were turned in by witnesses outraged by blasphemous words or behavior.

Lacking adequate manpower to police the populace and enforce its authority, the Inquisition relied on a combination of self-discipline and denunciations to uncover potential transgressors. Staffed by clerics, usually trained in law, and advised by theologians, the Holy Office relied on an unpaid administration of commissioners and familiars. The former, mostly secular clerics, functioned as deputies for the tribunals in the district towns; the latter, requiring proof of pure blood, acted as lay protectors of the tribunal. Since familiars enjoyed considerable fiscal and judicial exemptions, these positions were sought after and became in due course the domain of the elites. In Galicia, the Inquisition created a closed social group, recruited from urban elites in royal service and rural nobility: family, clientage, and faction transformed the Galician Holy Office into a bulwark of noble privilege in the seventeenth century, sapping its original spirit. The "infiltration" of the Inquisition by social elites contributed to its decline in the eighteenth century; no longer an institution at the forefront of the battle for Catholic orthodoxy, the Holy Office had become just another institution of social privilege in the Old Regime.

The negative image of the Inquisition has obscured a fundamental fact: it was Spanish Catholicism that created the Inquisition and not the other way round. Until the end of the old regime, Spain remained a deeply religious society. More than half of all books published in Spain between 1500 and 1670 dealt with religion (5,835 religious titles versus 5,450 non-religious subjects): biblical exegesis, scholastic theology, histories of religious orders, doctrinal treatises, texts of Church councils and synods, hagiographies, and religious biographies. One may compare this proportion with book production in Venice, the center of Italian printing: in Venice, the percentage of religious books in overall production increased from 16 percent in the 1550s to 35 percent in 1605–07, an impressive increase in a Catholic society, but still below the proportion in Spain. The bulk of this literature was in the vernacular, which meant it was accessible to a large segment of the population; in Catalonia, in fact, Catalan flourished as the language of Counter-Reformation literature.

Representing a vast effort at teaching Christian doctrines, the printed sermons, devotional prints, and catechisms reflected the intense campaign to evangelize "the Indies" within Spain itself. In Castile, the heartland of Spanish Catholicism and empire, indoctrination seemed to have achieved impressive results, judging from the interrogations of the Toledo Inquisition. When questioned on the knowledge of prayers (Pater, Ave, Credo, Salve) and the Ten Commandments, the common people showed they had learned the basic tenets of Christian doctrine by 1600. Before 1550, only 37 percent questioned could recite all four prayers; by the 1580s and 1590s 68 percent were able to; and 82 percent of all questioned in the first half of the seventeenth century knew all four prayers. Whereas only 40 percent knew the Ten Commandments between 1565 and 1584, some 77 percent had memorized their Decalogue by the middle of the seventeenth century. Indoctrination made great progress among both artisans and peasants: before 1550 only 17 percent of all peasants and 42 percent of artisans could recite the four prayers; by the first half of the seventeenth century, the comparative percentages were 74 and 91. These results, impressive when compared to Tridentine reform in other Catholic lands, must not be taken as representative of all of Spain. In Galicia, Catalonia, and other peripheral regions, there were reports of persistent ignorance of doctrine and hostility to the clergy well into the eighteenth century. In Castile, however, the presence of Catholic fervor seemed indisputable. A religion deeply connected to a society of estates,

Catholicism mediated potential disruptions in society in three ways: it provided an understanding for collective and historical identity; it regulated social mobility by absorbing successful mercantile families back into the society of estates; and it offered rituals and symbols for individuals at the moment of their death.

In his treatise *Diálogos familiares de la agricultura cristiana* (1589), the Franciscan Juan de Pineda divided Spanish society into farmers, artisans, men of war, learned men, courtiers, and clerics, adding that "each of these estates requires a belief that is different from the others." United in their abhorrence of things foreign and heretical, Catholicism shaped a common identity for a society that rejected Italian saints and disliked Roman abuses. Castilian, as it was claimed by Quevedo, represented the language of divinity; and the Spanish Empire, based on the Castilian heartland, seemed to embody the fulfillment of God's will on earth. This exalted and mystical image of Spanish imperialism was not limited to Spain: even Tommaso Campanella, a Neapolitan Dominican and visionary imprisoned for his anti-Spanish activities, wrote a treatise on the divine purpose behind Spanish expansion. At times of disasters, as in 1588, the king and nation went into collective penance, blaming the destruction of the Armada on the collective sins of the nation. A current of apocalypticism echoed in Spanish writings well into the early nineteenth century, especially during periods of political crisis. The best known work of this genre, the *Anticristo* (1604) by the Dominican Tomás de Maluenda (1565–1628), was reprinted in 1621 and 1647, when Spain faced one reverse after another in wars.

Left out of Pineda's description of estates, merchants in sixteenth-century Spain played an important role in Catholic renewal. Simon Ruíz, one of the leading merchants at Medina del Campo, the leading fair in Spain, established a hospital in his home town. Another rich merchant from Medina del Campo, Antonio de Acosta, brought up a son, José (1540–1600), who would become famous as a Jesuit missionary in Peru. Many merchant families, in fact, sent sons and daughters into the clergy; their *converso* origins testified rather to the identification with the goals of Catholic society. The story of Teresa of Avila may be taken as emblematic: of *converso* ancestry, Teresa substituted nobility of spirit for purity of blood in recruiting for her convent reforms, a movement to which two merchants – Alonso de Avila and Martin Ramírez in Toledo – contributed handsomely. Mercantile profit served as metaphor for spiritual gain in a letter of Francisco Xavier, written in 1548 in Goa: in it he recommended "a most valuable merchandise" neglected by European merchants in Malacca and China, "the conscience of souls."

Back in Spain, this merchandise was eagerly sought after and exchanged. Money poured into charities (hospitals, poor relief, and orphanages) and religious foundations; religious art work, devotional prints, and pious books fed a growing market for the divine. But it was in the realm of dying that the largest transactions between material and spiritual capital took place. Struck repeatedly by plagues and famines, the population of Spain (as in Europe) fell by perhaps one-third between 1580 and 1650. Castile, burdened with more taxes, suffered the most. Concomitant with this grim demographic decline was the Tridentine Church's campaign against traditional superstitions: the familial wakes and offerings to the dead. Unhinged from traditional bearings of family and kin, the faithful stood before Death, protected only by the rituals offered by the Church. As traditional cycle masses for the dead declined (they were criticized as derived from pagan beliefs), endowments for requiem and devotional masses sharply increased. In Cuenca, the number of masses specified in testaments tripled between 1605 and 1635; in Barcelona, there was an eightfold increase in masses for the dead between the sixteenth and seventeenth centuries. By 1700, some 3,000 masses for the dead were said daily in Barcelona. In a period of rising prices, the cost of masses rose faster than the average price index (300 percent versus 250 percent between 1531 and 1600 in Cuenca), creating more positions and better pay for chantry priests. Thus, while the population in the diocese of Cuenca dropped 40 percent between 1591 and 1654, the number of priests doubled. Over the long run, enormous resources passed from the sector of material production into the realm of spiritual production: in Cuenca in the middle of the eighteenth century, 57 percent of properties and 44 percent of the land belonged to the Church. At a time when the glory of Spanish arms existed only in memory and when her economic resources were drained, great multitudes still flocked to the sermons of the itinerant Jesuit preacher, Pedro de Calatayud (1689–1773) and millions of chantry masses were read every day for an empire of departed souls.

Italy

Commenting on the foundation of the Collegio dei Cinesi in Naples, a seminary established in 1732 for the education of Chinese priests, the cameralist Carlo Antonio Broggia (1698–1767) wrote to the archivist and *érudit* Ludovico Antonio Muratori in 1746 that "one ought to, for the sake of God, think of providing first and well for the needs of the Chinese peasants," adding further "there is no people [*plebe*] more barbaric and ignorant than our own. And to what do we owe this if not the insufficient number of clerics ready to teach and instruct them?" This letter, written in the age of reason, betrayed the profound disdain of the educated elites for popular customs and religion in the Kingdom of Naples. Italy, of course, was not a single country before the middle of the nineteenth century; and the chasm between North and South, a recurrent theme in the history of the peninsula, structured the different histories of Tridentine reform.

Politically, early modern Italy was dominated by Spain: viceroys governed Naples, Sicily, and Milan in the name of Spanish kings; the Spanish ambassador in Rome manipulated papal elections and shaped papal diplomacy; Spanish patronage supported the Medici duchy of Florence; only Piedmont and Venice were able to negotiate an independent course in politics. The differences between North and South depended not so much on the extent of Spanish domination in the Mezzogiorno, as liberal Italian historiography had depicted, blaming Spain and the Counter-Reformation for Italian backwardness. Rather, the human geography of the North, with its extensive roads and dense urbanization, favored the extension of state and ecclesiastical authority, a crucial factor in Catholic reform. The Mezzogiorno, in contrast, with its latifundia of sheep farms and commercial crops, its weak urban communes and strong barons, was a region centered on an overgrown capital city, Naples (one of the largest cities in early modern Europe), which siphoned off the material and human resources of the provinces.

The reforms of Carlo Borromeo in Milan provided a model for Tridentine Catholicism in all Italian dioceses: the bishop, acting as legislator, promulgated new ecclesiastical laws in provincial and synodal councils; in his role as judge, he enforced clerical discipline, combated heresy, and improved popular morals. As Borromeo himself learned in numerous confrontations, a Tridentine bishop needed the support of secular authorities in overcoming obstacles to reform. An implicit alliance between the early modern state and the Catholic hierarchy developed in central and northern Italy, targeting the people for social discipline and moral instruction.

In Venice and Florence, the state supported voluntary charities – the confraternities, pilgrim hospices, hospitals, foundling houses, and the *monti di pietà* – by reorganization and financial subsidies in times of crisis. Originating in the medieval communes, the diversity and strength of public charities became a special feature of Italian urban life in the 1520s, when the miseries of war rekindled traditional charity and nourished a reform movement that flowed through the watershed of Trent. Catholic reform channeled traditional charity in two ways: aid was extended to groups previously neglected – the mad, beggars, abandoned infants, prisoners, and prostitutes living on the margins of urban society; and it emphasized the moral and behavioral change of charity recipients. The boards of charitable institutions and the new religious orders devoted to the poor often drew their personnel and contributions from the urban elites; in Venice, voluntary offices on charity committees provided a measure of civic participation and political power to wealthy citizens otherwise excluded from the oligarchic institutions of the Republic. Through acts of charity, a lay spiritual elite discovered clerical vocations, furnishing new strength to the work of Catholic renewal. A few examples should suffice: the Somaschi Order was founded in this milieu of lay charity; de Lellis moved from a group working in a confraternity hospital to found a new religious order; and the *monte di pietà* in Naples, established in 1602 by seven noblemen who did charitable work in the Hospital for the Incurables, was governed by a board of noblemen, two of whom entered the Jesuit and Theatine orders later in life.

Christian charity, sustained by the better parts of society and supervised by the state, reflected a mixture of pity and fear toward the poor; it aimed to provide relief for the destitute, train the indolent for work, instill Christian discipline in the immoral, and render the rebellious submissive. But, by the 1590s, even the impressive growth in voluntary charity could not keep pace with the demand for relief. It has been estimated that average bread consumption may have declined about 30 percent and meat consumption by 25 percent in seventeenth-century Rome. The demographic havoc wrought by the recurrent plagues from the 1590s to the 1650s reflected a susceptible population weakened by the increasing poverty of the previous decades.

Able to alleviate only the superficial symptoms of structural poverty, the Catholic states in early modern Italy achieved greater successes in eradicating heresy and disciplining the clergy. For Carlo Emanuele I, duke of Savoy, the fight against heresy and for Catholic orthodoxy was also a battle against political dissent, a view shared by the Medici Cosimo I, grand duke of Tuscany, who saw Catholic reform as the best medicine for social and political disorder. In the "Serene Republic" of Venice, the Senate exercised a vigilant censorship on printers and booksellers, and crushed religious dissent, executing scores of Anabaptists (mostly recruited from the artisanry) in the second half of the sixteenth century. In the Kingdom of Naples, the state mercilessly hunted down peaceful Waldensians, killing some and driving the survivors into exile.

By stressing the centrality of the parish church and episcopal jurisdiction, Tridentine reform provided a powerful framework for the consolidation of state authority. There was a congruence in the duchy of Savoy between areas where parish sacramental life was the strongest and where ducal authority exercised the greatest authority. In subordinating family chapels, local saint cults, confraternities, and popular religious practices to the linear authority of the ecclesiastical hierarchy, Tridentine Catholicism reinforced all forms of institutionalized central authority at the expense of informal social power – kin, family, voluntary and corporate associations, with their local, dispersed worldviews that had appropriated religion for their own uses. Gradually and persistently, the new ecclesiastical administration (the bishop-legislator and his officials), supported by the state, redirected sacramental life from family chapels to parish churches, promoted confraternities dedicated to the universal cults of the Holy Sacrament and the Virgin Mary at the expense of local saint cults, and rendered the complex social groupings of early modern society into uniform units of souls in parish registers, more pliant to the social and moral discipline demanded by the Tridentine Church and the early modern state. Emblematic of this development was a record of the Inquisition in Faenza, a tribunal with jurisdiction over Romagna in the Papal States: the "Book of the Records of the Inquisition" enumerated the population of the parishes, the confessants, communicants, and heretics from 1596 to 1778, furnishing indispensable information for the agents of moral and social discipline.

The success of reform bishops thus depended less on their personal piety and rigor than on the recourse to coercive institutions. In northern dioceses, Tridentine reform gradually bore fruit under the energetic intervention of dedicated bishops: Feltre della Rovere, archbishop of Rimini (1565–78), Antonio Altoriti, archbishop of Florence, and Gabriele Paleotti, archbishop of Bologna, were some of the leading bishops contemporaneous with Borromeo who visited their diocese, disciplined the clergy, and introduced Tridentine reforms. Pastors of similar caliber were not lacking in the South: Belisario Balduino, bishop of Larino, Scipione Gesualdo, archbishop of Conza, and Lelio Brancaccio, archbishop of Taranto, all labored to apply Tridentine reforms to their dioceses. However, unlike in central and northern Italy, bishops in the Mezzogiorno encountered far greater opposition. Peculiar to the clergy in the Kingdom of Naples was the *chiesa ricettizie*, characterized by collegiate churches, corporate privileges, and the exclusion of clerics from outside the diocese from holding benefices. Of the 3,734 parishes in the Kingdom of Naples, 1,087 were collegiately organized. Reminiscent of the pre-Tridentine Church, local elites controlled ecclesiastical benefices as family resources: in the small diocese of Larino during the seventeenth century, for example, the laity held the right to nominate all parish priests; the bishop had none. Whether representing the interests of local feudal barons or the urban elites, the local churches in the Mezzogiorno reflected the quasi immobile socio-political structures of a refeudalized society, eschewing the control of a weak central viceregal authority in

Naples. (The powerful alliance of Neapolitan elites frustrated even the introduction of the Inquisition on the Spanish model – i.e., as a royal institution – and limited its operations through episcopal courts.)

The distance between Tridentine ideals and local practices in the South was further accentuated by the background of most bishops: most received their sees through royal or papal nominations and the majority were of Neapolitan or Spanish origins or came from the North. All bishops at Taranto until the end of the seventeenth century, for example, were foreign to the diocese. Non-residence still plagued this post-Tridentine diocese: Cardinal Gerolamo de Corrigio, archbishop of Taranto (1569–74), never set foot in his diocese; in the province of Otranto, only two-thirds of all bishops resided in their diocese until they died; many retired to Naples, where all material and cultural resources of the kingdom were concentrated. Naturally, reform bishops proceeded cautiously, making many compromises with entrenched interests, since the papacy was unable to back up their authority in many disputes with universities, chapters, and lay patrons. An intransigent man such as Lelio Brancaccio, archbishop of Taranto (1574–99), a client of the Carafa family who had been shaped by the religious zeal of the Carafa pope, antagonized most of his clergy and flock during his episcopate. Worn down by opposition, he retired to Naples in 1597 and governed his diocese through vicars until his death.

Judged solely by the measures of Tridentine decrees, Catholic reform met with very limited success in southern Italy: clerical concubinage was common until the middle of the eighteenth century; seminaries trained only a small fraction of the clergy; the laity by and large refused to see marriage as a sacrament, observing merely its outward form; and most elements of popular religion were never eradicated. Even so, the Church flourished: the number of monasteries more than doubled in Lecce between 1550 and 1620; and the ratio of clerics to the general population in the provinces of Otranto and Bari was the highest in the Italian peninsula. A comparison of the two archbishoprics of Otranto and Milan, however, reveals a fundamental difference in clerical vocations: whereas only 49 percent of the 7,684 clerics in Otranto in 1669 were ordained priests, the proportion of ordained priests in the overall clerical population in Milan kept climbing. Moreover, the ratio of priests to the laity also improved; it increased from one priest for 260 souls under Carlo Borromeo to one priest for 124 souls in 1766. The single most important reason for this increase was the growing demand for pastoral service and the larger parochial legacies. Obviously, Catholic renewal in the Mezzogiorno was not based primarily on a reinvigorated parish life; rather, it was sustained by a synthesis of a popular magical religion and the Tridentine norms of the elites. The missionary, not the bishop, was the crucial figure in this transformation.

Together with Andalusia and southwestern France, the Mezzogiorno enjoyed the distinction of being one of three regions in Catholic Europe that were the focus of internal missions. The Jesuits were the first in the field, in these "Indies" of Italy; they were followed by four other orders: the Congregation of the Pii Operai, founded in 1602 in Naples; the Congregation of the Fathers of the Mission, or the Lazarists, founded in 1627 by Vincent de Paul in France; the Apostolic Missions, founded in 1646 in Naples; and the Redemptorists, established by Alfonso de' Liguori in 1732. Based in Naples and the provincial cities, missionaries went on preaching expeditions to the small towns and villages of the kingdom, teaching catechism and calling for penance in tours that lasted between seven and thirty days.

The Jesuits set the tone for these theatrical and emotional missions, imitated by the subsequent orders except for the missionaries of the Pii Operai, who consciously adopted a more sober and practical style. Arriving in a town or village, the missionaries carried the cross at dusk through the streets of the community, clamoring for the populace to repent their sins. In sermon after sermon, they preached the fire and brimstone of damnation before proclaiming the sweet redemptory graces of Christ's suffering. Terrified and moved by these vivid tableaux of Christian faith, the community confessed *en masse* and took communion; sinners repented; husbands and wives were reconciled; children renewed their obedience; and families locked in mortal feuding clasped one another in forgiveness and peace. At times, the missionaries established confraternities to continue the work of moral regeneration after their departure; occasionally, they ran into opposition, when they lashed out at the scandalous lives of local clerics and notables; nearly always, they were welcomed in provincial towns and villages, where the monotony of life was relieved in these seasons of redeeming theater. For the authorities these mission tours helped to calm potential unrests, acting as a catharsis for the release of tension: the redemptorists pacified popular unrest in Calabria; the Lazarists reconciled feuding factions in the remotest provinces of the kingdom; and the fathers of the Apostolic Missions preached against sedition during the 1647 anti-Spanish revolt in Naples. For the bishops, the missions supplemented diocesan visitations and tapped the emotions of the populace for greater participation in the official liturgies of the Church. For the communities, these missions dissolved the hardened boundaries of class and factions; in the tears of repentance, nobles and peasants humbled themselves before the Redeemer and the missionary pulpit. These heightened moments of sacramental life repaired the fissures in the social body, so prone to factionalism and violence, and created a civic–sacral space that the parishes had failed to provide.

These rural missions, undertaken throughout the seventeenth and eighteenth centuries, inspired another effort to implement Catholic reform. A new campaign to evangelize the countryside was undertaken in the 1680s. Cardinal Innico Caracciolo, archbishop of Naples, and Vincenzo Maria Orsini, bishop of Benevento, were the leading figures. This campaign of Christianization went hand in hand with the viceregal government's efforts to suppress bandits and anarchic barons. In Larino, Bishop Giuseppe Catalani (1686–1703) reorganized parish and clerical life in a diocese ruined by bandits and feuds. His work was taken up by Bishop Carlo Maria Pianetti (1706–25). The diocesan seminary, established in 1564 but plagued by insufficient funds until 1690, began to bear fruit, turning out learned priests in sufficient numbers throughout the eighteenth century. Everywhere in the south, Catholic renewal drew on the confluence of popular devotion and official rituals: acting as mediators between two cultures, the clergy adapted the rites of the Church to popular demands for healing. In the eighteenth century the people of the Mezzogiorno honored their saints and near-saints for their sanctity and powers for healing. Theirs was a religion increasingly alien and ridiculous to the elites in Naples, turning to a new rationalism and asceticism under the new Bourbon dynasty, embarrassed by the emotionalism of popular rituals and by the "barbarity" of their own peasants.

4 The militant Church

In the struggle between Catholics and Protestants, most of western and central Europe, wedged in between the solidly Protestant North (Sweden, Denmark, England, and the United Provinces) and the Catholic Mediterranean, became a battlefield in the clash of faiths. Whether by arms, polemics, or persuasion, Catholicism turned the tide of the Protestant Reformation in the heartland of Europe: in the Holy Roman Empire, the Counter-Reformation withstood the challenge of the second wave of reform, the Calvinist Reformation, battling Protestants and stabilizing the boundaries between the confessions in the first half of the seventeenth century, before scoring with a handful of prominent conversions in the age of the Baroque; in the Spanish Netherlands, Protestant heresy, rooted out by repression and exile, was replaced by a Catholicism more firmly based on spiritual and ecclesiastical revival; in Poland, a land dominated by the nobility where toleration encouraged many Christian sects and confessions, the Counter-Reformation recovered nearly all of the lost ground by the seventeenth century, thanks largely to the effort of the Jesuits; in France, where the Protestant opposition won religious toleration and military security in 1598, the Counter-Reformation in the seventeenth century went on the offensive in the name of unity of faith and loyalty to the monarchy, ending finally in the 1685 revocation of toleration and the forced conversion of the Calvinist minority. In comparing the progress of Catholicism in these lands of militant Counter-Reformation, we will examine the socio-political matrix that supported the forces of Catholic renewal.

Poland

In 1558, the Italian Protestant, Lelio Socinus, who was in exile in Poland, wrote to Calvin in Geneva; he reported that, in the Polish Diet, many Catholic noblemen supported religious toleration because they considered religious liberty the foundation of political liberties. Aristocratic liberties, in fact, appeared as a recurring theme in this vast and complex realm, and structured the interplay of religious and political history. Ruled by a weak monarchy that owed its election to the nobility, the Kingdom of Poland in the sixteenth century included four distinct regions (Great Poland, Small Poland, Prussia, and Lithuania); five ethnic/linguistic groups (Poles, Germans, Lithuanians, Jews, and Ruthenians); and four major Christian Churches (Catholic, Lutheran, Calvinist, and Orthodox) and Judaism, plus a host of Christian sects such as the Anabaptists and Unitarians. Religious affiliation, not surprisingly, followed strong geographic and social contours. The Protestant Reformation spread in two waves. During the early decades of the sixteenth century, the Lutheran reform made substantial progress among the German-speaking populace, which, outside Prussia, tended to concentrate in towns. In mid-century, the Calvinist reform won many adherents among Polish speakers, particularly among the nobility; at the same time, Anabaptism, Unitarianism, and other forms of religious sectarianism and dissidence also found a hospitable reception. By the 1560s, therefore, one could find dense clusters of Protestantism: Prussia, centered on the towns of Gdansk (Danzig) and Torun, was heavily Lutheran, except for the Polish-speaking nobility; in Great and Small Poland and in Lithuania, there were 600–650 Calvinist temples in 1572, roughly one-sixth the number of Catholic parishes, with Protestantism claiming some 250 noble families in Great Poland (12–13 percent) as well as the allegiance of the German urban classes. Overall, with the exception of Prussia, one-sixth of the nobility was Protestant; the percentage was lower for the urban middle classes and extremely low for the peasantry. In the towns, except for Gdansk, they were a minority but politically well represented in Cracow, Poznan, Lublin, and Vilnius (Vilna).

Even before the conclusion of the Council of Trent, a handful of Polish bishops had resisted Protestant incursions: they published synodal decrees, disciplined dissident clerics, and tried to reform the clergy; Mikolaj Dzierzgowski, archbishop of Gniezno (Gnesen) (1548–59) was perhaps the most zealous example. But the real impetus for the Counter-Reformation came only in the 1560s, in the person of Stanislas Hosius, together with the papal nuncios and the Society of Jesus; and it would receive the strongest imprint from Italian religiosity and culture.

Stanislas Hosius (1504–79), son of a German immigrant father and a Polish mother, had studied in Italy before he entered into the diplomatic service of Polish kings. Appointed successively bishop of Kulm (1549) and Ermland (1551), Hosius composed a widely published treatise to defend the Catholic faith. Elevated to the purple in 1561, Hosius was one of the papal presidents in the concluding period of the Council of Trent.

In his role as middleman between Cracow and Rome, the Polish monarchy and the papacy, Hosius introduced the Society of Jesus to Poland and worked closely with the papal nuncios in combating Protestantism. Even though Poland was one of the first Catholic countries to accept the decrees of the Council of Trent in 1564, King Sigismund failed to have the Diet pass a law to repress the Polish Brethren, the Anti-Trinitarians, and the Anabaptists, sects that were anathema to the major Protestant Churches of central and western Europe as well. This policy of toleration, defended in the name of noble liberties, was supported by Catholics steeped in an older tradition of Erasmian philosophy, such as Archbishop Jacob Uchanski, the primate of Poland. Although suspected by Pope Paul IV of heresy, Uchanski was no Protestant; in the 1570s he insisted on the election of a Catholic monarch and personally saw to the reform of his archdiocese. But a more militant Counter-Reformation stance would come only with a younger generation raised in a different tradition – young Polish noblemen educated in the Jesuit college in Rome who returned to assume the chief ecclesiastical and secular positions in their native land. Forty-four of them had studied in Rome between 1565 and 1586, in addition to others educated in the Jesuit colleges that were being established in many Polish towns.

With the Roman connection, and with the marriage of Bona Sforza to King Sigismund III (1587–1632), Italian culture – language and Roman Catholicism – began to replace German as the predominant culture among the Polish ruling elites. The writings of St. Teresa were first introduced after 1598 in Italian editions; and the first convent of Discalced Carmelites (1605) consisted of immigrant Italian and Spanish nuns. Like the Spanish monarchs, who supported the Teresian reform, the Polish monarchy after 1576 became a staunch supporter of the Counter-Reformation in alliance with the Jesuits. King Stefan Batory (1576–80) elevated the Jesuit college in Vilnius to an university; Sigismund III, of the Swedish Vasa dynasty, was called the "Jesuit King"; his son Wladyslaw IV (1632–48) continued to favor the fathers of the Society, of whom his younger brother, Jan II Kazimierz (1648–68), was a member and a cardinal before he renounced his clerical vows with the blessing of Innocent X to assume the Polish throne.

The Jesuits themselves multiplied rapidly: in 1576 an autonomous Polish province was established; in 1608, it split into two provinces, for Poland and Lithuania; the five colleges in 1576 had increased to thirty-two in 1648; and their numbers jumped from 60 in 1574 to 570 in 1606 and to 1,390 in 1648. The best and the brightest were attracted to the new order, both bourgeois and noble: Jacob Wujek (1541–96), great scholar and theologian, came from a small town; Stanislas Kostka

(1550–68), the teenage novice-saint, hailed from an important noble family that had provided hereditary palatines of Pomerania and castellans of Gdansk; Stanislas Warszewicki (1530–91), tutor of Sigismund, had a father who was castellan of Warsaw; Piotr Skarga (1536–1612), court preacher to Sigismund III, was born near Warsaw to the minor nobility. Besides working as preachers, confessors, professors, and writers, the Jesuits also trained several generations of Polish bishops (see chap. 7) who would shape the Catholic renewal.

In spite of religious toleration, the Catholic recovery was not without violence. From the 1560s to the 1630s, repeated clashes marked the heightened tensions between militant Catholics and Protestants in the royal towns. In Poznan, the churches of the Lutherans and Bohemian Brethren were burned in 1606, 1614, and 1616; in Vilnius, the Calvinist temple was burned down twice before it was finally sacked in 1639; and the Lublin Calvinist temple was destroyed in 1633 after four attacks between 1611 and 1627. The most serious incidents occurred in Cracow, where between 1580s and 1613 religious clashes led to several armed confrontations and scores of casualties. Nothing, however, approached the scale of violence in France, as we shall see later. The dominant climate of religious toleration meant that Catholicism advanced more out of persuasion than coercion. With royal patronage, Jesuit education, and a strengthened monarchy in the seventeenth century, Roman Catholicism represented an elite culture that gradually wooed away the Protestant nobility: it created links to a glorious international culture and opened doors to royal patronage and ecclesiastical appointments. The history of the Catholic renewal in early modern Poland was to a large extent the story of the Polish nobility; the Counter-Reformation, consequently, left intact the social foundations of noble liberties. Piotr Skarga's sermons before the Diets, in which he excoriated the unchristian exploitation of serfs, remained words that merely echoed in the cloistered walkways of the convents and colleges, great landlords in a society built on unfree labor.

The Catholic Netherlands

Archduke Albert, appointed with his wife Isabella by Philip II in 1596 to govern the Low Countries, strongly supported the renewal of Catholicism. And, although Albert upheld the duty of every Christian to confess and receive communion at Easter, he opposed the bishop of Tournai's plan to check every household for compliance, telling the papal nuncio Frangipani that the measure "would remind one of the Inquisition, which is not practiced in Belgium." One might add that it was

Madrid's attempt to enforce religious conformity a generation earlier that helped to spark the rebellion that divided the seventeen provinces in the Low Countries. The Catholic Low Countries in the age of the Counter-Reformation included the area which is today Belgium, Luxembourg, and a strip of northern France. It was divided into two major polities: the independent ecclesiastical principality of Liège, part of the Holy Roman Empire, French-speaking; and the southern provinces that remained loyal to the Habsburgs, which, while constituting part of the dynastic heritage, retained their local rights, languages, and character. Belgium (to adopt a modern nomenclature for the sake of simplicity) was the site of many military conflicts in the early modern era: between the rebels and the royal troops until the 1630s, between Spain and France from the 1630s to 1660, and again between Louis XIV and his enemies from the 1680s to 1715. Part of Francophone Belgium was annexed to France; the remaining provinces passed to Austrian possession after 1715. Given this military and political turbulence, the Catholic renewal in the southern provinces seemed particularly remarkable.

Whereas the northern provinces broke away to form an independent Protestant polity, the south acquired a powerful Catholic identity that would shape its subsequent history. An indicator of Counter-Reformation fervor was surely the strength of the Society of Jesus. The initial province, called Lower Germany, was divided in 1612 into two provinces: Flandro-Belgium and Gallo-Belgium, reflecting the linguistic divisions of the land. Taking off from the 1590s, the number of Jesuits rose from 420 in 1595 to a peak strength of 1,574 in 1626, which was maintained for more than three decades. To put these figures in perspective, there were as many Jesuits in Belgium at the height of the Counter-Reformation as there were in Poland, a country ten times greater in size and several times in population. The 1626 figure of 1,574 Belgian Jesuits can also be compared to the 2,156 French, 2,283 German, and the 2,962 Spanish Jesuits, from much larger countries and populations.

The success of the Belgian Jesuits represented merely the most visible progress of Catholic renewal. During the seventeenth and early eighteenth centuries, the clergy constituted the only growing part of the population. In Antwerp, the largest city in Belgium, the number of clerics increased slightly between 1645 and 1716 (from 1,000 regulars, 250 beguines, plus seculars to 1,100 regulars and others), but the overall population had declined. While the clergy constituted only 1 percent of the total Antwerp population in 1526, they formed 1.75 percent in 1645 and 2.1 percent in 1716. In Lille, five new male and twelve new female religious orders were established between 1588 and 1667; the number of regular clergy increased from 390 in 1588 to 962 in 1695. This overall growth was all the more remarkable since it occurred during a period of demographic and economic decline. As in Spain, one can discern a significant shift of resources to religion in the Catholic society of the southern provinces. Some figures concerning confraternity membership, communion, devotional prints, and catechism schools should illustrate this point. In 1626, in the province of Flandro-Belgium some 13,727 laypeople were enrolled in Jesuit sodalities; in Antwerp alone, the Jesuits enrolled 3,800 laypeople in their sodalities in 1664, with another 7,750 registered in the Confraternity of St. Barbara, a pious association for the promotion of a holy death. In the 1660s about one-sixth of the population in Antwerp, reputedly the most pious city, was enrolled in confraternities. In Lille, the second largest city after Antwerp, the eucharistic confraternity enrolled 3,000 members between 1635 and 1645 and the Marian sodalities enrolled another 3,000. As a tool for piety in the confraternities, devotional prints (see chap. 10) with pictures and prayers had large pressruns and millions were produced in early modern Antwerp. The encouragement of frequent communion by the Jesuits showed spectacular results, according to their own reports: in 1626 the Jesuits gave communion to 24,000 in their Antwerp church (out of a total population of c. 60,000); in Lille, a city of 40,000, the number of communicants for all feastdays in 1626 was 130,000 and in 1640 it rose to 200,000. In teaching Christian doctrine to the young, the central government collaborated with local authorities and the clergy in luring children to free Sunday schools with bread and coins: in Lille in the middle of the seventeenth century, some 50 percent of all children (3,000–4,000) between seven and seventeen were taught catechism in Sunday schools or by schools run by the religious orders; in 1630 Antwerp the figure was 4,000–5,000.

These measures of success, resulting from a mixture of persuasion and coercion, reflected the close cooperation between secular and clerical authorities. The archdukes themselves set the tone: Albert and Isabella were patrons to the new religious orders of the Counter-Reformation, promoting the Jesuits, the Capuchins, and the Recollects, introducing the Discalced Carmelites from Spain, and keeping a Carmelite confessor (Thomas de Jesús) and Jesuit preachers at court. Isabella, in particular, was eager in promoting female religious orders. Sixteen of her ladies-in-waiting joined the Poor Clares; and Isabella herself dressed as a Franciscan tertiary after the death of her husband and co-regent in 1621. Imitating piety at the court in Brussels, the elites replicated lay patronage of Catholic renewal on a small scale over the densely populated and urbanized landscape of Belgium. Linked by family, class, and sentiment, the secular and clerical elites created a Catholic society loyal to Madrid and Rome. Royalism and Catholicism became inseparable. The Jesuit Leonardus Lessius praised the institution of monarchy in his *De justitia et jure* (1621); his fellow father Carolus Scribani equated the prince with the defender of Catholic social hierarchy in his treatise *Politico-Christianus* (1624); in Louvain, the Jesuits at the college staged a play decrying "Perfidious Gaul" in 1645; and in Ghent they dramatized the Virgin Mary as the warrior of the House of Habsburg.

In matters of faith, servants of the monarchy lent a ready hand in disciplining recalcitrant clergy and laity. Staffed by judicial officers and noblemen, the provincial councils became the chief instruments of social discipline. The secular courts prosecuted a litany of offenses, blurring the boundary between sin and crime in their pursuit of religious and social discipline. Ordinances from the archducal court to the local magistracy proceeded against clerical concubinage, Protestant heresy, blasphemy, sorcery, infanticide, and a large range of sexual offenses (adultery, prostitution, sodomy, incest, bigamy, and bestiality). To the coercive measures (executions, whippings, banishments, imprisonment, exile, and fines) we must add the admonitory and milder measures of episcopal discipline. Over the course of the seventeenth century, as the evidence from diocesan visitations have shown, the largely dedicated and conscientious Belgian bishops raised clerical standards, increased lay recourse to the sacraments, and improved the status and economic conditions of the Church. In spite of the tensions between Jansenist bishops and the Jesuits, Catholic reform succeeded brilliantly. Surcharged with religious energy, Belgium became an export land of Catholic renewal. Antwerp, the center of printing in northern Europe, produced devotional prints for the devout in the entire Catholic world, and books in Spanish, English, and Gaelic for polemics and propaganda. Louvain and Douai, the two university towns, received numerous Catholic exiles from England, Ireland, and the United Provinces. From the towns and villages of Belgium, young men became missionaries to Holland, the Spanish Americas, and China. And in Brussels and many towns, English and Irish Catholic exiles formed communities and cherished visions of reclaiming their own lands.

France

Even more intensely than in central Europe, the struggle between Protestant and Catholic in France assumed a savagery that reflected the full horrors of a civil war. For more than three decades, from the first outbreak of religious warfare in 1562 to the Edict of Nantes of 1598, the body politic was torn asunder by assassinations, massacres, sieges, and field campaigns. When Henry of Navarre, the Calvinist successor to the throne, converted to Catholicism and won the support of most of his countrymen against the opposition of the ultramontane Catholic League, he granted his former co-religionists *de jure* toleration in 1598, reserving for the Huguenots large regions of western and southern France under their effective administration and military control. The history of Catholic renewal in seventeenth-century France unfolded, therefore, against this Calvinist backdrop. From the ascension of Louis XIII to the throne and the hegemony of his favorite, Cardinal Richelieu, royal policy and the Counter-Reformation cause advanced hand in hand. To turn back the tide of Calvinism implied the extension of royal, centralized control over the rebellious provinces; to exalt the glory of the monarchy meant a redistribution of royal patronage to favor conversions among the leading Calvinist nobility; to assure the territorial integrity of the Gallican Catholic Church necessitated conquests and sieges. All this culminated some seventy years later in the restoration of monarchical power in the person of Louis XIV and in the 1685 revocation of the Edict of Nantes, by whose fiat the country once again returned to one faith, one law, and one king.

The identification between monarchy and Catholicism in France enjoyed a venerable tradition. The French episcopacy had defined itself since the fourteenth century as distinct and independent from Rome; and the ideology of Gallicanism, subscribed to by lay and ecclesiastical elites, posited the monarchy as the best defender of the special status and interests of the French Church. The advocates of Gallicanism, therefore, identified two sources of rivalry: the Huguenot minority at home, linked to international Calvinism and supported by the Dutch and the English; and the ultramontane, partisans of Rome and papacy, who espoused a militant Catholicism over the interests of the French monarchy and nation. I will first analyze the relationship between these alternative currents to Gallicanism and then examine the progress and difficulties of Catholic renewal.

The fight against Calvinism and ultramontane Catholicism preoccupied the French monarchy until the 1630s. During the wars of religion, the militant Catholic League allied itself with Spain, the traditional enemy, placing religious over political allegiance. By no means all Catholics accepted Henri IV's conversion; and Catholic pamphlets justifying regicide during the days of the Catholic League echoed earlier Calvinist political rhetoric in the aftermath of the Massacre of St. Bartholomew (1572). The assassination of Henri IV by a former student of the Jesuits in 1610 discredited militant Catholicism. The Parlement of Paris condemned the Jesuit theorists of regicide, Juan Mariana and Alfonso Suárez; and the Estates General of 1614, with the support of the clergy, passed a resolution affirming the divine origins of kingship and denying the popes any right in deposing monarchs. But a Catholic opposition to the "Most Christian King" Louis XIII and his favorite, Cardinal Richelieu, consolidated during the 1620s and 1630s, when French policy placed the reason of state over religion in supporting Protestant allies against the archenemy, Habsburg Catholic Spain. Coalesced around the queen mother, Marie de' Medici, the opposition to Richelieu clamored for an united Counter-Reformation front against all Protestants. This party of opposition, called the devouts (as opposed to the *politique* faction around Richelieu), collapsed as the cardinal-minister consolidated his power. Yet it would be mistaken to ignore the genuine commitment to religious reform on the part of Richelieu, whose first priority was the strengthening of the French monarchy.

In the long run, Richelieu's policy succeeded brilliantly. By identifying royalism with Catholicism, the court defined the terms under which the Calvinist minority must demonstrate its loyalty. Their reputation as potential rebels, borne out by the rebellions of the Calvinist lords (the duke of Rohan in 1621–29; the duke of Montmorency in 1631) eventually undermined the political autonomy of the entire Protestant community. Precisely this strategy was undertaken by Richelieu and his confessor, the Capuchin Joseph du Tremblay, in launching missions in the Protestant province of Poitou. In imputing disloyalty to Protestant dissent, the Capuchin preachers intensified tensions in a confessionally mixed society; in withholding royal patronage from Protestant notables, the government pressured the nobility to convert. Faced with divided loyalties, many Protestant communities remained neutral during Rohan's rebellion. Some, such as Henri duc de la Trémoille, the leader of one of the leading aristocratic clans in Poitou, converted to Catholicism in 1628 in submission to the king. This personal gesture, in the presence of the royal army besieging La Rochelle, a rebellious Calvinist town in collusion with the English, was rewarded by Louis XIII with an important office.

The renewal of religious warfare in the 1620s marked the turning point. Each passing decade witnessed increasing desertions from the ranks of the Protestant elites. Conversion, in turn, was rewarded by new honors and offices, thus further nibbling away at the edges of the Calvinist communities. With the outbreak of the English Civil War and the execution of King Charles I by a Protestant Parliament, rebellion and Calvinism became more firmly linked in the eyes of the French, even though the Huguenot communities demonstrated their loyalty to the crown during the Fronde. Royalism aside, simple demography was also working for the Catholic cause. In areas with minority Protestant populations, such as in Agen in Aquitaine, this steady loss to the majority Catholic population implied a demographic trend that would eventually result in the extinction of Calvinism. Only in majority Calvinist areas, such as Montauban and Nîmes, could demography withstand the political pressures of the monarchy. To speak of a general Catholic renewal in seventeenth-century France belies the enormous geographic diversity of the country, a complexity accentuated by the different experiences of Protestant reform in the sixteenth century.

There were 139 dioceses in early modern France, divided into large and wealthy northern ones – the archdiocese of Rouen had 1,388 parishes; Bourges, Chartres, and Limoges had some 800 each – but many bishoprics in the south, like their Italian counterparts, had only twenty to thirty parishes. To map the progress of Tridentine reform, one needs to divide the area of contemporary France into its political components in the early modern period. The decrees and canons of the Council of Trent were never officially accepted in the Kingdom of France; the Parlement of Paris and other opponents of papal rights considered the provisions injurious to Gallican liberties. In spite of repeated petitions by the French clergy, Henri IV and Louis XIII refused to publicize the Tridentine decrees; their only official endorsement was in 1615 during a separate meeting of the Second Estate, in which the exasperated French prelates voted to accept the constitution of Catholic reform.

In contrast to the French realm, the Duchy of Lorraine with its capital in Nancy and the papal enclave in Provence centered in Avignon owed allegiance to Rome and the Tridentine reform. The university at Pont-à-Mousson, established by Duke Charles III and Cardinal Charles I of Lorraine in 1572 and entrusted to the Jesuits, was the only ultramontane university in a French-speaking country. Catholic piety in Lorraine, manifest in Marian devotion, confraternities, and Roman allegiance, was heavily shaped by the Jesuits, who were under constant suspicion in neighboring France for their loyalty to Rome. A similar fidelity to Rome prevailed in Avignon. The governance by papal legates (usually Italians) and the proximity to Italy made Avignon into a conduit of Catholic reform for France: the Borromean reform, the new Italian religious orders, and the school for Christian doctrine all received an Avignonese imprint before their dissemination in France.

Avignon was important to the French Church for another reason: it represented the only Catholic stronghold in the heavily Protestant Provence and Languedoc. The decline of Catholicism in the south was confirmed by seventeenth-century diocesan visitation reports, which painted a picture of deserted parish churches and an understaffed clergy. The geography of Catholic renewal showed therefore a stark contrast between regions, demonstrated by a comparison between the Parisian region and the diocese of Nîmes in the south.

Pierre de Valernod, bishop of Nîmes (1598–1625), was the first prelate to restore Catholicism in this Languedocian diocese. His first visitation in 1611, to the western and mountainous part of his extensive diocese, revealed the devastations of the religious wars: of sixty-six churches inspected, twenty-two were totally and twenty-four partially destroyed; the parish clergy, mediocre and undisciplined, had simply abandoned twenty-three parishes. The same visitation record revealed both a numerical and a social predominance of Calvinists. In Nîmes itself, the 3,000 Catholics formed a minority among the 11,000–12,000 Calvinists; in the countryside, 2,000 Catholic households stood against 1,500 Calvinist. Socially, the Protestants numbered heavily among the judicial, mercantile, and artisanal elites, whereas Catholics were divided between a small nobility and a mass of peasants, farm-workers, and shepherds. In a society dominated politically by Calvinists, where mixed marriages were tolerated, Catholic conversions to Protestantism not uncommon (the consistorial records of the Calvinist synod recorded 450 converts between 1600 and 1620), and the traditional Catholic elites (the canons of the cathedral and colleges) indifferent to reform, Bishop Valernod had to bring in Jesuits and Capuchins in order to reinvigorate the Catholic faith. Father Pierre Coton, a famous Jesuit preacher, visited from Paris and succeeded in converting several Protestant notables, who subsequently received patronage in the capital. The competition between the confessions produced acute tension between 1600 and 1621, but in spite of rumors of armed conflicts, the daily contacts between Protestants and Catholics, their social, economic, and family ties prevented outbreaks of serious violence. During the rebellions of the duke of Rohan (1621–29) and the duke of Montmorency (1632), Protestant rebels destroyed Catholic churches, killed priests, and chased away many Catholics, but the worst excesses were prevented by a moderate party of bourgeois Calvinists, who opposed the military adventurism of Calvinist noblemen and militant artisans.

The suppression of the Calvinist magnates heralded a new attempt at Catholic renewal, one directed from Paris and inspired by royalism and central control. Anthime Denis Cohon, twice bishop of Nîmes (1634–44, 1655–70), a client of Richelieu, represented that particular French phenomenon, the reforming and political bishop. Seeing himself as a servant of the king, Bishop Cohon equated royalism with Catholicism. As the first French speaker appointed to this southern diocese, Cohon built a royal chapel in the cathedral, decorated with the symbols of royal and Catholic authority: the arms of France, the fleurs-de-lis, and images of Charlemagne and St. Louis. A resident bishop, Cohon imitated Borromeo in carrying out diocesan reform but his personal conduct was not beyond scandal. The Calvinist Church, even after the royal victory in 1629, maintained its strength, winning 509 conversions from Catholics between 1652 and 1672. Nîmes was evolving into a bi-confessional community: the persistence of mixed marriages, conversions in both directions, parity of Catholic and Protestant city councilors, and the juxtaposition of both Protestants and Catholics on the faculty of the college pointed to a model more similar to that of the Holy Roman Empire than France.

Under the direction of Richelieu and Mazarin, the French monarchy preferred persuasion to coercion in dealing with the Protestant minority. Capuchin missions were established by royal patronage in Languedoc after 1629; and the friars ("the poor man's Jesuits," as they were called) undertook preaching missions in the Protestant mountains of the Cévennes while the Jesuits worked the Calvinist notables in the towns and the Ursulines aimed at girls of the elites. Highly publicized conversions aside, the Catholic reform made slow progress in Nîmes. In 1663, there were still 76,000 Protestants versus 34,000 Catholics in the diocese; in the city, the numbers were respectively 12,000 and 8,000. Conversions to Protestantism and mixed marriages continued, despite the harsher interpretation of the Edict of Nantes by Louis XIV. These restrictions culminated in the forced conversions of 1679, a massive missionary campaign immediately followed, ending in the revocation of the edict of toleration in 1685. Protestantism in the Languedoc, however, survived royal repression even after 1685, partly due to its internal cohesion and partly due to the weakness of Catholic reform. The attempt to create a disciplined, Tridentine clergy met with great resistance. A seminary was founded only under the episcopates of Jacques Séguier (1671–87) and Esprit Flechier (1676–1710), the former a brother of the royal chancellor and a doctor of the Sorbonne, the latter son of a candlemaker and a member of the Académie française. Both bishops, northerners and rationalists, failed to transform the traditional Catholics of Languedoc into the new Catholics of a royal France.

The difficulties of Catholic reform in Nîmes reflected its geographical, political, and cultural distance from Paris, the center from which royal power and a new spirit of French Catholicism emanated. Catholic renewal took a very different path in the diocese of Chartres, much closer to the capital. Two reform bishops, Léonor d'Estampes de Valençay (1620–41) and Jacques Lescot (1641–56), embodied the two social groups behind the Catholic reform in France: the first was a courtier-bishop, an agent for Richelieu; the latter, son of a city councilor from St. Quentin, was professor at the Sorbonne and Richelieu's confessor. Together, they carried out diocesan visits, established the new religious orders, and tried to discipline the clergy. Between 1620 and 1650, a series of diocesan visitations managed to produce a more sober and celibate clergy. In a diocese relatively free of Protestants, the Catholic reform aimed at purifying traditional Catholicism of its popular "superstitions." The clergy was the target during the first half of the seventeenth century: episcopal officials, for example, investigated pastors who practiced popular healing in 1628, 1630, and 1651. In the second half of the century, it was the turn of the laity. Synodal decrees condemned clandestine marriages, regulated confraternities, guided processions, censored the profaning of cemeteries, and generally admonished the people, with mixed results, to practice a purified Tridentine Catholicism.

Nowhere was Catholic renewal and the pomp of the Gallican Church more apparent than in Paris. The diocese, first created in 1622, represented the wealthiest in France. It included some of the most prestigious convents in the kingdom: the Benedictine monasteries of St. Denis and St. Germain-des-Prés, and the Cistercian nunnery of Port-Royal, which became synonymous with Jansenism. Clerical reform received a great boost from the work of Vincent de Paul, a dedicated priest and client of the aristocratic Gondi family, from whose ranks came the first archbishop of Paris, Jean-François de Gondi (1622–54). The rural missions founded by Vincent de Paul, supported by the Catholic elites of the capital, steadily improved the quality of the secular clergy; the proximity of the Sorbonne also supplied an increasingly larger proportion of the new clergy, educated, disciplined, and Tridentine. Two specifically new French orders sprang forth in this milieu of the Parisian devouts: Cardinal Bérulle's Oratorians, modeled on the Oratory of Filippo Neri, and the Congregation of Jesus and Mary, founded by a student of the Oratorians, Jean Eudes.

By the second half of the century, rural missions were supplemented by catechism schools. By the 1690s, every parish in the archdeanery of Paris had one catechism school for boys, but only one in all for girls; teaching Christian doctrine to girls seemed to be mainly a task of the female religious orders. A combination of indoctrination, exhortation, and control ensured greater sacramental attendance. In 1672, for example, only 112 parishioners out of an estimated 50,000 communicants in the diocese refused to take the obligatory communion. Conformity, however, did not imply spiritual fervor. That was restricted to a small elite. The example of the Parisian region demonstrates a high degree of sacramental conformity and a functioning but mediocre clergy. The degree of Catholicity, however, should not be measured against the ideal norms set by Trent, or by the hypercritical comments of some preachers and missionaries. In comparison to other dioceses, Paris, Chartres, and Rennes, among others, figured among the more fervent spots. Yet even in Brittany, with strong attachments to Catholicism, the religion of the people failed to measure up to the expectations of the Counter-Reformation elites. Despite the waves of rural missions (1630s–70s), the diocesan visitations, and the new religious orders, the Parlement at Rennes still complained in 1720 of indifference to the office of the mass, when the people preferred drink and dance to the salvation of their souls. Alongside the Marian Jesuit sodalities for the spiritual and social elites, the people continued their devotions to traditional shrines and saints, ignoring the new heroes of the Counter-Reformation for saints that healed their pains and disease.

Catholic renewal and restoration of royal authority became synonymous in France. An implicit alliance between monarchy and episcopacy shaped the character of the Gallican Church. Despite occasional divisions (over Jansenism, or over Cardinal de Retz, archbishop of Paris, who intrigued against Mazarin during the Fronde), the French episcopacy depended on royal power to combat Protestantism and promote Catholic reform. This dependence was underlined by royal patronage, since almost all bishops and abbots were clients of the king or powerful courtiers. Ecclesiastical dignities in the Gallican Church, in fact, served as spoils for the nobility and the judicial elites, who received awards for royal service. We need to note only a few examples: François, Cardinal de Joyeuse, archbishop of Rouen, and dean of the Second Estate in 1614, was of royal blood and the son of the governor of Languedoc; Henri de Bourbon, bishop of Metz and abbot of the prestigious Benedictine monastery St. Germain des Près from 1623 to 1668, was an illegitimate son of Henri IV; and many bishoprics passed from uncle to nephew, such as the Bonzy at Béziers, the Villars at Vienne, the Gondi in Paris, the Sourdis in Bordeaux, and the Harlays at Rouen. This sacred alliance between monarchy and nobility, sealed on the altar of Catholic renewal and defended by the rhetoric of Gallican liberties, was perhaps best summed up by François Bosquet, bishop of Montpellier, who expounded on royal power to the young Louis XIV: "[the power] of the Most Christian King, animated by an almost sacerdotal spirit given by holy anointment, serves the glory of the Kingdom of Jesus Christ, in defending by force the violence which ecclesiastical discipline cannot repress." These were words indeed that presaged the famous encomium of absolute monarchy, espoused by Bishop Bossuet to glorify the reign of Louis XIV.

Germany, Austria, Bohemia

By the end of the sixteenth century, it seemed that the Reformation, unleashed by the writings of the Saxon friar Martin Luther, had just about engulfed the Holy Roman Empire. All of North Germany was lost for Catholicism, except for the Bishopric of Münster; Bohemia, the land of the Hussites and Bohemian Brethren, was largely Protestant; in the middle Rhine, the Palatinate threatened as a bulwark of Protestantism, first as a Lutheran, then a Calvinist principality; in the Southwest, the Duchy of Württemberg and many imperial cities remained staunchly Lutheran; and Protestants flourished even in the hereditary lands of the Habsburgs. Among the seven imperial electors, three were Catholic (the archbishops of Mainz, Trier, and Cologne), three were Protestant (the electors of Brandenburg, Saxony, and the Palatinate), and one (the king of Bohemia) was to pass from the Catholic to the Protestant camp in 1618, a moment that would spark off the Thirty Years War. Further down the hierarchy of imperial estates, Catholic allegiance was confined mainly to the prince-bishops (Würzburg, Bamberg, Münster, Paderborn, Speyer, and Worms being the most prominent), with the notable exception of the duke of Bavaria. Among the Imperial Knights, Protestant allegiance prevailed, even in Franconia where they were nominally vassals of the prince-bishop of Würzburg. For the cities represented in the imperial Diet, fewer than one-third remained Catholic, most of them small agrarian towns in the Southwest and Alsace; among the larger imperial cities no more than one person in ten was Catholic, the most important exceptions being Cologne and Aachen.

We need to think of Catholic renewal in central Europe as two distinct phenomena. In terms of Catholic reform, Tridentine norms did not begin to be established until the early seventeenth century; most measures were implemented after the 1660s and saw fruition only in the eighteenth century; and several reforms, such as the removal of pluralism and clandestine marriages, made little headway at all. Yet a revived Catholic identity was very much in evidence. It took shape in politico-confessional consciousness, as in the formation of a League of Catholic Princes in the empire in the 1590s in defense against a new wave of Calvinist militancy. It demarcated social and geographical boundaries, as citizenship in Catholic cities came to be defined by confessional allegiance, as in Cologne in 1617, and as Catholic peasants in the diocese of Speyer proclaimed their differences from Protestant neighbors, even when they resisted the disciplining measures of Tridentine reforms. Alongside the new Catholicism of Trent, exemplified by reform bishops, Jesuits, and discipline, existed a traditional Catholicism that defended corporate privileges and devotional customs. Everywhere in central Europe, these contending impulses determined the shape of Catholic renewal.

Overwhelmed by the success of the early Reformation movement, the

Catholic Church in the empire began to respond only in the 1540s. The first impulses came from the cities, among an urban Catholic patriciate still loyal to tradition. Johannes Gropper, canon in Cologne and member of the patriciate, was the best-known example. He composed two catechisms in the 1540s, opposed Protestant candidates in the archiepiscopal election, and brought in Jesuits, who made Cologne their first and one of their strongest German strongholds. Although the Religious Peace of Augsburg stabilized the confessional boundary in 1555, Catholic renewal in the spirit of Trent gathered momentum only in the 1580s. The strength of Protestantism represented only part of the problem. Strong resistance to reform was offered by traditional Catholicism, especially by the entrenched corporate interests embodied in the imperial Church (*die Reichskirche*), that collective of bishops, abbots, and other ecclesiastical prelates whose rights were guaranteed by the imperial constitution and who doggedly defended their autonomy and privileges against outside intervention. Like the Gallican Church, the imperial Church represented the interests of the nobility and patriciate. Considered family patrimonies, benefices passed within a restricted elite; and their income was used to ensure a living commensurate with class. As a result, the reform of the clergy envisioned by Trent remained largely a dead letter: clerical concubinage persisted until the early seventeenth century, and even later for members of the clerical elites; pluralism remained a common practice, even among bishops dedicated to Catholic reform, such as the two Bavarian archbishops of Cologne, Ernst and Ferdinand, uncle and nephew; the Tridentine decrees were published in 1612 in Cologne, and the Roman missal only in 1625; the few seminaries established in the seventeenth century lacked sufficient funding and students; and the Tridentine prohibition of clandestine marriages, the decree "Tametsi," was unknown in some rural parishes in the diocese of Cologne as late as the 1660s.

Yet the Catholic renewal made steady progress. Three factors were responsible for this success: first, Counter-Reformation goals coincided with the interests of Catholic dynasties in centralizing the early modern state; second, the fervor of Catholic reform was sustained by a social/spiritual elite that staffed both the ranks of the new religious orders and the administration of the confessional state; third, the Counter-Reformation inspired a revival of traditional forms of Catholic piety and channeled popular devotion into forms more acceptable to Tridentine Catholicism. The first two processes developed in approximate simultaneity, starting in earnest in the 1570s, and endured until 1700; the revival of popular Catholicism took off slowly in the 1660s and reached its climax between 1700 and 1760. Thereafter, elite and popular religion parted ways, as the reforms under Maria Theresa and Joseph I led to the repudiation and destruction of the Counter-Reformation.

Dynastic and confessional interests dovetailed in Bavaria and Austria. Faced with a Protestant noble opposition in the estates, Duke Albrecht V suppressed noble liberties in 1564 and instituted a program of enforcing Catholic conformity and political centralization. A clerical Council, established in 1570, supervised and disciplined the clergy; the Jesuits, lavishly supported by the Wittelsbach dukes, founded colleges, took over the staffing of the university, and trained future generations of officials and clerics for Counter-Reformation Bavaria. Catholicity became the prerequisite for upward social mobility: certificates of confession and communion, to be obtained from the clergy, established qualification for positions on city councils and in the ducal government; the clerics themselves, inspired by Jesuit education and controlled by the state apparatus, in turn vouched for the religious conformity and reliability of the ducal officials. A dynastic cult evolved around the Wittelsbachs, depicting the dukes as moral, pious, Catholic princes, as suggested by the political treatise of the Jesuit Maximilian von Contzen, court confessor in Munich. When the Wittelsbachs assumed control of the northern bishoprics after 1585 (Cologne, Liège, Münster), the Bavarian model was likewise introduced: Archbishop Ferdinand of Cologne established the Church Council in 1601 to instill clerical discipline, an institution supplanted by the Officiate Court in 1616.

This image of the Catholic prince, the opponent of Machiavellian reason of state, was developed to perfection in Austrian Habsburg propaganda. Linked to a miraculous legend, and associated with cults of devotion to the eucharist, the crucifix, and the Virgin Mary, this *pietas Austriaca* was transformed into allegiance to the imperial institutions and loyalty to the dynasty. In Bohemia, a conflict played out in 1618 was similar to one in Bavaria fifty years earlier: a Protestant nobility, centered in the estates, opposing a Catholic monarch, was crushed by the clash of arms at the battle of White Mountain. In spite of the moderation of Prince Karl von Liechtenstein, the emperor's *Statthalter*, repression took a heavy toll. Executions, banishments, and confiscations struck down the Protestant nobility, while discrimination against Protestants imposed a harsh Counter-Reformation regime: in 1624, urban citizenship was restricted to Catholics; in 1626, the clergy was restored to the First Estate; and in 1627, all noble families were given six months to convert or to emigrate. Fifteen pairs of Jesuit and Capuchin missionaries visited Protestant areas and preached conversion; those who refused Catholic words were threatened with the quartering of troops. Such drastic measures obtained outward conformity and created the vision of

Catholic–Habsburg tyranny in nineteenth-century Czech nationalist historiography; they obscured the milder effort to renew Catholicism, exemplified by the founding of Jesuit colleges under the patronage of the Catholic magnates.

If the Counter-Reformation succeeded in Bohemia by force, Catholicism gained grounds in the heartland of the empire more by patronage and persuasion. As the empire recovered from the Thirty Years War, and as the Habsburgs enjoyed a resurgent prestige, the imperial court in Vienna was able to extend patronage beyond its traditional clients. Habsburg patronage, in addition to keeping an imperial city such as Überlingen in the Catholic orbit, exerted a greater pull in a re-ordered Holy Roman Empire. For a century after 1613, one Protestant prince after another converted to Catholicism, in search of territory, title, office, or conscience: Wolfgang Wilhelm, duke of Palatinate-Neuburg converted in 1613 to inherit the duchies of Jülich and Berg; Friedrich of Hesse-Darmstadt converted in 1636; Christoph Wilhelm of Brandenburg in the Thirty Years War, along with other prominent captives of Habsburg arms; Landgrave Ernst of Hesse-Rheinfels converted in 1651; Christian August of Sulzbach in 1656; Friedrich August, elector of Saxony in 1697; and Carl Alexander, later duke of Württemberg, in 1712. Others, less exalted figures, followed in their footsteps – Protestant magistrates, theologians, and professors – a process not unlike Huguenot defections to Catholicism and the monarchy in seventeenth-century France.

The Society of Jesus constituted one of the central forces behind the Catholic recovery in central Europe. Circumventing the privileged corporations of the imperial Church, the Jesuits trained a new breed of clergy and officials in their many colleges and in the Collegium Germanicum in Rome. From a modest beginning of half a dozen Jesuits in the college at Cologne (1544), the Society had grown to five provinces by 1630 (Upper Rhine, Lower Rhine, Upper Germany, Austria, and Bohemia) with close to three thousand members. In addition to the generations of young men educated at the Jesuit colleges in the empire, another 3,899 students graduated from the Collegium Germanicum in Rome between 1552 and 1797. Elected to episcopal sees, acquiring benefices, appointed as vicars, officials, and suffragan bishops, these Germanici, as the alumni were called, identified with the values of Tridentine Catholicism. They battled entrenched corporate interests, pushed through reforms, and fought Protestantism: in Breslau, they constituted the "Counter-Reformation" faction in the cathedral chapter; in Münster, they supported Christoph Bernhard von Galen, one of their own, against a rival episcopal candidate; in Cologne, Trier, and other bishoprics, they took helm at the episcopal government, setting the tone of Catholicism, at least from the top. They began to make a difference after the first decades of the seventeenth century. It was due to these Tridentine clerics that Tridentine reform achieved some measure of success after 1650.

Behind this Jesuit wave lay a significant social transformation: weakened in their ties to the civic communes, the elites in Catholic towns reoriented themselves to loyalties that transcended the city walls. The mercantile urban elite of the sixteenth century was slowly turning into an office-holding, judicial elite in the course of one or two generations. Service to the prince and to the universal Catholic Church provided both paths of social mobility as well as the symbols for a more glorious, transcendent consciousness. In Cologne, the new Tridentine Catholicism grew out of the ranks of the traditional Catholic elites; Johann Rhetius (1532–74), rector of the first Jesuit college, was the son of a five-term Cologne Bürgermeister. In Münster, the Counter-Reformation party first consolidated around the judicial elites in service of the government of the Wittelsbach archbishops (they were also bishops of Münster) during the 1580s; these newcomers in city politics, recent immigrants and socially successful, were joined one or two generations later by established Catholic elite families. In Munich, the leading proponent of the witch-hunt, the chancellor of the privy council Johann Sigmund Wagnereckh sent all three of his sons to the Jesuit order, one of whom, Heinrich, rose to prominence as university chancellor in Dillingen.

It was not all confrontation between the new Tridentine Catholicism and the old. True, the Counter-Reformation states instituted stricter mechanisms to enforce religious conformity: in Bavaria, bailiffs and priests certified mass attendance, confession, and communion, and thoroughly pursued dissent and witchcraft; in the bishopric of Cologne, diocesan visitations were supplemented by a reinvigorated synodal court that relied on informants and fines; in Salzburg, persistent resistance by Protestant peasants to the authority of the prince-bishop led to the expulsion of 17,000 in 1731. But there were unmistakable signs of Catholic renewal among the populace, even without coercion and discipline. Pilgrimage revived in the early decades of the seventeenth century. At first an urban movement, pilgrimages to the Marian shrine at Telgte or to the Holy Blood shrine at Walldürn spawned elaborate institutional practices: sodalities, confraternities, devotional prints, and pilgrimage medals connected these small town shrines to wider networks of Catholic communities. Ecclesiastical authorities quickly stepped in to keep "excesses" and "popular superstitions" in check, as Bishop von Galen in Münster succeeded in establishing clerical authority over the Telgte cult. In South

Germany, the common people imitated the piety of their rulers: the Marian shrine at Altötting, the site of Wittelsbach and Habsburg piety in the seventeenth century, became a popular destination in the eighteenth, alongside the shrines at Passau, Vierzehnheiligen, Benediktbeuren, and other lesser ones.

5 The martyred Church

In a geographic band across northwestern Europe ruled by Protestant regimes, Catholicism was outlawed, persecuted, and repressed, much like the experience of the erstwhile Protestant dissidence that had become the official Church in England,[1] Ireland, and the northern Low Countries. Caught in the dynastic and confessional conflicts that shaped Europe from 1570 to 1650, Catholics faced divided political and religious loyalties. In England, a minority plotted to overthrow the Protestant regime with the help of foreign arms, dreaming of restoring a Catholic monarchy while the majority stayed loyal to a government that persecuted them. In Ireland, the Counter-Reformation channeled resentment against English conquest into a religio-political struggle that gave identity to a nascent Catholic Irish nation. In the Netherlands, the large Catholic population, sustained by missions from the Catholic south, achieved a *modus vivendi* with the new republic, in which an official Calvinist Church and religious toleration existed side by side. In all three countries, Catholicism was shaped by the strength of the laity and characterized by a weak ecclesiastical hierarchy, strong kinship and communal structures, and the primacy of missions over uniform parish life.

England

Elizabeth's ascension to the throne in 1558 dashed the hopes of a Catholic restoration in England. The short years of Mary's reign and the rigor of her repression of Protestants did not endear Catholicism to the English population. Early Elizabethan Catholicism, though it cut across all social classes, was heavily elitist: almost half of the English exiles to the Continent and those persecuted under the anti-Catholic legislations came from landowning classes. Its upper-class character further enhanced by the severe persecutions during the latter years of Elizabeth's

[1] In this chapter, "England" refers to England and Wales.

reign, English Catholicism became in the seventeenth century a minority religion dominated by the gentry.

The history of Catholicism in early modern England can be divided into three periods: an initial period from the 1560s to the 1620s marked by growth, persecutions, martyrdom, and exceptional elan; a middle period of stability followed by decline from the 1630s to 1700; and a final period of recovery and stability during the eighteenth century leading to the end of discrimination in the nineteenth century.

During the last decades of the sixteenth century, the fate of English Catholicism reflected the larger confessional and dynastic struggles in Europe. In the 1560s, English Catholic exiles in the Spanish Low Countries wrote many anti-government and anti-Protestant tracts that were smuggled back into their homeland, repeating a pattern that characterized English Protestant dissent in an earlier generation. Led by intellectuals, the exiles included more than one hundred former fellows and dons from Oxford, many dissatisfied with the spiritual vacuity of the Anglican Church and the political expediency of the Elizabethan regime. In 1568, one of the exiles, William Allen (d. 1594), founded a college for English priests at Douai, which became one of the major seminaries for training missionaries. Its first graduate left for England in 1574; a total of 440 priests from the Douai College worked as missionaries in England between 1574 and 1603 and 98 of them were executed by the Elizabethan regime. The savagery of persecutions reflected the deep insecurity felt by the queen (who was herself religiously indifferent) and her advisors (who were ardent Protestants) in the face of internal rebellion and foreign invasions: in 1569 the Northern Rising under the duke of Northumberland raised the Catholic banner; in 1570 Pope Pius V excommunicated and deposed Elizabeth, giving implicit sanction to any Catholic to assassinate a heretical monarch; in the 1570s Gregory XIII sponsored fantastic schemes of invasion and assassination, resulting only in the desultory attempts to aid Irish resistance in 1578 and 1579; in the 1580s Spain and England confronted one another in the Low Countries; and in 1588 England faced and defeated a Spanish invasion.

Seen as potential traitors, English Catholics faced savage repressions. In the 1570s laws were passed requiring church attendance and the government kept census lists of Catholic recusants who were fined and imprisoned; further legislation forbade the ownership of papal writs; in 1581, after the conviction of the Jesuit missionary Edmund Campion on fabricated charges of treason, the regime declared the presence of Catholic clergy on English soil a capital offense; between the first execution in 1577 and Elizabeth's death in 1603, the regime executed 183 Catholics (including 123 priests) and fined, imprisoned, tortured, and deported thousands more. Tensions eased only in the last years of Elizabeth's reign when Clement VIII abandoned schemes to depose Elizabeth; under James I English Catholics were generally acknowledged as loyal subjects and the anti-Catholic legislation lost much of its rigor in application.

Not unlike the growth of the Protestant movement, the bloody repression under Elizabeth gave the Catholic cause charisma and the mission its martyr-heroes: the brilliant Oxford humanist-turned-missionary, Edmund Campion, the poet Robert Southwell, also a Jesuit, and many others. There was no lack of vocations. Catholic gentry and mercantile families sent their sons to be educated on the Continent; in addition to Douai, an English College in Rome under Jesuit supervision was established in 1576 and a college for English Catholics was financed by Philip II in Valladolid.

Danger gave glamor to the early missions. Dressed as merchants and tradesmen, missionary priests returned to England in disguise, trying to stay ahead of informants, spies, and agents of the government, traveling, staying, and ministering the sacraments in Catholic houses and manors, fed, supported, and hidden by a secret Catholic network. In hidden chapels and house attics, the priests heard confession, said mass, and gave spiritual counseling. The Counter-Reformation entered England not in the guise of reforming bishops, diocesan synods, and a strengthened sacramental life centered around the parish, but rather as an intensely individual spirituality.

Conditions improved after the savage repressions of the 1580s. In 1598 there were eighteen Jesuits in England; by 1607 their number had shot up to 130 and it would stay between 150 and 200 until the suppression of the Society. The dominance of the Jesuits should not eclipse the effort of other missionaries: in addition to a small but important Benedictine presence, the secular clergy supplied more than half of the mission's personnel. At first under the direction of the Jesuits, the secular clergy, increasingly irritated by the political bad press of the Jesuits, was placed under the archpriest, George Blackwell, nominated by Rome in 1598. His nomination did not end friction between the Jesuits and the secular priests; only the appointment of William Bishop and Richard Smith as successive bishops of Chalcedon (1623–31) smoothed over the problems of different missionary jurisdictions. The English Catholic community could count about 300 priests in 1603, a number that reached its peak strength of 750 in 1634. The crisis of the Civil War in the 1640s and the so-called Popish Plot in 1678 reduced the size of the clergy, which recovered to a stable level of 400–500 priests during the eighteenth century.

The recruitment of missionaries went through three distinct periods.

Until 1610, students at the continental English seminaries were drawn about equal parts from the gentry and the commons: at the Roman seminary sons of gentry comprised 47 percent of the students as against 53 percent for those from a commoner background; in Valladolid the percentages were 49 percent versus 51 percent. By the early seventeenth century, the social origins of English missionaries had become mostly gentry: in the 1610s, two-thirds of the students in Rome came from gentry family; in the 1650s, three-quarters were gentry. The trend was reversed only toward the end of the century, the result of more scholarships for needy students and apparently declining vocations among the gentry: the students at Douai between 1691 and 1750 included only 37 percent gentry, the rest being commoners.

Repression and discrimination necessarily limited the size of the English Catholic community. An estimate puts the number of Catholic communicants in 1603 at 30,000, out of a population of 2.5 million; the community grew rapidly to about 60,000 in 1641 and stabilized at around 80,000 in 1770. At no time did the English Catholic community represent more than a small fraction of the population. Separated from their neighbors by feasts and fasts, addicted to popish priests and mass, as their hostile countrymen saw it, English Catholics grew distinctly apart in a realm where Protestant identity came to signify nationhood. Geographically strongest in the north (from Lancashire and Yorkshire to the Scottish border), the social profile of English Catholicism took shape during the early years of persecution. Deprived of an ecclesiastical structure, English Catholicism resembled the many Protestant sects that sprang up during the English Civil War: kinship, household, and charismatic leadership gave tone to its contours.

Women, in particular, played a crucial role in the early decades. In York, the wives of Catholic tradesmen were outspoken in adhering to their faith. Among the gentry, women again featured prominently. Many Protestant or conformist gentlemen had Catholic wives; government legislation to have householders pay fines for their recusant spouses met with strong opposition. Among the Catholic gentry, wives presided over the household, raising children in the Roman faith, supervising the observance of fasting, arranging for the visits of priests, and proselytizing among servants and tenants. Perhaps the most famous example of strong Catholic matriarchs was Dorothy Lawson (1580–1632), whose father, Sir Henry Constable, was one of the wealthiest men in the North and M.P. for Yorkshire, and whose mother, Margaret Dormer, used one of the many remote family estates as a hideout for priests. After her marriage to Roger Lawson in 1597, Dorothy Lawson converted her mother-in-law and most of her family. Her husband, however, remained a Protestant and practiced law in London while Dorothy retired with her children to a family estate near Newcastle, which became a center for Jesuit missions in the northeast. Lawson's background was similar to that of Mary Ward, also the daughter of Yorkshire Catholic gentry, whose evangelical zeal on the Continent was nurtured in the female religious activism in the English North. The importance of women was also revealed by the testimonies of many English students at the continental seminaries, who attributed family and maternal influence to their vocations. This era of Catholic matriarchy ended in the 1620s with the amelioration of the recusancy laws, enabling Catholic patriarchs to assert greater authority in their households. In any event, kinship solidarity and household discipline seemed paramount. Adherence to Catholic faith radiated from the authority of the Catholic householders to their children, servants, and tenants; early modern English Catholicism assumed its special social and spatial shape in clusters of local groups centered on a gentleman's household. This was a Catholic revival that domesticated the missionary priests, who depended on the financial support and protection of the gentry.

The Netherlands

Conditions for Catholicism in the early modern Dutch Republic resembled the English case with two significant differences: first, the repressive measures were much less severe, both in actual legislation and in application; second, unlike in England, Catholics in the United Provinces composed a large part of the population, being in the majority during the early years of the revolt against Spain and still constituting some 48 percent of the population in 1650. Still, on the surface of things, Catholics faced many hardships. Like their English co-religionists they were deprived by law of many public rights. The first anti-Catholic *placat* passed by the States-General in 1581 outlawed Catholic worship in churches and private houses, forbade the wearing of clerical garb, closed Catholic schools, and suppressed Catholic writings; infractions were punished with fines, which were increased to confiscation of property after the assassination of William of Orange in 1584. Anti-Catholic legislation continued into the eighteenth century; provincial and local authorities regularly published anti-Catholic *placats*, including further prohibition against sending Catholic children to be educated abroad. The rigor of these measures was attenuated by the absence of a strong central government and by the voluntary nature of the official or public Calvinist Church. In Holland, the most populous and prosperous province, anti-Catholic legislation was applied with moderation, but in Zeeland,

Drenthe, Groningen, and the Generality Lands (the area to the south conquered from the Spanish Low Countries in the early seventeenth century), repression was harsher: Catholics were compelled to be married and to have their children baptized by Calvinist preachers, and had to attend their sermons.

In the central provinces of the Republic, nonetheless, the authorities overlooked numerous infractions for a fee. Venality and toleration seemed to go hand in hand, decried many Calvinist preachers, but the practice was institutionalized. Magistrates collected these fees, called *recognities*, to allow the visit of a Catholic missionary or to grant permission for the construction of a Catholic church; later, more extensive concessions were given in exchange for *composities*, by which a Catholic community would pay yearly fees for the right of worship. In spite of prohibitions by the States-General and the States of Holland, magistrates continued to collect *recognities* and *composities* in exchange for the *de facto* recognition of Catholicism. The Dutch ruling classes found repression distasteful, for theirs was a republic born out of resistance to religious intolerance. Some, especially in the towns of Holland, found Catholicism attractive; in 1620–25, several hundred patricians, who had supported the recently disgraced faction of Remonstrants in the Calvinist Church, converted to Catholicism. Moreover, the regents themselves benefited personally from these practices: in 1643, the States of Holland appointed Lord van Wimmenum, the bailiff of Rijnland, to investigate the enforcement of anti-Catholic legislation, not knowing that the bailiff himself had taken thousands in guldens. In 1651 the Synod of the Calvinist Church petitioned the States-General to enforce the *placats*; in 1656 and 1666 the States-General imposed fines on officials who "composed" with Catholics. Renewed in 1730, 1735, 1755, and 1760, this *placat* remained a dead letter; the old practices continued.

Shielded from the full rigor of anti-Catholic legislation, the Dutch Catholic community was further sustained by missionaries from the Spanish Netherlands. Entrusted to the Jesuit Sasbout Vosmeer, appointed apostolic vicar by the pope, the Holland mission nevertheless used mostly secular priests for fear that the "Spanish character" of the Jesuits would give provocation in the North. The conclusion of the twelve-year truce in 1609 between Spain and the Netherlands facilitated missionary work. In 1616, there were 219 priests in the Dutch Republic (200 seculars, 15 Jesuits, and 4 Franciscans); by 1642, the missionaries numbered 500 (360 seculars, 74 Jesuits, and the rest from other religious orders). Born in the north, these missionaries typically went to study in the Catholic south; after their return, family and friendship networks facilitated their ministry.

Similar to the English case, Dutch Catholicism also developed its own special geographical and social character. Strongly represented in the towns of Holland and Utrecht (where toleration was common), Catholicism formed a solid bloc in the conquered Generality Lands of Brabant. In Den Bosch, for example, the population strongly resisted Protestant evangelization; in 1700, some 140 out of 194 parishes in the diocese remained Catholic and relied on missionaries from the south for the sacraments. Socially, Dutch Catholicism found adherents among the elites and the rural populace, in contrast to the strong Protestant loyalties of the merchants, tradesmen, and laborers of Holland towns, and the rich peasants and fisherfolk of Zeeland. Besides its attraction for the patriciate, Catholicism also counted many adherents and converts among the intellectual elites: the painters Rembrandt, Frans Hals, Hendrick de Keyser, and Johannes Vermeer, the poet Joost van den Vondel, and the Leiden professor Petrus Bertius. Between 1640 and 1700, Catholicism attracted a small but steady number of converts from the clerical, academic, and social elites of the Dutch Republic. Outside the big towns, clientage played an important role. With the exception of the solidly Catholic Generality Lands, pockets of Catholicism often clustered around the patronage and protection of a local lord.

Like the English Catholics, Dutch Catholics developed a strong devotion to their martyrs, especially the monks at Gorcum massacred by Calvinist Sea Beggars during the initial uprising against Spain. *The History of the Gorcum Martyrs*, written by Willem Estius, was published in 1603; promoted vigorously by the Jesuits, the cult was approved by the Congregation of Rites in 1621 and by the papacy in 1675.

Ireland

In 1542 two Jesuit missionaries – a Frenchman and a Spaniard – visited Ireland via Scotland. The fathers were unimpressed. They thought the Irish barbarous, immoral, and their observance of Christian rituals a far cry from continental standards. Yet fifty years later, Catholic Ireland would stand in the forefront of the militant Counter-Reformation. In this predominantly Catholic land, allegiance to Rome came to be identified with tradition; and the goals of the Tridentine Church would provide an ideology for armed resistance against foreign conquest by Protestant England.

Not all Catholics, however, identified England as the enemy. The Old English – descendants of Anglo-Norman conquest centered in Dublin and surrounding towns – tried to balance their Catholicism with allegiance to the English monarchy; the Old Irish – Gaelic speakers with strong traditional clan ties – oscillated between resigned acceptance of English lordship and armed resistance. During the last quarter of the sixteenth century, a new wave of English plantations, justified in the name of Christianizing an uncivilized people, acted as a catalyst to the volatile mix of religion and politics. The official Protestant Church, however, commanded little allegiance beyond the officials, settlers, and soldiers of the Elizabethan regime. With the establishment of an official Protestant Church of Ireland and with the coming of continental Catholic missionaries, the Irish gentry, like their English Catholic counterparts, began to send their sons abroad for education. The first Irish abroad came mostly from Old English families and were included among the students at the Douai seminary for English priests, which became the model for the subsequent foundations of Irish colleges on the Continent.

The 1590s represented a turning point. The defeat of the northern earls in the Nine Years' War (1594–1603), an anti-English and anti-Protestant uprising in Ulster under the leadership of Hugh O'Neill and aided by Spain, led to a massive exile. Deprived of their land and livelihood, the Irish lords and their retainers sought patronage and protection on the Continent with the Habsburgs. Further repressive measures by the English regime drove large numbers of Catholic clerics abroad, a movement that turned into a torrent after the crushing of another, larger uprising in 1652. Between 1590 and 1681 no fewer than twenty Irish colleges were established on the Continent. The largest numbers were in the Spanish Netherlands: in Antwerp, Louvain, Nieuwpoort, Dunkirk, Ypres, Lille, St.-Omer, Brussels, Tournai, and Douai; others were founded in Spain, France, and Italy. Hundreds of Irish priests received their training in these continental seminaries, where they absorbed the teachings of the Tridentine Church and returned home as bearers of a new militant Catholicism. By 1613, Douai had sent 149 priests back to Ireland; the College of St. Patrick at Salamanca, endowed by Philip II, had sent back 148. Of the 800 diocesan priests in Ireland at this time, the majority had been trained on the Continent. The Irish clergy abroad served as transmitters of the Counter-Reformation. The first Tridentine catechism in the Gaelic language, for example, was translated from the Spanish by the Franciscan Flaithrí O Maoil Chonaire (Florence Conry); the first printed Gaelic catechism, the *Teagasg Críosdaithe* (1611), was adapted from Cardinal Bellarmine's catechism by the Franciscan Bonaventure O'Hussey and printed in Antwerp; still other religious writings and devotional treatises in Gaelic were published in Antwerp, Brussels, and Louvain. This last named university town in the Spanish Netherlands became the center for Catholic Gaelic literature, thanks to the Irish friars.

From the pen of these exiled Irish clerics came a new historical interpretation that extolled Catholicism and Gaelic civilization. In the major work of history, the *Foras Feasa ar Eirinn* (History of Ireland), written by Geoffrey Keating in the 1630s, an Old English priest educated at Bordeaux, Irish society before the Norman invasion was portrayed as Christian and civilized. This golden age of the Gaelic past, made to harmonize with the values of Tridentine Catholicism, was said to exemplify a moral standard consonant with the demands of the Counter-Reformation Church. Keating argued furthermore that the recent English conquerors, like the Scandinavian invaders of earlier times, would eventually be expelled. Counter-Reformation polemic bolstered the sense of national pride. A passage in the catechism by Bonaventure O'Hussey illustrates this sentiment:

> It is beyond all reason that the old holy fathers of the Church Ambrose, Augustine, Jerome, Gregory . . . or St. Patrick who brought Ireland to the faith . . . who performed miracles, or other Irish saints such as Colm Chill, Bridget, Ciaran, and many more besides whose holiness and miraculous deeds cannot be verified, should be accused of going astray in their faith . . . that Luther whose master is the devil . . . should have correct and precise knowledge of his faith.

A Catholic Gaelic culture was also enshrined as the locus of resistance to Protestant English conquest in the ecclesiastical history, the *Acta sanctorum Hiberniae*, written in the 1640s by the Irish Franciscan John Colgan in Louvain. Ireland, a holy land, had bred saints and scholars for centuries; and this idyllic history was only temporarily interrupted by the English conquest and the English Reformation.

Many of the exiled Irish clerics were connected with the elites of Gaelic Ireland. Some, notably Florence Conry, founder of the Irish Franciscan college in Louvain, had participated in the rising of the northern earls in 1601. Others descended from families of hereditary poets, traditional clients of the powerful Irish lords. The ideology of Catholic resistance reflected the closely knitted clerical–military network among the Irish exiles in the Spanish Netherlands. The defeated Irish lords and their retainers found employment in the Army of Flanders: between 1586 and 1621, more than 5,000 Irish mustered in the Spanish army; many served directly in an Irish regiment formed in 1605 by Henry O'Neill, son of Hugh, the earl of Tyrone. Henry himself had been the pupil of Hugh MacCaughwell, guardian of the Franciscan college St. Anthony's in Louvain and chief chaplain of the Irish regiment. In fact, the O'Neill network connected not only soldiery and clergy, but also Brussels and Madrid. In addition to the O'Neills and MacCaughwell, other prominent members included Conry, who advised the Spanish court on Irish politics, Eugene MacMahon, archbishop of Dublin, and the Franciscan

Robert Chamberlain, educated at Salamanca and Louvain and serving as personal chaplain to Hugh O'Neill. The Irish regiment and the militant friars constituted thus the best hope for foreign intervention among the militant Catholics at home, as well as an instrument of warfare and diplomacy for the Spanish Habsburgs. Many other family ties pointed to a wider network between Irish arms and the Gaelic cross: Cecilia and Eleanor Dillon, two founding members of the Irish Poor Clares in Gravelines in 1625, were sisters to James Dillon, a captain in the Irish regiment; four of the other five founding Poor Clares also had relatives in the Army of Flanders. Whereas Louvain shone as the intellectual center of Irish exile, Brussels accommodated the Irish exile community, clustered in the parishes of St. Michael, St. Eude, and St. Catherine.

No wonder the regime in Dublin viewed Catholic clergy as ringleaders in the rebellion against English authority. In 1605 and 1611, it banned all foreign missionaries; in 1612 it executed Cornelius O'Devany, bishop of Down; in 1617 it banned all Irish clergy who had studied abroad; between 1641 and 1652, it executed scores of clerics during the suppression of the Irish Uprising; and it exiled more than 1,000 priests after the Irish forces at the last stronghold of Galway surrendered in 1652. The Flemish connection concocted many insurrections: the chief conspirator in the 1605 Gunpowder Plot to blow up the Houses of Parliament and King James I, Guy Fawkes, had served in the Army of Flanders; the 1641 Uprising in Ireland was led by Owen Roe O'Neill and Thomas Preston, two veterans of the Army of Flanders; and many of the Catholic clergy at Kilkenny who supported the insurgent Catholic Confederacy against Dublin had been trained in the Belgian colleges.

Not all Catholics in Ireland supported the violent overthrow of English rule. The Old English, in particular, feared provoking greater religious restrictions. In the peaceful decades between the Nine Years' War and the 1641 Uprising, Catholic missionaries went about their work with little interference. The government in Dublin was too weak to enforce its authority in all corners of the land; and the people stood solidly behind their clergy. These decades of Catholic renewal brought into sharp focus the conflict between two kinds of Catholicism, one Gaelic, traditional, oral, ritual, focused on kinship obligations; the other continental, Tridentine, textual, sacramental, centered on individual culpability. These underlying tensions became manifest in the ecclesiastical politics between 1618 and 1650.

Before 1618, English repression rendered impossible a resident Irish episcopacy. But the accommodation between the papacy and the Stuart monarchy allowed for a greater degree of religious toleration, a move welcomed by the Old English in Ireland. In 1618, David Rothe was appointed bishop of Ossory; in the following years, many of the vacant sees were also filled, mostly with Old English Catholics. The reconstituted Irish episcopacy saw its task as the peaceful introduction of Tridentine reform, a process to be safeguarded by political loyalty to the English monarchy and intended to eradicate the superstitious and, in its views, the uncivilized ways of Gaelic Ireland. Upholding an ideal Catholic hierarchy centered on episcopal governance and an orderly parish life, the bishops tried to assert their authority, sanctioned by the Council of Trent, over the laity and the regular clergy. Espousing discipline, morality, and sobriety, theirs was a religion of towns, so well tested in the metropolitan centers of continental Catholic Europe. Traditional Gaelic society, in contrast, was shaped by its rural character, deeply attached to kinship and clan loyalties, and embedding religious rituals in larger kin and group solidarities. In this traditional world, the friars, particularly the Franciscans, played an integral role, serving as holy men to kin groups, mediating feuds, and facilitating the travel of departed kinsmen from this world to the next. Conflicts over ecclesiastical jurisdiction between the religious orders and bishops, a pattern common enough in post-Tridentine Catholicism, thus assumed the nature of a larger cultural conflict. Rituals and sacraments became flashpoints: in confession, the Tridentine clergy stressed the contrition of the individual sinner as against the satisfaction due the offended party; in marriage they inserted clerical authority into the traditional arrangement between kin groups; in burials, they decried the licentiousness and feasting that accompanied funeral wakes by which a kin group affirmed its solidarity over death. Visitation reports by bishops and foreign-trained priests painted a picture of religious observance far from the standards established by Tridentine Catholicism.

The resumption of war between Spain and England in 1625 accentuated the divisions within Irish Catholicism. Opposing five loyal Old English bishops and the Old English Catholic gentry stood four pro-Spanish bishops and the partisans of Ulster, clients of the exiled earl of Tyrone. On one side was the hope of greater royal toleration at the price of obedience; on the other, the vision of a full restoration of Catholic Ireland, the eradication of English Protestantism, and the removal of the plantations. Disunity persisted during the uprising in the 1640s and the call to overthrow the Stuart monarchy by the papal nuncio in Ireland, Cardinal Rinuccini, hardly bridged the gap. In any event, the clash of arms decided the cause of religion. Massacres of English Protestants during the early stages of the Uprising fueled the Black Legend of Catholic perfidy and cruelty. Protestant hatred condemned all Catholics. Oliver Cromwell's victorious army carried out savage reprisals; and the

Commonwealth confiscated land from many Catholics, Old Irish and Old English alike. Dealt a severe blow, Catholicism in Ireland recovered slowly after the restoration in 1660. A disciplined, Tridentine Catholicism might have made slow progress against kinship solidarity and traditional religion, but the Counter-Reformation had given a nascent national consciousness to a people martyred for their religion and resistance.

6 The papal curia

In 1529 Gasparo Contarini, Venetian ambassador to Rome and a future cardinal of the Church, addressed the following speech to Clement VII:

> Do you not think, Your Holiness, that the good of Christendom is this little temporal state which the Church has acquired? Before it was a state, it was the Church and the best Church. The Church is the university of all Christians. This state is like the state of a prince of Italy attached to the Church. Therefore, Your Holiness, you must principally obtain the good of the true Church, which consists of the peace and tranquility of Christians, and postpone for now everything in connection with the temporal state.

Contarini's discourse reflected the view of the Catholic reform party, but the call to forsake the temporal interests of the papacy for spirituality fell on deaf ears. During the Council of Trent defenders of the papacy limited reforms to "the members" of the Church, leaving the reform of "the head" to the papacy itself. But that reform – carried out in fitful measures and dependent on the personal asceticism of the popes – was long in coming. While the general moral tone in the Roman curia after Trent turned more ascetic, dignified, and saintly (one pope, Pius V, was even canonized in 1712), the institutional development between the Renaissance and the Baroque papacy showed a remarkable continuity. Two trends were central: first, the transformation of the papacy into an absolute monarchy, with the attendant development of a papal court (the curia) and a more centralized administration within the Papal States, drawing upon the service of the feudal nobility and the emerging urban elites; second, the intermingling of temporal and spiritual realms, reflecting the combination of the two sometimes contradictory roles of the pontiff, as prince of an Italian state and the supreme pastor of the universal Church. The internal logic of the papal curia, as a socio-political system, as it were, largely negated the reforms of Trent.

Who were the popes? Between 1540 and 1770 twenty-nine men wore the tiara. All were Italians. A breakdown of their geographic origins yields the dominant position of central and northern Italy (see table 6.1). Four popes each came from Rome and Bologna, the two largest cities in the

Table 6.1. *Geographic origins of the popes 1540–1770*

Region	Number of popes
Papal States	12
Tuscany	8
Duchy of Milan	4
Naples	3
Republic of Venice	2

Papal States; three from Florence and two from Siena, Tuscan cities with long ties to the papacy, and two from Venice.

While the early modern popes came from different social backgrounds, only two (Pius V and Sixtus V) had humble origins. The rest hailed from families of the ruling elite: the Farnese Paul III traced his descent from a famous *condottiere* dynasty and raised his family to ducal status during his reign; the Carafa Paul IV came from a Neapolitan baronial lineage; Gregory XV's father was the count of Pompeio; the dei Conti Innocent XIII and the Orsini Benedict XIII were sons of dukes; the Castagna (Urban VII), Rospigliosi (Clement IX), Ottoboni (Alexander VIII), Pignatelli (Innocent XII), Albani (Clement XI), Corsini (Clement XII), and Rezzonico (Clement XIII) were nobles; the urban patriciate – bankers, jurists, professors, merchants, officials, notaries – supplied Julius III, Marcellus II, Pius IV, Gregory XIII, Gregory XIV, Innocent IX, Clement VIII, Leo XI, Paul V, Urban VIII, Innocent X, Alexander VII, Clement X, and Innocent XI, the largest contingent, with fourteen out of twenty-nine popes.

The aristocratic character of the papacy became more marked during the Baroque period; the only two popes from humble backgrounds – Pius V (1566–72) and Sixtus V (1585–90) – were elected in the aftermath of Trent and embodied the spirit of the Counter-Reformation. They proved the exceptions to the rule. After 1590 the papacy became the exclusive preserve of the Italian elites. During the Baroque, the path to the cardinalate and ultimately the papal throne passed through a series of recognized markers, and progress was facilitated by family status, wealth, connections, and talent, as one 1621 observer in Rome remarked, "cardinals are elevated out of family, merit, wealth, and nomination by princes." A typical curriculum vitae for the Baroque popes might look something like this: born into a well-connected family, the young aspirant, after his initial studies, would pursue a legal education; his first position in the curia having been secured by a kinsman or patron, whether by succession (a kinsman resigning his office), purchase, or nomination, the young man would prove himself in a series of offices, slowly climbing the ladder of success in the papal administration – from the two great courts of the rota and the camera or a lesser governorship to nunciatures and small bishoprics, followed by greater governorships and more prestigious nunciatures – until receiving the purple. Once one was elevated into the college of cardinals, the political connections built up over a lifetime, in addition to character and ability, would determine one's chances of being included among the *papabili* (those deemed electable in the papal conclave).

There existed, naturally, variations to this standard pattern of advancement: Alessandro Farnese (Paul III) was elevated to the cardinalate thanks to his sister Giulia, the mistress to Alexander VI; Michele Ghislieri (Pius V), who distinguished himself through his implacable orthodoxy and his work as head of the Roman Inquisition, was elected primarily for his saintly reputation. If these two men represented respectively the worldly Renaissance and ascetic Counter-Reformation papacy, the majority of early modern popes eschewed these extremes: they were more likely to be canon lawyers, whose private lives did not give rise to scandal, steeped in long years of papal administration and diplomacy, and astute in the politics of patronage in the Roman curia. The importance of jurisprudence is reflected in their educational background: nineteen popes held doctorates in canon and Roman law; five were humanists; and only three experts in theology.

Another way of interpreting this preponderance of jurists is to say that the pope of the Baroque era was more likely to be a secular cleric, trained in canon law, and rose through service in the papal curia. Only four of the twenty-nine popes came from religious orders: Paul IV was a co-founder of the Theatines; the Dominicans supplied two, Pius V and Benedict XIII, and the Franciscans one, Sixtus V. It is significant that the only two popes from humble social origins (Pius V and Sixtus V) were mendicant friars, whereas the eighteenth-century Dominican pope, Benedict XIII (1724–30) represented the exception to the rule: he accepted papal election reluctantly and only upon the urging of the superior of his order; his deviation from the pattern of the *papabili* only underscored his distinction, being the son of the duke of Gravina, of the illustrious Roman clan Orsini, with two popes among his ancestors.

Taken as a whole, one can discern a transformation in the character of the papacy: from the more worldly Renaissance papal court, with its strong humanist and artistic interests, dominated by a handful of princely families, and often ridden by scandals, to a short-lived Counter-Reformation papacy in the second half of the sixteenth century, austere and ascetic, privileging theology and Inquisition, to a papacy of the Baroque era when the career of a pope ran through the stages of jurist, courtier, administrator, diplomat, and cardinal, and when the papal curia became the institution of social advancement for the aristocracy and urban patriciate of Italy.

Yet these changes belied an underlying institutional continuity in the history of the papacy between the late fifteenth and late seventeenth centuries. An ecclesiastical career at the top, and in general the development of the papacy into an absolutist monarchy, cannot be understood without taking into consideration the family strategies of the Italian ruling classes. Behind many papal elections were stories of family success: the attainment of supreme ecclesiastical glory was built upon the astute accumulation of wealth, the patient cultivation of patronage, and the investment in office, sustained by different kin and carried out over generations. When an individual was elevated to the throne of St. Peter, it was expected that he would seal the fortunes of his family by lavish gifts and favors. The phenomenon of nepotism, as we will see, survived the Tridentine reforms by more than a century.

Not only did the papacy recruit from the most elevated classes in early modern Italy, the papal curia also served as an institution for social advancement. The Farnese, Boncompagnis, Perettis, Sfondratis, Aldobrandinis, Borghese, and Barberinis shed their social roots as *condottieri*, merchants, farm-workers, patricians, lawyers, and professors to acquire land and title, becoming the new nobility of early modern Italy. The example of the Borghese is instructive; the transformation from the urban professional classes to landed nobility occurred within two generations and found its crowning moment in the election of Camillo Borghese as Paul V in 1605.

The 52-year-old Cardinal Borghese was a compromise candidate. Pope Clement VIII died in March 1605. Among the *papabili*, Borghese was considered too young; but the two rival factions led by Cardinals Montalto and Aldobrandini canceled out their own candidates. When finally a Medici (from the cadet branch) was elected as Leo XI, he ruled for less than one month. In the following conclave, Cardinal Borghese turned out to be the only candidate acceptable to all factions; his election represented the unexpected triumph of a brilliant family strategy that had carefully cultivated patrons and accumulated wealth.

The father of Camillo, Marcantonio Borghese (1504–74), was born in Siena. After his studies, he lectured on law at the university and represented his native city on a diplomatic mission in 1537 to Cosimo I, duke of Tuscany. It was the beginning of his clientage to the Medicis, from which his family would reap rich rewards. In the same year he followed a relative to Rome to practice law. In 1547 he became a lawyer for the Consistory, one of the most important lay lawyers in the Roman curia. After the death of his first wife in 1549, he married into a Roman patrician family; Camillo was one of seven children. Retained in diplomatic service by Siena, Spain, and France, Marcantonio's talents also won the approval of Paul III and Julius III. His success laid a solid financial basis for his family. In 1558, Marcantonio purchased the office of a knight of St. Peter for his five-year-old son Camillo; in 1568, in reward for his father's service, Philip II granted Camillo a stipend from the bishopric of Catania, for which the young man received first tonsure. After studying in Perugia, Camillo returned to Rome in 1572, where his father had purchased for him an office at the Signatura. In 1577 he was consecrated priest; in 1581 he became a datary in the Penitentiary. Meanwhile, his older brother Orazio pursued a parallel lay career in the Roman curia, purchasing different offices, including that of the rectorship of the University of Rome, the Sapienza. The Borghese siblings pursued a common strategy of family advancement, investing in offices, land, and marriage. During the 1580s Camillo invested at least 6,000 scudi in six offices; two sisters married into the Roman patriciate; one brother married nobility; and a family chapel was established in imitation of the custom of the Roman aristocracy.

A decisive turn came in 1588. In that year, Orazio purchased the office of chamber-auditor (one of the highest financial offices) for the large sum of 60,000 scudi, which he financed mostly on credit; and Camillo was appointed vice-legate to Bologna, the second largest city in the Papal States and the site of the most prestigious Italian university. His three-year tenure at Bologna won him important contacts: in his office Camillo corresponded with princes and prelates; he personally saw to the establishment of a college at the university endowed by Sixtus V; and he became a client of the grand duke of Tuscany. In 1590 his older brother Orazio died at the age of thirty-seven. Roman custom dictated that purchased offices reverted to the pope upon the death of their incumbents. The Borghese, having indebted the family to raise the purchase capital, had not yet recovered their investment from the income of the office of chamber-auditor. The family faced a major financial blow. Thanks to the intervention of the Medicis, Pope Gregory XIV granted Camillo the right to succeed to the office. In 1593 he served as special nuncio to Philip II. His official mission was to gain Spanish monies to support an imperial campaign against the Ottomans; privately, he carried out personal commissions for the Roman aristocracy, gaining favors for Cardinals Montalto and Aldobrandini at the Spanish court. This mission vastly expanded his contacts; his account of favors now included a wide network of princes and prelates. In his six years as chamber-auditor Camillo had recouped the investments made in the original purchase; elevated to the college of cardinals in 1596, he received several episcopal benefices, which he "resigned" to kinsmen and clients. As the *de facto* head of the Holy Office in 1600, Cardinal Borghese disposed of even more offices and income for his own expanding clientele. In 1605, the brothers began constructing what came to be the Palazzo Borghese; the purchase of a villa and large tracts of land in the Frascati further consolidated their noble status.

After his election, the Borghese rose even further in the social ladder: Francesco, an older brother, became captain-general of the papal guard, governor of Borgo, castellan of Ascolli, and admiral of the papal galleys; another brother, Giovanni Battista, was appointed castellan of Castelangelo and Ancona; a nephew, Scipione Caffarelli, was elevated to the cardinalate and changed his family name to Borghese; princes and prelates showered the family with monies and gifts. Although his two brothers never gained real political power (that was reserved to the cardinal-nephew Scipione), the Borghese prospered during the years of Paul V. When Giovanni Battista died in 1609, his assets totaled over one million scudi. Even the distant cousins in Siena received some rewards: the pope's namesake received the archbishopric of Siena. Paul V, however, focused his largess on his brother's son, Marcantonio, the only male heir to the Borghese. The young Marcantonio married an Orsini, one of the two grandest Roman clans; in 1620, his uncle, the pope, acquired for him the title of a Spanish grandee, in exchange for elevating Ferdinand, King Philip III's ten-year-old son, to the cardinalate and granting him the income of the archbishopric of Toledo, the richest in Spain. The Borghese had transformed themselves from an elite urban family of local renown into one of the great aristocratic clans of early modern Italy.

The rise of the Borghese illustrated the significance of patronage. Like all early modern states, the papacy, as a socio-political system, also functioned on patronage for the articulation of power and the distribution of offices. A central part to this system of patronage was the institution of the cardinal-nephew. Even in the early Church, office-holding and kinship had been closely connected. The popes of the Middle Ages regularly granted favors and honors to their kinsfolk, something universally expected and accepted. Since the supreme pontiff combined in his person both spiritual and temporal powers, it often happened that many popes possessed neither the inclination nor the aptitude for the exercise of political power. To protect themselves against factional intrigues, and to carry out a policy free of the manipulations of foreign powers, the popes needed trusted political advisors, whom they found among their kinsfolk. The figure of the cardinal-nephew, necessary as it was during the Renaissance, when the Papal States competed as one among different players in the arena of Italian politics, quickly became detrimental to the prestige of the papacy itself during the pontificate of Alexander VI (1492–1503), when his son Cesare Borgia, ruthless in the pursuit of power, served as the model in Machiavelli's treatise on the exercise of power, *The Prince*. Clement VII (1523–34), a Medici and cousin of Leo X, was the last of the cardinal-nephews elected to the papacy. A new spirit turned with the Council of Trent: in spite of his ambition and the grandeur of his household, Alessandro Farnese, "cardinal-nephew" (he was in fact the pope's grandson) under Paul III, failed three times to become pope (in 1565, 1572, and 1585).

The cardinal-nephew acted as a vice-pope: he formulated foreign policy, directed the state secretariat (often serving also as the secretary of state), corresponded with all nuncios, and, after the creation of the congregations of cardinals in 1588, also oversaw the expanded papal administration. That nepotism in itself was not necessarily corrupt was testified by Carlo Borromeo (1538–84), elevated by his uncle Pius IV to the purple at a young age, and whose personal conversion led him to the role of an exemplary Counter-Reformation bishop. Nevertheless, the limited tenure of the cardinal-nephew, whose power waned at the death of the reigning pope, dictated a logic of family politics that undermined reform, leading to the frenzied accumulation of benefices during the reign of the pope for redistribution to kinsmen. Cardinal Ludovisi, nephew of Gregory XV, died in 1632, having accumulated the benefices of the archbishopric of Bologna, twenty-three abbeys, the vice-chancellorship of the Church, and the directorship of the Signatura, most of which were redistributed to seventeen kinsmen. While the accumulation of benefices at the highest level of the Church made a mockery of the Tridentine injunction against pluralism, the practice of "resignation" (whereby the holder of a benefice resigned his office to another for a pension) perpetuated simony (the sale of Church offices) in essence if not in name. For clerical elites, there existed little distinction in practice between Church and family property. The single greatest privilege enjoyed by the cardinal-nephew was the right to make wills (*facultas testandi*), by which he could dispose of incomes from benefices in a personal testament to lay members of his family.

The cardinal-nephew, then, represented the tip of a social group that fed on the resources of the Church. Again, the Borghese served as an example: their family servants bore the arms of papal troops and were exempted from taxes; their vassals could not be tried in other courts, except for crimes of heresy and capital offenses; the nephews received a total of 758,495 silver scudi in cash from the pope; between 1605 and 1620 the nephews acquired 158 and a half offices and titles (8 percent through purchase and 92 percent as gifts); the family purchased fifty-one pieces of land around Rome; and Cardinal Borghese, an avid art and book collector, acquired an enormous private collection, including 416 books from the Vatican library. Through the institution of nepotism, the enormous resources of the Papal States constituted a patrimony for partial redistribution to rising families (through tax exemption, accumulation of benefits, gifts, and appointments to offices), who, in turn, constituted a new nobility by avidly acquiring titles and land. Bourgeois families, particularly the urban patriciate from the larger cities, having made their money in commerce and finance, bought land from the old baronial families, indebted by the need to raise ever more ruinous dowries and the gap between stable rental income and rising prices. Nepotism in the papal curia represented the fulcrum of this social movement.

Various attempts after Trent to suppress nepotism succeeded in checking only temporarily the excesses of this system; it was not until 1692 that nepotism was abolished by Innocent XII. A crisis in papal finances led directly to its suppression. To understand the reform of 1692 we need to examine briefly the structure of politics in the Papal States.

If the medieval papacy was an innovator in administration, as many historians have argued, the early modern papacy represented the precursor of the modern state. It had a standing army; it instituted a permanent direct tax in 1543; it created the first permanent diplomatic corps; it centralized administration and suppressed local autonomy; and it sponsored mercantilism by developing roads, ports, industry, and trade.

Parallel to the centralization of administration in the Papal States was the concentration of authority in the papal monarch. Having survived the challenge of Church Councils in the early fifteenth century, the pope's greatest ecclesiastical rival lay in the collective authority of the cardinals. After Sixtus IV (1471–84), the collective strength of the college was much diluted by rapid expansion in its overall numbers, as successive popes elevated their partisans to the purple in order to bolster their own political authority. The membership of the college of cardinals rose from twenty-four in 1415 under Martin V to seventy in 1586, when the number was fixed by Sixtus V. By the early sixteenth century, cardinals were recognized as the inner circle in the papal court: Paolo Cortese's treatise, *De cardinalatu* (1510), published about the same time as Castiglione's *Book of the Courtier*, listed several qualities to these princes of the Church that echoed those of their secular counterparts. Indeed, among the ranks of the cardinals were numerous members of the most illustrious princely houses of Italy; during the sixteenth century the college of cardinals counted eight Carafas, eight della Roveres, seven Medicis, seven Gonzagas, four Colonnas, and four Farnese. Yet while the Italian aristocracy found its way into the innermost corridors of power in the papal curia (by 1600 more than four-fifths of cardinals were Italians), the college of cardinals gradually lost its authority as a senate in checking the powers of the papal monarch and was itself coopted into the machinery of papal government. After the middle of the sixteenth century, popes seldom consulted the assembled cardinals (confining their counselors, instead, to their cardinal-nephews); their transformation into leading officials of the Papal States was completed in 1588 when Sixtus V remodeled the secretariat of state, creating fifteen permanent congregations of cardinals, six to oversee temporal affairs (for food supplies, the navy, the relief of taxes, the university, roads–bridges–water, and counsel), and the rest in charge of spiritual affairs (for the Inquisition, the Signatura, new churches, rites, the Index, the application of the Council of Trent, regular clergy, secular prelates, and printing).

Capping a complex institution that supervised both the temporal affairs of the Papal States and the spiritual affairs of the universal Church, the congregations, as their nomenclature made clear, reflected the dual nature of the papal monarchy, described as "one body and two souls" by a historian. Three courts attended to the litigation of the universal Church: the Penitentiary handled cases of conscience and theology; the Signatura, divided into a section on justice and another on grace, functioned as an appellate court for religious cases; and the rota served as both a first and appellate court in mixed religious and civil cases. Four institutions dealt with finance and paperwork: the chancery, presided by a cardinal, employed a small army of abbreviators, glossators, correctors, computators, and bullators to prepare, certify, and send out apostolic letters; the datary was in charge of concessions of benefices, marital dispensations, and sales of offices; the apostolic chamber controlled both papal finances and that of the universal Church; the secretariat of state, eclipsed during the sixteenth century by the office of the cardinal-nephew, grew in importance during the next century and absorbed the functions of the cardinal-nephew in 1676. Other offices pertained to the secular rule of the pontiff: the prefect and governor attended to the administration of the city of Rome, while six legates served as regional governors in the Papal States (Bologna, Marches of Ancona, Romagna, Umbria, Patrimonio, and Campagna), and governors administered localities. In diplomacy, the papacy appointed permanent ambassadors in Catholic countries. This institution, which first developed at the end of the fifteenth century, acquired a new significance because of the Protestant challenge; nuncios in Cologne, Brussels, Munich, Madrid, and Vienna worked closely with the leading Catholic powers to stem Protestantism, while protecting the interests of the papacy and sending back to Rome a constant stream of ecclesio-political reports.

To finance the building of the Papal States and to advance the cause of the universal Church, the papacy relied on the time-honored methods of raising revenues in early modern Europe: taxation and the sale of offices. Although military expenditures of the papacy represented only a fraction of the enormous sums that consumed Habsburg, Valois, and Bourbon purses, the popes also spent considerable sums furthering the cause of the Counter-Reformation: in addition to engaging its galleys and troops at Lepanto against the Ottomans (1571), the papacy also provided subsidies for Spanish arms; generous sums went to support other causes in Catholic diplomacy and arms – for the Catholic League in France, for imperial troops in Hungary fighting Turks, and, in smaller measures, to support the numerous Catholic exiles from Protestant Europe. As ecclesiastical revenues from other countries dried up in the sixteenth century (whether due to the Reformation or concessions to Catholic sovereigns), taxation increased heavily in the Papal States, sparing neither clergy nor laity. The burden of taxes drove many beyond the law: under the protection of feudal barons, bandits infested the countryside of Romagna and Ancona, attacking merchants, extorting protection, and venging violence on behalf of their baronial patrons. Repeated and occasionally savage attempts at suppression only held banditry in check; neither feudal barons nor bandits were completely domesticated by the early modern papal state. Its ability to tax restricted by feudal lords and social outcasts, the papacy used the public debt (*monti*) as security for the sale of offices.

Like other early modern states, the papacy mortgaged away its financial future in the sale of offices. In 1520 the 2,232 offices sold had a net worth of 2.5 million ducats; in 1565, the number of offices sold had risen to 3,635 and their value to 3.3 million. In addition to buying offices in anticipation of their income, the public debt was another favorite instrument of investment among the elites. The 1619 papal budget showed that almost 50 percent of all expenditure went into interest payment on the public debt.

Aside from these time-honored institutions, the early modern papacy adopted mercantilist policies to advance trade and industry: marshes were drained, the port at Civitavecchia was enlarged, road and bridges were maintained, and the great alum mines at Tolfa were systematically exploited. An indispensable product in the production of dye and hence textiles, alum represented the most lucrative product in the early modern papacy. Its exploitation was farmed out to entrepreneurs; and most of the products were sold to the Netherlands for its textile industry. The century 1550 to 1650 was the most productive period at Tolfa; revenues from exports helped to maintain the financial health of the Papal States, transforming in the process the face of Rome, as popes and cardinals added churches, palaces, squares, bridges, and roads to make the city into the capital of the Catholic world.

Fortunes turned in the 1640s. Drawn into a petty war against the Farnese over Castro, a papal fief, Urban VIII was defeated by a coalition formed by France, Tuscany, Venice, and Modena. The exhausted papal treasuries were not replenished, and as alum production at Tolfa steadily declined, the financial crisis forced a reform of the papal curia. To curb expenditure, Innocent XI (1676–89) reduced offices and stipends and drastically reduced the economies of the papal curia, but his cardinals resisted any attempts to do away with nepotism; in 1692, by the bull *Romanum decet pontificem*, Innocent XII (1691–1700) decreed that popes should never grant estates, offices, or revenues to relatives. Financial exigencies, more than the fervor for reform, finally dealt the death blow to nepotism.

Gone were the days when the pope led his army into battle, clad in armor and flanked by banners of the priest-king as in the time of the Old Testament; the warrior pope Julius II (1503–13) – that intrepid conqueror of Perugia and Bologna, that target of Erasmus's biting satire – was succeeded by more sedentary and peace-loving pontiffs, who, nonetheless, defended their monarchical authority with equal zeal. Sensitive to lay intervention in ecclesiastical affairs, the post-Tridentine Catholic Church extolled clerical authority; in the Papal States this led to the clericalization of the state, with a confusing mix of temporal and spiritual jurisdictions. These contradictions were manifest in three areas: sale of offices, episcopal jurisdiction, and the use of the interdict.

In the long lists of abuses ascribed to the Roman curia by the fathers of the Council of Trent (not to mention Protestants), simony and pluralism ranked at the top. Yet these practices persisted. As the supreme shepherd of the universal Church, the pope would have desired reforms regarding Church benefices – witness the efforts by Pius V and Sixtus V to implement the reform decrees of the Council of Trent – but as the monarch of the Papal States, it would have required the popes to have an iron will (and a lack of realism) to undercut the very financial and social foundations of their own rule. In any event, the papacy's mixed powers provided a *raison d'être*: defending the venality of office against the possible charge of simony, Giovanni Battista de Luca, a seventeenth-century jurist at the papal curia, argued that the profits from the sale of offices did not represent an exploitation of the spiritual by the temporal; rather, the purely ecclesiastical incomes of the papacy fell short of its obligations in the spiritual realm, and hence the pope was exploiting the temporal state in order to meet the needs of the universal Latin Church. More than just a clever argument, de Luca's discourse points to a central feature in papal finances: during the seventeenth century there was a net outflow of money from the papacy to northern Europe in support of the Catholic cause, reversing the trend during the Renaissance.

To tap the resources of the state for the needs of the Church, the papacy exercised strong central rule, limiting local autonomy, abolishing privileges, and exacting obedience. In their double roles as clerics and administrators, the legates and governors exercised more effective authority than their counterparts in secular states; for them, the question of conflicting Church and state jurisdictions never arose. This theocracy, potentially more effective than its secular counterparts, in instilling Christian discipline among the people, worked at times against the interest of Catholic reform. Bologna was a case in point. The archbishop of Bologna, Gabriele Paleotti (1522–97), later a cardinal, exemplified the Tridentine bishop: a resident pastor, he promulgated the decrees of Trent, held diocesan synods, and worked to discipline the clergy and educate the laity. His episcopal authority, however, was consistently undermined by the wide powers granted to the legates and governors by the papal curia. From 1566 to 1570, Archbishop Paleotti repeatedly complained to Rome about violations of his ecclesiastical jurisdiction by Governor Doria on numerous issues – the visitation of monasteries, supervision of the regular clergy, discipline in church, the observance of feastdays, and the judgment and imprisonment of clergy. In spite of appeals to his friend Carlo Borromeo, Paleotti's complaints went largely unanswered. Matters came to a head in 1569 when a canon at the cathedral refused Paleotti's order to say mass and, when censured, appealed to the governor. Doria accepted the case, touching off a strong protest by Paleotti. In the end Rome supported the archbishop, forcing the canon to seek public pardon.

Although Paleotti won Rome's backing in enforcing Tridentine reform in this one case, he failed to assert the autonomy of episcopal jurisdiction in principle. For the Roman curia, an autonomous bishop was dangerous for the internal politics of the Papal States; the papacy acted in ways similar to the Spanish government in Milan when challenged by the reform jurisdictions of Archbishop Borromeo. For the rest of his episcopacy, Paleotti had to contend with truncated episcopal authority. In 1578 the papal legate to Bologna Cesi was given jurisdiction over both ecclesiastical and civil cases, thereby abrogating the jurisdiction of the bishop's court; in response to Paleotti's protest, Cardinal Boncompagni wrote:

"Since Signor Cardinal Cesi is also an ordinary to His Holiness, it does not seem right that there should be any difference between the secular court and ecclesiastical one." In the Papal States, Tridentine rules were subordinated to the interests of the theocratic monarchy.

If theocracy ruled effectively within the Papal States, it proved fragile when confronted by secular Catholic powers. Inspired by an elevated sense of papal prerogatives, Paul V excommunicated the Senate of the Republic of Venice and placed the city under an interdict in 1606. The quarrel began when the Venetian government arrested two clerics for buying land without prior permission. The pope protested this infringement of clerical immunity and, when rebuffed, pronounced the ban. Declaring the interdict invalid, the Venetian Senate demanded loyalty from the clergy; the majority continued to administer sacraments and say mass, while those who refused, notably the Jesuits, were expelled from the Republic. A pamphlet war ensued: the Servite theologian Paolo Sarpi (1552–1623) defended Venetian republicanism and sharply criticized papal intervention during the Council of Trent; the papal position was taken up by Cardinal Roberto Bellarmino (1542–1621), an eminent Jesuit theologian, and Cardinal Cesare Baronius (1538–1607), the author of a monumental history of the Church. Religion was not at issue (the Venetian government pursued Protestants with vigor, abhorring heretics as potential rebels); the interdict of 1606 represented rather the contest between two Catholic states, one theocratic in constitution, the other republican, but both claiming jurisdiction over ecclesiastical and secular realms. Thanks to French mediation, Venice and Rome settled their differences in 1607; by freeing the two clerics, Venice conceded nothing (the Jesuits were banned until 1656), and papal prestige took a beating.

Papal authority declined precipitously during the seventeenth century. Hemmed in between France and Spain, Bourbon and Habsburg, in politics the papacy was a minor player commanding modest resources; in religion, its assertion of spiritual supremacy in the Catholic world was compromised by a series of concordats that conceded extensive rights of clerical appointments to Catholic monarchs. The reason of state, a philosophy espoused alike by Catholic and Protestant princes in their exercise of statecraft, increasingly made the theocratic pretensions of the papacy irrelevant. At the peace negotiations in Münster that ended the Thirty Years War, the papal nuncio, Fabio Chigi (the future Alexander VII), was largely ignored when he protested the far-reaching concessions to German Protestants in the imperial constitution.

Brushed aside in the empire, the papacy found its authority also challenged in France; disputes over Church appointments and papal supremacy dragged on through the reign of five popes. The conflict began as a personal hostility against Alexander VII on the part of the French minister Cardinal Mazarin during the Fronde: a noble faction led by Cardinal de Retz plotted against Mazarin and the boy king Louis XIV, and when the revolt failed, Retz fled to Rome. In later years, Louis XIV still resented papal protection of his former enemies; in 1664, on the pretext of a minor incident at the French embassy in Rome, he occupied the papal territories of Avignon and Venaissin. As a gesture of reconciliation, Alexander's successor, Clement IX, granted the French king a free hand in Church appointments, but relations deteriorated under the pontificate of Clement X when the Sun King appropriated Church incomes to pay for his wars. In 1673 and 1675, Louis XIV claimed regalia – the right over all ecclesiastical appointments in France and the income of vacant sees and abbeys; in 1682, the French clergy rallied in support of their royal master, declaring in the Four Gallican Articles that the pope had no authority over kings or in temporal affairs. Good relations were restored only by Innocent XII (1691–1700), who recognized the Gallican arrangements.

Its political insignificance notwithstanding, the Baroque papacy presided over a heroic Catholicism, peopled with missionaries, martyrs, converts, and living saints. The eighteenth-century papacy, in contrast, drew inward, conscious perhaps of a bygone age of greatness: politically, it wavered between Catholic powers in the wars of the Spanish and Austrian successions, failing to please anyone and alienating everyone in the process; intellectually, it condemned atheism and freemasonry, feeling lost in the rushing torrents of the Enlightenment; geographically, it unwittingly reversed the global mission of Catholicism, when Clement XI first prohibited the use of Chinese Rites, a measure confirmed by Benedict XIV in 1744 (see chap. 12) that led to the suppression of Catholicism in Ch'ing China. The century was not without its great popes – learned, pious, good-willed – especially Benedict XIV; but the questions that preoccupied the papacy seemed antiquated: the condemnations of Jansenism (see chap. 13), the promotion of cults (of the Virgin Mary and of the Sacred Heart of Jesus), and the canonization of saints. If the Baroque century was the time of living saints (whether in the flesh or in living memory), the canonization of saints during the eighteenth century seemed to signify the closing of an heroic age: Benedict XIV composed a classic study on the process of canonization (1734–38); Clement XII and Clement XIII elevated many to sainthood in the middle of the century; but the age nourished few who would themselves be canonized one day. Eighteenth-century Rome remained the site of the papacy and the capital of the Catholic world, its beautiful churches, palaces, bridges, fountains, and squares filled with nostalgia for a remembered age of charisma.

7 Bishops and priests

"What is the bishop but the sun of his diocese, a man totally inflamed, totally dedicated to approaching the soul of Christ by his constant example and frequent preaching of the Word?" This encomium was written by the Portuguese Dominican Bartolomeu dos Martires, archbishop of Braga, one of the most fervent spokesmen for the dignity of the episcopal office during the final session of the Council of Trent. While sojourning in Rome during and after the conclusion of the Council in 1563–64, Archbishop Bartolomeu befriended the cardinal-nephew, Carlo Borromeo, who would himself become the model Tridentine bishop.

Born in 1538 as the second son of Count Giberto Borromeo, Carlo followed a career typical of the privileged: destined for ecclesiastical office as a younger son of the nobility, he was tonsured at the age of seven in order to receive the income of a nearby abbey; after his initial education in Milan at the palace of his family, he continued in the study of law at Pavia, obtaining the doctorate in both canon and Roman law in 1559 at the age of twenty-one. A shy, studious youth (resulting from his speech impediment), Carlo lost his mother at the age of nine and his father just before his graduation. Yet he was not without patrons. In 1560, the newly elected Pius IV called his sister's son to Rome, lavishing offices and titles upon the young man, making him into his confidant, advisor, and secretary of state. Created cardinal on January 31, 1560, Borromeo was ordained subdeacon and deacon on December 21 in the same year, just a little over twenty-two years old. A creature of the Roman curia, the young cardinal-nephew personified the system that came under intense criticism from the Church fathers at Trent. When his uncle convoked the third meeting of the Council in December 1560, Borromeo served as middleman between the papal legates and the pope, evaluating reports, dictating letters, passing on instructions, and generally defending the papacy's interests against the bishops calling for reform of the head of the Church. If the Council served as Borromeo's apprenticeship in theology, an academy he founded in Rome, the so-called "Vatican Nights" – attended by leading humanists and curialists to discourse on various learned subjects – furthered his humanist education.

The winter of 1562 was a turning point for Carlo Borromeo. In November, Carlo's elder brother Francesco died unexpectedly. Deeply attached to his brother, Carlo was devastated; the family, without a male heir, faced a crisis. Urged by his relatives (including the pope) to marry, Borromeo agonized over his indetermination. Francesco's death shattered, it seemed, the world of patronage and glory that the young cardinal had known; and after undergoing the *Spiritual Exercises* with the Jesuit Ribera, Borromeo decided on being ordained priest, celebrating his first mass at St. Peter's and his second at the Jesuit church. This personal conversion made Borromeo somewhat of an oddity in the papal curia: not only did he renounce the gold- and silverware and the fine fares at table, Borromeo drastically reduced the size of his household and adopted an austere and severe piety that struck the papal court as extreme. His change thus coincided with the conclusion of the Council of Trent; taking its reforms to heart, Borromeo, upon his nomination to the see of Milan in May 1564, decided to fulfill the injunction of episcopal residence and forsake the papal curia. His work on the Roman breviary, catechism, and missal having been completed, Borromeo entered Milan in a triumphal procession in 1565, the first archbishop to actually reside in his diocese in eighty years.

The largest diocese in Italy, the metropolitanate of Milan comprised fifteen bishoprics and extended over six territories – the Spanish Duchy of Milan, the Republic of Genoa, the Papal States, the Republic of Venice, the Swiss Confederation, and the Grison. The wealthiest city in northern Italy, Milan stood at the crossroads of North and South, East and West, a strategic node in the Spanish possessions that linked the two houses of Habsburg and the base for Spanish troop movements to the Low Countries. The new archbishop of Milan, a Renaissance prelate and a Counter-Reformation convert, united in his person many contradictions: shaped by the optimistic humanism of his youth, the mature Borromeo expressed deep pessimism over sinful human nature; having reached the apex of the curial system as cardinal-nephew, Borromeo the pastor turned to episcopal models deeply critical of Rome; dedicated to the promotion of Christian piety, the shepherd of his flock nonetheless distrusted lay spirituality and sought to administer, control, and legislate the Christian folk. This reticent man became the most expressive sign of the Catholic renewal, channeling different currents of reform into his diocese and turning Milan into a laboratory for disciplining the clergy and the laity.

His most trusted assistant, the vicar-general Niccolò Ormaneto, had been an associate of Bishop Giberti of Verona, one of the early advocates of Catholic reform before Trent. With Ormaneto's experience in diocesan reform, the new archbishop adapted Gibertian methods that consisted of disciplining the clergy and indoctrinating the laity. The principle was simple: the bishop's spiritual jurisdiction was to be supreme and unchallenged. The methods, stipulated by the Council fathers at Trent, were straightforward: the regular convention of provincial councils and diocesan synods under the presidency of the bishop to promulgate the reform decrees and to discuss particular problems of pastoral care; the uses of the ecclesiastical court to correct clerical misbehavior; and the carrying out of parish visitations to gather information on ecclesiastical property, clerical behavior, and lay conformity. If the plan of Tridentine reform seemed simple in theory, in practice the obstacles were complicated. In every diocese, the reform bishop found his assertion of spiritual authority challenged *de facto* and *de jure*: the canons of his own cathedral chapter might ignore admonishments to improve moral behavior and keep divine office; collegiate churches and monasteries might resist episcopal visitations and disciplinary measures, claiming papal exemptions or privileges; regular religious orders might refuse obedience to the bishop, pleading a greater obedience to their order superiors; the majority of benefices often eluded the bishop's patronage, the right of nomination being in the hands of ecclesiastical and lay patrons; and the secular authorities tended to resent the arrogation of authority by the reform bishop, whose zeal seemed to extend ecclesiastical liberties at the cost of secular jurisdiction.

Borromeo faced all these obstacles in Milan. Under the Visconti and Sforza dukes, civil authority had a large say in ecclesiastical affairs; the dukes nominated candidates to the see and ducal officials helped supervise clerical discipline. When the Duchy passed to Spain, these practices continued: as the most influential man in the Spanish Church, Philip II appointed his bishops and inquisitors; as the king's regent in Milan, the governor jealously guarded the royal prerogative in the defense of the Catholic faith. Unbending in his newfound piety, Borromeo soon antagonized the civil authorities; the governor suspected his political motives and the Milanese Senate resented his intervention with their patronage over ecclesiastical offices. Supported by his uncle, Borromeo confronted the governor in defense of ecclesiastical dignity. There were mutual recriminations, and clashes between episcopal servants and the governor's troops, leading to excommunication. Gradually tempers simmered down. After the death of his uncle in 1565 and with Gregory XIII after 1572 less sympathetic to his confrontational tactics, Borromeo learned to compromise. His rising popularity, on the other hand, gave cause to the

Spanish authorities to exercise restraint, particularly after the archbishop escaped an assassination attempt in 1569, when a friar from the Humiliati Order, which was resisting Borromeo's reform discipline, fired a shot that brushed Borromeo's side while he was saying mass in the house chapel of the episcopal palace. This incident, subsequently celebrated as divine intervention in his hagiography, bolstered Borromeo's saintly reputation in Milan. His was a saintliness addicted to hard work.

In the nineteen years of his office, Borromeo convoked six provincial councils and eleven synods; during these sessions, the implementation of the Tridentine reforms was discussed, individual difficulties in the parishes resolved, and episcopal instructions on indoctrination, liturgy, and worship disseminated. The legislation and instructions, collected in the *Acta Ecclesiae Mediolanensis* (Acts of the Church of Milan), first published in 1582 and reprinted many times, provided the blueprint for the dissemination of the Borromean reform. True to his humanist education, Borromeo relied on the printing press; immediately after his arrival, he established a printing press in Milan to publish the texts necessary to disseminate Catholic reform – the new breviary, missal, catechism, and the acts of the synods and councils. The Word was announced: Borromeo preached tirelessly from the pulpit (overcoming his speech impediment), wrote numerous pastoral letters, and gave uncounted instructions (his correspondence numbered some 60,000 letters!). Information was gathered: the archbishop and his officials regularly visited parishes and monasteries, gathering facts on the financial and physical conditions of ecclesiastical institutions, the spiritual condition of pastors and convent inmates, the nature and state of worship, and, in the case of the parishes, the presence of heretics and confraternities and the *status animae* of the laity – recording data on baptism, catechism, confession, communion, and marriage.

More than ever before, the archbishop of Milan corrected the behavior and probed the conscience of his flock. The key to reform, however, was a better-disciplined and -educated clergy. The modern confessional, whose invention is sometimes erroneously attributed to Borromeo, represented a device not so much to explore the innermost recesses of conscience but to discourage sexual harassment of female parishioners by confessors. Elaborating upon a practice initiated by Bishop Giberti, Borromeo's confessional (the earliest model simply with a grill separating the chair of the confessor and the kneeling bench for the confessant) prevented physical contact between confessor and penitent, leading, in later evolutions, to anonymity and impersonality in the confession of sins.

To improve clerical training and in accordance with Tridentine decree, Borromeo established three seminaries: one for training the clergy of the city of Milan, the second for instructing clergy for rural parishes, and the third for missionary priests to Switzerland, a project dear to his heart. Dissatisfied with the slow reform of clerical standards, in 1579 Borromeo founded a new community of priests – the oblates of Saint Ambrose – who would form the inner clerical elite of his reform.

In a sermon preached in 1569, Borromeo compared the constituent parts of the Church to celestial and earthly hierarchies: the bishops, in this analogy, corresponded to the first order of angels, the seraphim and cherubim closest to God. Needless to say, this elevated sense of ecclesiastical dignity reserved a less exalted place for the laity. When Borromeo arrived in Milan, earlier Catholic reform had already established an extensive network to teach catechism. The first school of Christian doctrine was founded in 1536 by the chaplain Castellino da Castello, the son of an artisan; in 1539 a lay confraternity joined him; and by 1563 the movement counted 200 clerical and lay members, teaching 2,000 girls and boys Christian doctrine in thirty-three schools. Hostile to the teaching of Christian doctrine by the laity, Borromeo incorporated the schools after Castellino's death in 1566, placing them under clerical direction and making the instruction of catechism his own project; in the year of Borromeo's death, the diocese of Milan boasted 740 schools with 3,000 teachers and 40,000 pupils in a diocese of 560,000 souls.

Remembered for his manifold contributions, the late archbishop represented different things to different men: the Milanese juriconsult Giovanni Pietro Bimio praised his humanity, justice, prudence, temperance, and fortitude, virtues resplendent of humanists; Giovanni Francesco Bonomi, bishop of Vercelli, celebrated him as an epic hero in Vergilian meters; other bishops dedicated to reform invoked his memory and imitated his example; and the papacy employed him as a figure to emphasize loyalty to Rome, depicting Borromeo, in the canonization ceremony of 1610, in his regalia as a cardinal and not as a bishop. But for the people of Milan, their archbishop was perhaps best remembered as the indomitable pastor, who stayed at his post during the 1576 plague while most authorities fled the city, mobilizing friars and priests to care for the afflicted, organizing *lazaretti* to receive the sick, and comforting the dying.

Tridentine reforms reached a highwater mark in Milan under Borromeo. The waves of reform failed to reach many stagnant pools; and although Catholic reforms in the seventeenth and eighteenth centuries pushed beyond Borromeo's achievements here and there, they came in ebb and flow and took longer, unlike the focused goals and concentrated energy in Borromeo's Milan. But even in Milan Borromeo's achievements could not be maintained: provisions in the *Acts of the Milanese Church* remained unimplemented after the archbishop's death and the impetus of reform simply petered out. Tridentine reform did not pick up steam again until the episcopacy of his cousin, Federico Borromeo (1601–31), who labored to preserve the memory and work of his illustrious kinsman. For the Catholic episcopacy three sources nourished the many streams of reform: Trent provided the historic moment and canonical prescriptions, the theory and emotion, one might say; Rome established institutions for the training of a new clerical elite, the practice and the brain; and Milan represented the synthesis of the two in action.

The impetus of reform was felt early in Spain. In Trent, Spanish bishops argued strongly for the duty of episcopal residence and a greater authority to deal with clerical disobedience. As the largest foreign contingent at the Council, many Spanish prelates returned to their sees, fired with enthusiasm to implement the reform decrees. Such was the case with Bishop Alvaro de Moscoso (1550–61) and Bishop Diego Ramírez de Sedeño (1561–73) of Pamplona, Archbishop Francisco de Mendoza of Burgos, and Bishop Miguel Muñoz (1547–53) and Bishop Bernardo de Fresneda (1562–71) of Cuenca, among others. Supported by Philip II, Spanish bishops flexed their muscles. In Cuenca, Bishop Fresneda solicited reports on clerical abuses and convoked a diocesan synod in 1566 to announce the Tridentine decrees. To overcome the hostility of the clergy, led by the cathedral canons, archpriests, and the beneficed clergy, Bishop Fresneda coaxed and coerced, citing papal and royal authority to back up his own. The opposition having been overcome, Bishop Fresneda possessed two instruments to correct clerical behavior: the ecclesiastical courts and the Inquisition. The former he staffed with reliable men – the vicar-general and other ecclesiastical officials, dedicated to reform and loyal to episcopal authority; the latter, a royal institution with a mixed lay and clerical staff, functioned as an auxiliary institution outside the bishop's control. Tridentine reform of the clergy, meant, in practice, the criminalization of clerical behavior hitherto undefined, tolerated, or unprosecuted: drinking, whoring, gaming – the spectrum of crimes ranged from swearing, brawling, and concubinage to murder. Between the 1560s and 1600 the number of cases prosecuted at the episcopal court shot up by six times; the Inquisition also encouraged denunciations of clerical misconduct during the same decades.

Outside Spain, the Milanese model was also decisive. The writings of Borromeo and his diocesan legislation served as blueprints for many reform bishops: Jacomo Sacrato, bishop of Carpentras (1572–92) in the papal enclave of Avignon, adapted his 1584 synodal statutes from the 1565 provincial statutes of Milan, while his ordinance of 1592 was almost a copy of Borromeo's 1573 *Instruction on the Construction of Churches*; and in France, the assembly of bishops meeting in Melun (1579) voted to adopt the decrees of Trent and the 1565 Milanese statutes, which served in turn as a model for the statutes of provincial councils held in France between 1581 and 1594.

The Tridentine reforms, however, proceeded slowly and unevenly in France, due to Gallican opposition to the papacy; it was not until 1615 that the Second Estate officially adopted the Tridentine decrees. It was in two regions on France's frontier – Lorraine and Avignon – that the Catholic reform gained a quicker pace. Already in 1564 Bishop Nicolas Psaume called the Jesuits to Verdun to help reform the Church; in 1572, Duke Charles III and Cardinal Charles of Lorraine founded and entrusted the new university at Pont-à-Mousson to the Jesuits, an institution that would train all subsequent bishops in Lorraine, including Cardinal de Vaudémont, who modeled himself after Borromeo. In Avignon, the humanist bishop of Carpentras Jacques Sadolet inspired later reform bishops, including his nephew Jacomo Sacrato (1572–84), who adopted the Roman breviary and missal and introduced the confessional in 1584. Two archbishops of Avignon dedicated to clerical reform – Francesco Maria Tarugi and Gio-Francesco Bordini – were disciples of Neri in Rome.

In contrast, the episcopacy in central Europe was far from reliable. As princes of the Holy Roman Empire, German bishops often behaved more as rulers than as pastors. Until the 1580s all archbishops of Cologne had lovers: Gebhard Truchsess von Waldburg planned to marry his mistress, the Countess Agnes von Mansfeld and turn the bishopric into a hereditary principality; defeated in battle, he was succeeded by Ernst von Wittelsbach, a son of the Bavarian duke, who also had a mistress of noble rank. The Tridentine spirit came only in the person of another Wittelsbach, Ernst's nephew, in 1612, but Archbishop Ferdinand, albeit a staunch partisan of Catholic renewal, was a strange embodiment of the Tridentine spirit, being a notorious pluralist who held the bishoprics of Freising, Münster, and Liège. The German bishops were a decidedly mixed lot. While zealous reformers used their political power to advance the Catholic cause – men such as Bishop Otto von Truchsess of Augsburg and Bishop Julius Echter von Mespelbrünn of Würzburg – the other prince-bishops were more princes than prelates. During most of the seventeenth century, two bishops of Strasburg – Archduke Leopold-Wilhelm (1625–63) and Franz Egon von Fürstenberg (1663–82) – hardly set foot in their dioceses.

Since all bishops owed their nominations to patronage, political appointments as such did not necessarily imply unwillingness to reform. In fact, many reform bishops in France were political creatures: the first two reform bishops of Chartres were both clients of the royal minister – Honor d'Estampes de Valençay (1620–41) served as Richelieu's agent and his successor; Jacques Lescot (1641–56), professor at the Sorbonne, used to be Richelieu's confessor – and in Nîmes, the first reform bishop, Anthime Denis Cohon (1634–44, 1655–70), another client of Richelieu, executed his master's religious and political policies. In Rennes, Bishop La Motte-Houdancourt (1642–61) was *aumonier* of Anne of Austria, and Bishop Le Tonnelier de Breteuil (1725–32) was master of the Royal Chapel; in St. Malo, Bishop Achille de Harlay (1632–46) was one-time ambassador to Istanbul, while Bishop François de Villemontée (1658–70) had served as intendant of Poitou. In France as in Spain, royalism and Catholic reform were perfectly compatible goals. In the Spanish Netherlands, royal patronage again worked for reform; two bishops of Tournai, Jean Vendeville and Michel d'Esne, had been respectively privy counselor in Brussels and page at the court of Philip II; together, they steered the diocese in the path of Catholic renewal during the crucial years 1588 to 1647. There were many such examples. The political bishop emerged as a figure in northern Europe, where dynastic interest, Catholic religion, and the struggle with Protestants produced a powerful politico-religious mix that shaped prelates of the Church. Some, as we have seen, were nobility, spawning veritable episcopal dynasties, such as the four Madruzzos, uncles and nephews, who occupied the see of Trent without interruption between 1539 and 1658. Others worked their way up from humbler backgrounds, such as the ambitious and ruthless archbishop of Prague, Cardinal Harrach, one of the most prominent figures in Counter-Reformation Austria.

If patronage was the rule of appointment (the dignity of episcopal office required after all either noble birth or bourgeois talent) and piety the disposition of the individual, it remained nonetheless essential for Rome to secure the loyalty of bishops in lands contested by Protestantism. The instrument for inculcating allegiance to the papacy and Roman Catholicism lay in the different colleges in Rome staffed by Jesuits. The mission of the German College (Hungarians were admitted later), founded in 1552, was "to serve as a Trojan Horse to introduce Catholicism into Germany," in the words of Cardinal Morone, who had extensive dealings with German Lutherans. During the early modern period, the German College was the single most important institution for the formation of the cream of the German secular clergy: it educated many young noblemen and sons of urban patricians, who became prelates, vicar-generals, and leading ecclesiastical officials of the imperial Church. Bishop Christoph Bernhard von Galen, who implemented the Tridentine decrees in Münster, was an alumnus of the German College, as were the members of the reform faction in the bishopric of Breslau, who pushed through Tridentine reform over the opposition of the traditional clergy. Altogether, between 1560 and 1803 (when German ecclesiastical polities were secularized), some 18 percent of all bishops in the empire were alumni of the German College; in Austria, the percentage for the same period rose to almost 30 percent. The German College exerted an equally powerful influence in the entourage of the bishops: in the second half of the seventeenth century, alumni of the college formed almost one-quarter of all cathedral canons in bishoprics of the empire and provided many personnel for the highest administrators (suffragan bishops, officials, and vicar-generals) in the episcopal curia who often planned and executed the steps for reform.

If the German College represented the Trojan Horse for the Counter-Reformation in the Holy Roman Empire, the Jesuit Roman College served as the catapult that breached the walls of the Polish Reformation. With the exception of Cardinal Hosius, the Polish episcopacy at mid-century was remarkably tolerant of the different religious movements that competed for adherents: Bishop Uchanski (1502–81), primate of Poland, came under suspicion of Protestant sympathy during the pontificate of Paul IV, but he enjoyed the backing of King Sigismund. A new episcopacy shaped in the image of Trent began to assume power in the 1570s, due to the fervor of Cardinal Hosius and the Society of Jesus established a decade earlier in Poland. Many students who had trained first in Jesuit colleges in Poland and later at the Roman College assumed high ecclesiastical offices: Peter Kostka, bishop of Chetmno (1574–95), a cousin of the young Jesuit saint Stanislas; Jerome Rozdrazewski, bishop of Cujavie (1581–1600); George Radziwill (1556–1600) – prince, Protestant, convert – ordained in 1580, elevated to cardinal in 1584, and consecrated bishop of Cracow in 1592; Bernard Maciejowski, bishop of Cracow, cardinal, and primate of Poland (1606–08); Benedict Woyna, bishop of Vilnius (1600–15); Martin Szyszkowski, bishop of Cracow (1616–30); Paul Wotucki, bishop of Cujavie (1616–22); and in fact all bishops of Gniezno and Cracow during the seventeenth century had been students at the Jesuit Roman College.

What the Borromean legislation entailed was the reduction of the complex and contradictory sets of practices and exceptions governing the pre-Tridentine secular clergy to a more rational and simplified set of rules. The clergy before Trent constituted a highly amorphous body: to be a clerk implied, above all, having a particular legal status, being subject to canon law and ecclesiastical courts and exempt from taxation and secular jurisdiction; it also conferred the right to receive income from ecclesiastical property and office. The vast majority of clergy, after simple tonsure, never advanced to receive major orders (subdeaconery, deaconery, and priesthood); they did not say mass, discharged no pastoral duties, and commonly wore no distinctive clerical garb; presented by family for tonsure, they drew on the Church's resources for scholarships, income, and positions. As late as the 1570s the ratio of subdeacons to the tonsured in the diocese of Carpentras was only 6.4 percent, but by the first decade of the seventeenth century, the ratio rose to 30.4 percent, indicating a vast improvement in real clerical vocation. Among the elites of the secular clergy – the canons of cathedral and collegiate chapters – many never received major orders and lived more or less openly as secular laymen.

For those ordained and entrusted with the care of souls, there was little uniformity in training: the 1579–81 visitation records in the diocese of Trent revealed that, of 214 parish clergy, only 6 had doctorates and many barely knew their Latin; moreover, only 29 clerics (13.5 percent) owned any books. Until the late sixteenth century, the ecclesiastical hierarchy exercised little control over ordination: tests were not required, a standard of theological knowledge not stipulated, and investigations into vocation and background of the candidates did not exist. Dispensations were granted readily. The large number of ordinations bespoke lack of control: in Avignon, 575 subdeacons were ordained in 1532, and another 486 in 1538. A similar situation also obtained regarding the clergy in Naples between 1650 and 1740: about 60 percent of the clergy never received more than minor orders; and some 40 percent of all tonsures occurred between the ages of seven and fourteen, indicating family strategy to draw on ecclesiastical resources rather than genuine vocations. The ecclesiastical hierarchy resembled a two-tier structure in which the upper echelons were reserved for the elites and the lower ranks were open to competition, with education, patronage, and luck all playing a role.

The crucial point was the benefice, defined as a sacred office to which the Church has attached the perpetual right to receive revenues from ecclesiastical properties. The beneficed clergy ranged from the parish priest with a modest living to great prelates with incomes of princes, but they all ranked above the masses of unbeneficed clergy in search of income and security – the numerous chaplains living off fees from saying endowed masses and administering sacraments, often commuting between different parishes and chapels. Since many of these benefices and private masses lay beyond episcopal jurisdiction, there was correspondingly little control the bishop could exercise over the proliferation of cults and variations of liturgy. Tridentine reform must be understood as the simultaneous attempt to increase episcopal discipline over the clergy and to unify the diverse liturgical practices; it aimed to create a better trained, morally unreproachable clergy using canonically approved liturgical texts – the Roman catechism, the Roman breviary, and the Roman missal – to celebrate feastdays approved by the official Church. The heart of this undertaking lay in the shaping of a professional clergy, more capable of resisting the infiltration of lay practices in sacramental life, better qualified to correct lay superstitions by teaching right doctrine and, on the whole, capable of guarding the holy from the profane and dispensing salvation to the laity.

Faced with the task of reforming the clergy, the bishops possessed several instruments, some long-standing, others provided by the decrees of the Council of Trent: the diocesan seminary to train a new clergy; the diocesan synod to communicate episcopal instructions and gather information from the pastoral field; the diocesan visitation to gather information and supervise parish life; and the ecclesiastical court to investigate and discipline clerical malefactors.

The Tridentine provision to establish diocesan seminaries under episcopal guidance reflected the limited authority of the bishop over clerical appointments; the right of nomination often lay with other ecclesiastical (cathedral chapter, collegiate churches, universities, abbeys) or lay patrons (princes, city governments, noble, patrician, or bourgeois family endowments). In Strasburg, for example, the bishop controlled only fifteen benefices in a diocese of 213 parishes in 1670; the nobility and urban patriciate effectively controlled the distribution of Church offices and income, frustrating several episcopal reforms since the late fifteenth century. In the small south German Catholic imperial city of Überlingen, all clerical nominations depended on the city council, none on the bishop of Constance. The seminary could work as a counterbalance, training a new breed of clergy dedicated to reform and obedient to episcopal instructions.

Borromean Milan aside, this Tridentine provision was by and large a failure. Several attempts were made in the diocese of Trent itself to implement the Tridentine decree to no avail: in the 1550s and 1560s Bishop Cristoforo Madruzzo (1539–67) wanted to bring in the Jesuits and establish a seminary along the model of the German College in Rome; in the 1580s and 1590s, his nephew and successor, Ludovico Madruzzo (1567–1600) considered turning alternatively the cathedral school and an abbey into the diocesan seminary; all effort floundered, however, due to insufficient funding and the opposition of the cathedral chapter. Very few diocesan seminaries were actually established in the two hundred years following Trent: in Cologne, out of his own income Archbishop Ferdinand opened a seminary in 1615 (with twelve scholarships) that was forced to close in 1646 when funding ran out; only in 1736 was a permanent seminary opened; in Naples, the seminary established in 1568 by Archbishop Alfonso Carafa was very limited in scope; in Paris, Archbishop Gondi wanted to establish a seminary in the suburb of St. Jacques in 1618 but gave up because he could not find money; only after 1642 were the first seminaries opened; in papal Avignon, three seminaries were founded in the dioceses of Carpentras, Cavillon, and Avignon between 1581 and 1586, but by 1618 only the one at Carpentras remained open, while the others had closed due to insufficient endowment. The first wave of foundations in the wake of Trent proved a fiasco; only in the late seventeenth century did renewed will and effort lead to more permanent establishments. That, however, was due to a new breed of clergy willing to support reform; diocesan seminaries thus owed their existence to a new Tridentine clergy and not the other way round.

A new breed of Tridentine clergy emerged gradually over several generations, shaped by episcopal discipline, improved income, and, above all, by Jesuit education. In many regions of northern Europe, Jesuit colleges and universities staffed by Jesuits trained the majority of the new Tridentine clergy; the university at Pont-à-Mousson in Lorraine, the university at Dillingen in Bavaria, the university at Douai in the Spanish Netherlands, and the German, English, and Irish Colleges were cases in point.

Better training went hand in hand with stricter control. Aside from the Jesuit institutions and the few diocesan seminaries, reform bishops possessed new or reinvigorated instruments for the discipline of the clergy. Several of these have been mentioned – the diocesan synod, the ecclesiastical court, and the visitation. Others included clerical congregations, such as the chapters for rural clergy in Würzburg that brought together country priests for regular consultation, reading, and retreat, all under the watchful eye of episcopal officials; or the Secret Congregation of Ordinants, created by Archbishop Innico Cardinal Caracciolo of Naples in 1680 to tighten clerical discipline; or the clerical council, a sort of department of the clergy staffed by secular and clerical officials and backed by the mixed authority of the prince-bishop, pioneered in Bavaria and later extended to Cologne and Münster by the Wittelsbach archbishops.

By the early decades of the seventeenth century the quality of the parish clergy had noticeably improved. First, the clergy had been by and large celibate. In the city of Überlingen, clerical concubinage was completely suppressed by the city council after 1580; in the diocese of Cuenca, younger parish priests in the generation of Trent (1540–65) were only half as likely to lapse into sins of the flesh than the generations born between 1479 and 1539 (10 versus 19 percent); in the city of Lille, the bishop of Tournai regularly condemned clerical sexuality between 1586 and 1667, even though there were only a handful of scandals; in Würzburg, the clergy was almost completely celibate by the middle of the seventeenth century; in the rural deanery of Tielt near Ghent between 1616 and 1650, some 7 percent of the parish priests lived with a maid (five out of sixty-eight) and another 7 percent came under suspicion, most of the culprits having reformed by the 1630s; and in the diocese of Cologne, clerical concubinage in urban parishes was wholly suppressed, although it lingered on in rural parishes.

Clerical celibacy was successful in cities for obvious reasons: episcopal authority lay close at hand; scrutiny by laypeople was inescapable; and traditional anticlericalism, on the part of merchants and artisans, made a morally unassailable clergy more urgent. The countryside was a different matter. Unlike their urban colleagues who drew cash incomes, rural priests received the bulk of their tithe in grain and many farmed their own plot to supplement income; the parish house functioned as a peasant household requiring collaborative labor, rendering the housekeeper more than just a sexual partner. This arrangement was commonly tolerated by the laity. Malicious gossip and denunciations arose only in specific instances: when the priest turned out to be a notorious womanizer instead of a good provider for his partner and children in a long-standing relationship, or when the women in question were quarrelsome and disliked by the parishioners. The pre-Tridentine rural clergy, in sum, did not differ very much from his neighbor and parishioner: he often lived with a woman, maintained a small farm, administered the sacraments, dressed otherwise like his parishioners after mass (sometimes even during mass), and socialized with them in taverns and weddings. Consequently, clerical celibacy was much harder to enforce in rural areas. In a relatively rural and mountainous diocese such as Trent, approximately 20 percent of the parish clergy lived in common-law marriages at the time of the Church Council; the situation only improved during the seventeenth century. In the Ahrgau, a rural district in the diocese of Cologne, five out of nineteen parish priests had common-law wives in 1628; the priest at Buschhoven (near Bonn) simply sent away his maid temporarily during diocesan visitations, a practice followed by his successor in the parish thirty-five years later. Clerical celibacy was not achieved in rural Cologne until the end of the seventeenth century.

A celibate priesthood created a stronger demarcation between clergy and laity, a distinction reinforced in the countryside by the different social backgrounds and higher incomes of the Tridentine clergy. The century following Trent saw a gradual and steady improvement in clerical income, a result partly of the rising price of grain and partly of the better administration of ecclesiastical benefices. In the rural deanery of Tielt, for example, clerical income rose 45 percent between 1622 and 1682. The scale of income corresponded to qualification and benefice: the best-paid clergy were university-trained priests in wealthy urban and rural wine-producing parishes; the worst were the chaplains in remote mountainous poor parishes. In Lille, the university-trained priest drew incomes between 1,500 and 4,000 livres, while the chaplains had between only 350 and 800 livres (supplemented by fees charged for performing sacraments); in the diocese of Paris, the great majority of parish priests in 1666 (360 out of 386) received incomes between 300 and 1,500 livres; in the diocese of Strasburg, the richest benefices in 1665–72 were located in cities in wine-producing communities, yielding annual incomes of over 200 florin (15 percent of all clergy), while the middling majority (55 percent) drew between 100–200 fl., and a substantial minority (30 percent) received less than 100 fl. in the poorest parishes in the mountains.

Given the great disparity between rich and poor parishes, it is possible perhaps to draw useful conclusions only based on specific examples. Sources from the deanery of Tielt in the Spanish Netherlands indicated two general trends: a substantial improvement in clerical income during the seventeenth century in absolute terms, and a relative improvement of clerical income over other trades in comparative terms. Not only did the income of the parish clergy increase 45 percent between 1623 and 1683, but this development occurred in a period of comparative price and wage stability. In seventeenth-century Bruges and Ghent, a skilled artisan (butcher and carpenter) could expect annual incomes of 38 pounds, his apprentice less than half that, and an average laborer on the farm under 20 pounds; the income of parish priests ranged from a minimum of 35 pounds established by the bishop to over 116 pounds in an urban parish. The best-paid parish priests were almost on a level with the best-paid middle-rank officials in the archducal government – the bailiff of Oudenaarde, the secretary of the Council of Brabant, or the first collector of the tolls of Flanders. They were a long way removed from the farming and neighborly priest one century ago.

Buttressed by better income, the dignity of the new Tridentine clergy also reflected a more elevated social profile. In Überlingen, more than half of the city's clergy after Trent had studied at the university and more sons from ruling families chose a clerical career after 1600; in Strasbourg, the lower clergy was recruited primarily from the semi-rural/semi-urban bourgeoisie, and a clerical career in the family served as a marker of upward social mobility; in rural Ahrgau and the deanery of Bonn (diocese Cologne), most clergy came from small towns, with fathers as lower- and middle-ranking officials, artisans, and small merchants, and occasionally as rich peasants, but very seldom from the independent peasantry with small farms; and in the rural deanery of Waas in the Spanish Netherlands all except a handful of parish priests in the 1670s were born in cities.

Rising income also spurred more clerical vocations. Again, Milan served as a model diocese. Under Carlo Borromeo in the 1590s, 2,101 priests tended 560,000 souls in the archdiocese; in 1689, the population of 590,000 was ministered by 3,302 priests; respective numbers for 1766 were 600,000 souls and 4,743 priests. The trend is obvious: while the population increased marginally between the late sixteenth and the late eighteenth centuries, the number of priests more than doubled; the ratio of priests to parishioners rose from 1 in 260 to 1 in 127. While Milan might have represented an optimal case, local studies of other dioceses indicate this was part of a larger development.

One of the most striking changes in the new Tridentine clergyman was precisely his urban background. The seventeenth-century rural parish priest in Lyons diocese was more likely to be urban-born, university-educated, and alien to the world and ways of his parishioners, maintaining the respectful and distrustful distance between clergy and laity, reinforced by urban disdain for country customs. The same degree of distance and disdain characterized the outlook of the Counter-Reformation Irish clergy toward the native priests, the former shaped by Tridentine precepts in Irish colleges on the Continent, the latter little distinguished from the kinsfolk they lived among. By pushing for clericalization in the life of the Church, Tridentine reform hastened the conquest of country by city: trained in colleges and universities located in cities, the city-born clergy brought to the rural folk a centralized liturgy and an urban outlook formed by book-learning. The urbanization of the Tridentine clergy was reflected in these figures: in the diocese of Cologne, the origins of 8,450 early modern clergy (subdeacons, deacons, and priests) out of 11,100 are known; more than 52 percent came from the six largest cities in the diocese, with the city of Cologne itself supplying 15.9 percent of all clerics; in the diocese of Naples, urbanization of the clergy reached an even higher degree, with 65.8 percent of all priests (1,215) between 1650 and 1675 natives of the capital city and 68.2 percent residing also in the capital.

It is important to remind ourselves that clerical discipline was imposed unevenly and with difficulty and forbearance. Local and regional conditions varied greatly, depending on the measure of episcopal and secular zeal. Even in the last quarter of the seventeenth century, there were still rural priests in the diocese of Paris who understood not a word of Latin. And scandals still haunted the clerical elites, such as the Abbot de Choisy

(1644–1724), a nobleman in the reign of Louis XIV, a cross-dresser, transvestite, and androgyne. But by the eighteenth century, it was rare for a parish priest to be without a library, however small, and the Abbot de Choisy, after a personal conversion, finished his life as a pious and austere cleric, writing a gigantic history of the Church and esteemed as the dean of the Académie française.

8 Counter-Reformation saints

Twenty-seven men and five women who lived between 1540 and 1770 were canonized as saints by the Church during the same period; another six received the preliminary recognition of beatification. Two countries supplied the overwhelming majority: eighteen saints were Italians, fourteen Spanish (including one from Peru), three French, one Savoyard, one German, and one Polish. All were members of the clergy. Except for six seculars (one pope, two archbishops, two bishops, and one priest), the rest belonged to religious orders. Although many congregations were represented, sanctity seemed to reside particularly in the new religious orders of the Counter-Reformation. Half of all saints (nineteen out of thirty-eight) hailed from new orders: the Jesuits led with six saints; the Capuchins came second with five, followed by the Theatines with three; the Visitadines, Oratorians, Somaschi, Piarists, and Lazarists each had one. To this group must be added five members of orders reformed in the spirit of Tridentine Catholicism, such as the Discalced Carmelites and Alcantarians (a Spanish reformed Franciscan congregation), bringing the saints belonging to Counter-Reformation congregations (as against the traditional religious orders) to a total of twenty-four or almost two-thirds of all saints.

Another way to look at our group of saints and near-saints is to examine their attributes, in other words, the personality traits and achievements recognized by the early modern Church. We can discern seven archetypes of saints: founder, reformer, mystic, bishop, missionary, social worker, and martyr.

The founder-saints constituted the largest group; they included both the original founders of new Counter-Reformation religious orders and a few of their close associates. There was Gaetano Thiene (1480–1547), co-founder of the Theatines (with Pope Paul IV), canonized in 1671 and his close associate Giovanni Marinoni (1490–1562), blessed in 1762; Ignatius was, of course, the founding father of the Jesuits, and Francisco Borgia (1510–72), duke of Gandia, Spanish grandee, and the third general of the Society, was the most prominent recruit in the early years of the new order, and his name lent it tremendous prestige; Filippo Neri (1515–95) established the Oratory of Divine Love in Rome; Girolamo Emiliani (1481–1537) instituted the congregation for the care of orphans that came to be called the Somaschi; the Frenchman Vincent de Paul (1580–1660) established the Lazarists; the Spaniard Joseph Calasanza (1556–1648) founded the teaching order of Piarists; and Jeanne Françoise de Chantal (1572–1641) was the founding mother of the Visitadines. When the ship of the Roman Church creaked under the roar of Protestant waves, these institution-builders of the Catholic Church saved the papacy from shipwreck.

Associated with the founder-saints were reformers of religious orders: the Spanish Franciscan hermit Peter of Alcantara (1499–1562) gave his name to a branch of reformed Franciscans that would eventually merge with the Observants; and Teresa of Avila (1515–82), who was encouraged by Peter of Alcantara, almost single-handedly reformed the Discalced Carmelites, founding convents of strict observance throughout Castile and whose success radiated from Spain to the other Catholic countries of Europe.

Teresa's reputation transcended that of an institution-builder, for she was justifiably the mystic-saint par excellence of Catholic renewal. Her mystical experiences (the meditations, temptations, distress, trances, visions, raptures, and union with the divine), set down in her autobiography and in a guide to meditation (*el camino real*), inspired others to sainthood. Women were prominent among the mystic-saints, as a group second in importance only to the founder-saints: Caterina dei Ricci (1522–90), an Italian Dominican nun and friend of Filippo Neri, enjoyed great repute during her lifetime for her mystical visions; the Italian Carmelite María Magdalena dei Pazzi (1566–1607) was reputed to possess supernatural powers; the Dominican nun Rosa of Lima (1586–1617) modeled herself on the fifteenth-century mystic-saint Catherine of Siena, and was the first saint from outside Europe to be canonized. They continued a long tradition of medieval female mystics, whose sanctity and reputed therapeutic powers aroused both admiration and suspicion on the part of the Church. For male mystic-saints healing also represented an essential attribute: Juan de la Cruz (1542–91), author of sublime poetry, belonged to the Carmelite order and considered himself a disciple of Teresa; the Italian Franciscan Giuseppe of Cupertino (1603–63) was venerated for his healing, mysticism, and levitation; and the mystical-healer Serafino (d. 1604), an Italian Capuchin laybrother, led an otherwise uneventful life.

The next group of saints exemplified the reforms set forth in the Council of Trent; they were the bishops who implemented the decrees, disciplined the clergy, and guided the laity. Like their founder-saint counterparts, bishop-saints also built institutions, albeit more as legislators and administrators than as charismatic leaders. Foremost among them was Carlo Borromeo (1538–1610), cardinal-nephew of Pius IV, who renounced the Roman curia to take up residence as archbishop of Milan; his reforms of the clergy, his synodal decrees, and his vigorous defense of ecclesiastical jurisdiction, enshrined in the legislation of the archdiocese of Milan, served as a blueprint for other Tridentine bishops in their own diocesan reforms; his personal asceticism and rigor earned him great respect if not affection; and in 1610 this model Tridentine bishop was the first Counter-Reformation saint to be canonized. Gregorio Barraigo (1625–97), bishop of Venice and later cardinal, modeled himself after Borromeo and was pronounced blessed in 1761. The Borromean model unified many qualities. The bishop as pastor inspired François de Sales (1567–1622) to renounce his inheritance (he was the eldest son of the seigneur de Nouvelles) and follow a clerical vocation that would elevate him to the see of Geneva; like Borromeo, he sponsored new female congregations and sent missionaries to Protestant Switzerland. The bishop as defender of orthodoxy shaped the careers of Michele Ghislieri (1504–72) and Toribio of Mogrobejo (1538–1606). As a zealous inquisitor in Como and Bergamo, the ascetic Ghislieri first came to the attention of Cardinal Carafa who, upon election to the papacy, elevated Ghislieri to be cardinal and inquisitor-general; elected in 1566 as pope, thanks to the support of the rigorist party led by Cardinal Borromeo, Pius V sharpened the powers of the Holy Office, expanded the competence of the Index, and turned Rome into a monastery. The other inquisitor-saint, the Spaniard Toribio, had served as inquisitor in Granada before his appointment as archbishop of Lima in Peru.

Missionary-saints equaled in number to the saintly bishops. Their heroic journeys, far from home, friends, and country, expanded the boundaries of Catholicism and excited the imagination of the Counter-Reformation; their labors reaped souls in exotic lands to balance the loss to Protestants in the heartland of Christianity. Francis Xavier (1505–52), one of Ignatius's earliest companions, was the most prominent: he journeyed to India, labored in the Portuguese dominions before sailing to Japan; hoping to gain entry into China, he died in the Portuguese enclave of Macao awaiting travel permission. As one of the favorite heroes of the Jesuits, who pushed hard for his canonization, Xavier's missionary enterprise was also undertaken by saints from the mendicant orders: the Spanish Observants could boast of Francisco Solano (1549–1610), who taught Christianity to the Indians of Peru; the Capuchins had Giuseppe of Leonessa (1556–1612), a missionary to Turkey (he met with no success), and Fidelis of Sigmaringen (alias Mark Rey, 1577–1622), who tried to convert Protestants in the Grison; the Dominicans celebrated Louis Betrand (1526–81), missionary among the Indians of Colombia; and at home, the Jesuit Jean-François Régis (1597–1640) labored among Huguenots in Languedoc and Auvergne; and the Augustinian friar Thomas of Villaneuva (1488–1555), archbishop of Valenica, tried to instruct and convert the poor Moriscos in his care.

Two remaining categories of saints seemed less significant for the Counter-Reformation Church: social worker and martyr. Among the former was Felix of Cantalice (1513–87), a laybrother of the Capuchin house in Rome – from peasant stock, of unschooled ignorance and apostolic simplicity, humble and dedicated to the care of the poor and sick, known by the mighty cardinals and befriended by the saintly Filippo Neri – who, in his apostolic poverty, served as a counter-example to the learning and splendor of the Roman curia, the glory and power of which reflected divine majesty. The other social-worker saint was also an Italian; rejected by the Jesuits on account of his poor health, Camillius of Lellis (1550–1614) dedicated his life to care for the sick in hospitals and, by forsaking glory, gained sanctity.

Only one saint died as a martyr. Giovanni of Prado (1584–1631), an Observant Franciscan missionary among the Christian captives on the Barbary coast killed by Muslim pirates. Why was there only one martyr-saint in the Counter-Reformation when hundreds if not thousands filled the annals of the early Church? Early modern Catholicism did not lack martyrs; far from it: Chancellor Thomas More and Bishop John Fisher beheaded in 1535 for refusing to swear allegiance to Henry VIII as the supreme head of the Anglican Church; the forty young Jesuits recruited for a mission to Brazil in 1570 thrown overboard when the French Calvinist corsairs captured their ship in the Bay of Biscay, sparing all lives but theirs; the friars at Gorcum, massacred by Dutch Calvinists in 1585; the English Jesuit missionaries to their Protestant homeland – betrayed, tortured, quartered, such as Robert Southwell (1561–95) and Edmund Campion (1540–81), remembered as saints in the history of English Catholicism; and the scores of European and Japanese Jesuits, together with thousands of Japanese Christians, burned, crucified, and suffocated in 1597 and during the seventeenth century in the most brutal repression of Christianity after the Roman caesars. Their memory was celebrated; yet their official sainthood was not proclaimed until the nineteenth and twentieth centuries.

There are two possible answers. The first is ideology. The Counter-Reformation Church saw itself as a Church militant and triumphant; the image of martyrdom, so well suited to the identity of the apostolic Church persecuted by pagan rulers, was not the self-image of the papal monarchy, heir to the theocratic imperium of late antiquity. John of Nepomuk, vicar-general to the archbishop of Prague, the only medieval martyr canonized by the early modern papacy, was killed in 1393 by King Wenceslas not for his refusal to divulge sins confessed by the queen, as legend would have it, but in a dispute over ecclesiastical appointment. Regarded nonetheless as the patron saint of confessors, he was depicted in this role in a painting by Crespi performing this sacrament in an invention of the Counter-Reformation, the confessional.

The second reason was ecclesiastical politics and papal administrative centralization. The process by which holy men and women were pronounced blessed and sainted is like the evangelist's description of the first apostles: many are called but few chosen. Distrustful of the proliferation of saint-cults during the Middle Ages, the post-Tridentine papacy centralized sainthood and made it uniform (like liturgy, doctrine, and ecclesiastical administration). During the Middle Ages the cults of saints were spontaneous, local, and at times fraudulent, as clerics fabricated miracles and the common folk, eager for healing, flocked to these shrines. Not a few were directed against the Jews, such as the cult of Little Simon of Trent, reputed to be ritually murdered by Jews in 1475, whose relics attracted the Council fathers, whose cult was sanctioned in 1588 by Sixtus V, and whose memory thus passed into that great scholarly monument of sanctity, the *Acta sanctorum*. Keenly aware of the potential for fraud and devotional excesses, the early modern papacy exercised great caution in granting sainthood: decision-making was centralized in Rome, unauthorized local cults prohibited, stringent criteria for the proof of holiness established, and extensive investigation instituted. These careful procedures, codified in the early eighteenth century by Pope Benedict XIV, guided the procedure of canonization for modern Catholicism. Rome was the key. For a candidate to attain sainthood, advocates needed to succeed: the odor of his sanctity, so to speak, had to permeate the papal curia; the strength of that fragrance in turn depended very much on the political backing for the dead candidates. A large majority of clerical martyrs in early modern Catholicism were Jesuits: the 1675 martyrology of the Society of Jesuits compiled by Mathias Tanner listed 304 fathers killed for their faith. Already criticized for their overweening influence, the huge number of martyrs from the Society would have overwhelmed the scales of the Church. Many Catholics did not need reminding that Jesuits and the Church were not synonymous in early modern Europe.

In a satirical pun on Ignatius, the Dutch Calvinist poet Jacobus Revius attributed the Jesuit's sanctity to the weapons of Spanish soldiery:

Ignatius the Spaniard, a former soldier, became the patron saint of soldiers, canonized as it were out of Spanish cannons, went the punning of the witty Dutchman. He was not wrong. Indeed, the politics of sainthood was the politics of patronage: thirty-two out of thirty-eight saints in early modern Catholicism came from Italy and Spain and its dominions, the two pillars of the Counter-Reformation. All except one saint (François de Sales) canonized during the seventeenth century came from Italy and Spain and its dominions; most gained sainthood due to the patronage of the papacy or the kings of Spain: Borromeo, Cajetan (Gaetano), and Neri belonged to the inner circle of the Roman curia; Ignatius, Xavier, Borgia, and Teresa were sponsored by the Spanish monarchy. After the early canonization of Carlo Borromeo in 1610, the Catholic world witnessed a glorious ceremony on March 12, 1622, in St. Peter's Basilica; five new saints were added to the liturgy of the Catholic Church: Ignatius of Loyola, Francis Xavier, Teresa of Avila, Filippo Neri, and Isidor Labrador, the twelfth-century peasant and patron saint of Madrid. It was a magnificent day for Spanish Catholicism: Xavier, the founder of Jesuit missions; Teresa, a national saint revered by King Philip II; Isidor, patron saint of Madrid, a city elevated in 1560 to be the capital of the Spanish empire and, for some, the Catholic world; and Ignatius, founder of the religious order that turned the fortunes of Catholicism. The canonizations in 1622 symbolized the close alliance between Spain and papacy in the opening years of the Thirty Years War; Gregory XV, the first Jesuit-trained pope, exhorted Spanish arms to roll back the boundaries of Protestantism. Papal goodwill aside, the sanctity of the Spanish saints had been some years in the making. We will examine that mobilization in the case of Ignatius.

When Ignatius died in 1556, his secretary Juan Alfonso de Polanco ordered a death mask and portraits to be made. Used for commemoration of their founder within the order, these early memorabilia reflected the tradition among the early Jesuits to model themselves after the first apostles. The rapid success of the Jesuits, however, aroused increasing opposition, particularly from the Dominicans and Theatines. To protect the still-young order from the Inquisition (under the authority of the Dominicans), it became more desirable to bolster the authority of the founding father; and as the figure of Ignatius receded from the living to the remembered, it acquired a mythical aura within the Society. In 1572, General Borgia commissioned the first biography of Ignatius; written by the Spanish Jesuit Pedro de Ribadeneyra, the small press run of 500 copies was limited to internal circulation. By the early 1580s Ignatius's life gave more than edification to the Jesuits: General Claudio Acquaviva asked Pope Gregory XIII to open the case for Ignatius's sanctity; in 1586, two biographies of Ignatius were in wide circulation; and in that same year, Ignatius's body was translated to the new church for the order, the Gesù. After the establishment of the congregation of rites in 1588, the Jesuits wanted official recognition for their founder. In 1594, the fifth general congregation of the Society voted to request the opening of the process of canonization; their request was supported in person by the Spanish ambassador and by letters from Philip II and Maria of Austria; their case was argued in the Roman curia by the first Jesuit cardinal, Francisco Toledo, freshly elevated to the purple. Clement VIII, however, denied the request in 1599 against the recommendation of the congregation of rites. The problem was that Ignatius had never been associated with miracles and healing, attributes traditionally ascribed to saints; Cardinal Toledo's argument, that Ignatius's merit lay in his great service to the Church, could not persuade the pope to place the rational before the miraculous.

Immediately, the Society began to fashion a miracle-working saint. Cardinals Toledo and Baronius, members of the Rites Congregation who had supported Ignatius's canonization, both visited his tomb at the Gesù, inaugurating the cult of devotion at Ignatius's tomb. In 1601, Ribadeneyra published a fuller biography of the Society's founder. Richly illustrated with woodcuts showing the saint's divine vocation (signified by his visions and the halo) and his miracles, this biography purported to represent the heroic Ignatius, already canonized in heaven. The campaign succeeded. In 1605 Pope Paul V opened the process of canonization. The Society redoubled its effort to propagate Ignatius's saintliness: in 1605, the Bavarian Jesuits published a booklet on Ignatius's life, illustrated with eighty engravings from drawings by the young Rubens, and with a prepared text on Ignatius's canonization, leaving blank only the name of the pope and the date of canonization. The 1605 *Life of Ignatius* combined two traditions – Ignatius as founder and Ignatius as miracle-worker; he was compared explicitly with Francis of Assisi, another founder-healer saint. After 1606 the Society published many Ignatian writings, often with representations of him as saint. The iconographic and iconological actions intensified after the papacy pronounced Ignatius blessed in 1609. Peter Paul Rubens, the greatest artist of the Counter-Reformation north of the Alps, was commissioned to paint several portraits of Ignatius for the cathedral in Antwerp and the Gesù in Rome. From Rubens's workshop came a gigantic painting (today in Vienna) that depicted Ignatius standing at the high altar, at the head of a long row of Jesuits, illuminated by divine light and casting demons out of the afflicted Christian flock. This dramatic representation was completed in time for the 1622 canonization, which was facilitated by the support of Cardinal Ludovisi, the papal nephew.

Strictly speaking, Ignatius's canonization contravened the decrees of the Council of Trent. The Council fathers prohibited all saint cults not sanctioned by the local bishop; sanctity, and its official recognition in canonization, was meant to reflect papal power. Thus the existence of an Ignatian cult within the Society of Jesus before 1622 was technically uncanonical, yet its very existence proved the saintliness of the candidate and built pressure for eventual canonization. For the three other Counter-Reformation saints canonized on the same day as Ignatius, unofficial cults were also in existence before 1622: Xavier was venerated within the Society for purported miracles and cures; a cult devoted to Neri had arisen in the Chiesa Nuova, the church of the Oratorians in Rome; and the Carmelites in Rome were also celebrating Teresa as a saint. Canonization was theater. The very moment of the ritual itself – presided by the pope and ranged by cardinals – represented merely the act. A great deal went on before the stage performance: the script, flyers, and broadsheets were printed, players found, roles rehearsed, and the stage constructed, just as pious biographies, engravings, woodcuts, and writings of the candidate had to be produced, sympathetic cardinals identified, and popes convinced. The audience came, attracted by a multitude of advertisements – the commemorative medals, paintings, engravings, and hagiographies. And like the drama of Catholic renewal, canonizations honored the heroes and heroines of the Church, narrating their lives, casting them in action against demons, heretics, and other enemies of the true faith.

Good theater was not cheap – the Visitation nuns at Annecy spent a fortune to get their founders Jeanne de Chantal and François de Sales canonized (they spent more than one-third of a million livres for François de Sales' canonization alone). Nor was the saintly theater wholesome, as in the drama of Teresa's body. Revered as a living saint during her last years, Teresa's body fell prey to relic-seekers as soon as her soul had departed for paradise. Since she died away from her home convent at Avila, a legal battle ensued for the honor of her burial. Repeatedly dug up, reburied, and examined for its sanctity, Teresa's body enjoyed no repose: little bits of her were amputated by ecclesiastical and lay dignitaries, or simply by those who felt a right and need to partake of her bodily sanctity. The actual state of the saint's body struck a poignant contrast to Bernini's famous sculpture, modeled after Teresa's own description of a mystical union with God, being pierced with the arrow of divine life. There, in art, Teresa's body appeared supple, beautiful, weightless, smitten unconscious by divine love; here, in death, it was fought over and cut up for relics. The flesh of saints embodied the deep paradox so central to Catholic salvation – the martyr's body racked by torture and mutilation and the incorruptible flesh of the saint; the repudiation of life in embrace of death and the subsequent triumph of eternal life.

In confronting this paradox, holy men and women fashioned their own sanctity: at the catacomb of St. Sebastian on the Appian Way, the only catacomb known to Rome at the time, Carlo Borromeo came and prayed; there also, Filippo Neri spent nights in reading, prayer, and meditation next to the bones of the early Christian martyrs. In 1578 the tomb of Priscilla, an early Christian woman, was discovered; further explorations eventually uncovered more than thirty catacombs. Rome was dumbfounded. It sat atop hallowed ground, of miles of underground tunnels connecting burial sites and refuges of the early Christian community; it felt the living tradition shaped by the blood of numerous martyrs, whose relics and their timely discovery seemed to testify to the truth of the papacy and the Catholic Church at an hour of need. Partly inspired by these early Christian monuments, and partly in response to Protestant challenge, Cardinal Baronius began work on his great history of the Church, *Ecclesiastical Annals*, the first volume of which appeared in 1588. In 1599, the wooden coffin of the early martyr St. Cecilia was opened (it had been sealed in the ninth century and forgotten in a Roman church); the body, still lifelike and undecomposed and seemingly asleep, created a great sensation and inspired a beautiful sculpture by Stefano Maderna and a painting by Nicolas Poussin. Like a volcano, the early Church suddenly erupted and shook the Catholic world of 1600; the blood of its martyrs flowed like lava over the parched landscape of Catholic renewal. The very earth itself came alive, suspending human time, announcing, as it were, a greater truth that transcended all materiality. In 1634, the Oratorian Severano published *Roma sotterranea*, communicating the decades of secret discoveries to the world. Suddenly, the very gates of history crumbled: after the last canonizations of the early sixteenth century sanctity again permeated the Church, holy men and women walked the earth, and the new saints of the Counter-Reformation took their place next to the saints of old in the revised liturgy and calendar of the Catholic Church.

A Catholic reader in early modern Europe had at his disposal several saints' lives, notably the popular medieval compilation, *The Golden Legend*, and the more scholarly work by the German Carthusian Lorenz Surius, *De probatis sanctorum historiis*, published in Cologne between 1570 and 1575 and known for its critical methods. There was nonetheless no comprehensive hagiography. Around 1600, a Jesuit professor at Tournai, Heribert Rosweyde (1569–1629), decided that he would launch a project to record and edit sources related to the lives of the saints.

Rosweyde, a native of Utrecht, had entered the Society in 1588; his passion for ecclesiastical antiquities, perhaps inflamed by the iconoclasm of the Calvinists of his native land, inspired him to search out monastic libraries in Hainaut and Flanders in search of manuscripts of saints' lives and passions of martyrs. Having secured permission from the superior of the Jesuit College at Antwerp, where he was transferred, Rosweyde published in 1607 a prospectus for his hagiographic project. It aimed to reconstruct the authenticity of ancient hagiographies by removing subsequent stylistic additions, philological impurities, and textual corruptions; to bring to print yet unpublished saints' lives; and to provide commentaries to explain incoherences and contradictions in the sources; all this would be arranged by the feastday of the saints, beginning with the first of January. Guided by humanist methods and Catholic piety, Rosweyde planned eighteen volumes for his hagiography, including an alphabetical catalogue, a biographical dictionary, and lists of the social, spiritual, and clerical conditions of the saints. He sent a copy of this prospectus to Cardinal Bellarmine in Rome. After reading the project proposal, the eminent cardinal was said to have exclaimed: "This man believes he is going to live another two centuries!" Bellarmine wrote back to discourage the project, stressing that many early sources were unreliable and had to be revised; he counseled Rosweyde to abandon the project. The professor, however, refused to give up ten years' labor, publishing an edition of *Lives of the Desert Fathers* in 1615 and struggling on until his death in 1629.

In 1630 a Jesuit by the name of Jean Bolland (1596–1665) at the college of Mechelen received orders to proceed to Antwerp in order to organize the papers left behind by Rosweyde. After examining the papers, Bolland continued with Rosweyde's unfinished work and would give his name to the most monumental project of scholarship in the Catholic Church. Happily for posterity, neither Bolland nor his superiors knew exactly what they were in for, but by 1635, overwhelmed by his task, Bolland called for help. Another Belgian Jesuit, Godefroid Henskens, joined him. In 1643, half a century after the initial design and eight years into the collaboration, the first two volumes covering the month of January were published in Antwerp. Bearing the title *Acta sanctorum* (Acts of the saints), the two folios totaled more than 2,500 pages; the next installment followed fifteen years later, covering February in three volumes. The world of scholarship, both Protestant and Catholic, greeted its publication with great acclaim. Pope Alexander VII extended an invitation. In place of the sickly Bolland, Henskens and a new collaborator, Daniel van Papenbroek, undertook the journey. Supported by papal approval, the two roamed Italy and France, forming contacts with scholars, spreading the fame of the hagiographers, visiting monasteries, cathedrals, and universities, prying loose manuscripts jealously guarded by monastic librarians. They returned to Antwerp with 1,400 "Lives of Saints" and "Passions of Martyrs," copied from manuscripts dispersed throughout Catholic Europe. Greek sources were added; the dimension grew; and the three volumes of the month of March were published in 1668, three years after Bolland's death. Henskens died in 1681, having worked on twenty-four volumes of the *Acta*.

During the last quarter of the century, the *Acta sanctorum*, under the editorship of Papenbroek, weathered a grave crisis. Working on the feastday of St. Albert (April 7), Latin patriarch of Jerusalem who wrote the Rule of the Carmelites, Papenbroek wrote a commentary based on historical sources that deviated from the legends of the saint fiercely held by the Carmelites. The publication of this volume incited a war of pamphlets that lasted for fifteen years. In 1693, the provincial of the Carmelites in Belgium published a scathing attack on the Jesuit hagiographer; in 1695, the Spanish Inquisition accused Papenbroek and the dead Henskens of numerous doctrinal errors and pronounced them heretics. Forced to justify himself in a painstakingly written refutation, Papenbroek sent a young associate to seek the support of Innocent XII in Rome. The pope admonished both parties to silence; and little by little, the reasoned arguments of the Bollandists mollified their opponents until the Spanish Inquisition rescinded its condemnation in 1715. Although the heroic age of Jesuit hagiography had passed, the *Acta sanctorum* was battered by a greater storm: the 1773 dissolution of the Society of Jesus halted work; and the French Revolution led to the dispersal of the collection. The project, restored in 1837, is finally nearing completion four centuries after its initial vision.

As advocates in the heavenly court, saints were tied to the devout on earth by a complex network, constructed from material things and immaterial memory; votive candles, pictures, engravings, books, feastdays, prayers, and visions bound saints to a network of clients who implored their intercession, for health, cures, and spiritual well-being. Sainthood thus sprang from the dialectic between the heroic individual and the community; and canonization was forged from interactions between the skeptical, cautious, and investigative institutional Church and the collective memory of local communities. A closer examination of the investigations carried out at the beginning of the canonization process can reveal the deeper social ties that nurtured the reputation of sanctity. Two cases for sainthood serve as examples. They concern two reputed saints from southern Italy in the region of Basilicate, both Franciscans, Domenico da Muro

(1632–83) and his disciple Bonaventura da Potenza (1651–1711). The case for Domenico was opened in 1694 and again in 1742 but did not lead to the desired results; that of Bonaventura opened in 1727 and was completed in 1737–40 and led to his beatification in 1775. There were many similarities between the two Franciscans: they came from the middling ranks of small Neapolitan towns; they worked exclusively in the region of Basilicate as ascetic friars, hearing confession, visiting convents, preaching to the common folk, and settling feuds; and both were said to have worked miracles healing the sick. Both were venerated after their death. Yet only one passed the first test of sainthood established by the ecclesiastical hierarchy. A comparison of their cases would reveal the differences between ecclesiastical and lay perceptions of sanctity.

The Congregation of Rites, established in 1588, was the official institution in charge of canonization. Its officials gathered testimonies from witnesses in formulaic questionnaires that ascertained three things: first, the civil and religious state of the witnesses, their place of origin and residence, age, ancestors, profession, date of last confession and communion, and the name of confessors; second, the ties between the witnesses and the candidate-saint regarding the theological virtues (faith, hope, and charity) and the cardinal virtues (prudence, justice, fortitude, and temperance); and third, the supernatural powers of the candidate such as effected miracles, clairvoyance, prophecies, etc. The first evidence was gathered within living memory of the friars' death – eleven years in the case of Domenico da Muro and sixteen for Bonaventura da Potenza – thus recording local oral legends for evaluation by the official Church. For Domenico seventy-five testimonies were gathered; for Bonaventura 162 faithful testified.

These testimonies established a direct relationship between devotion to the friars and their supernatural powers. The wife of a ropemaker in Amalfi, for example, told of her difficult labor, whereupon Domenico gave her a host cut into three pieces with the name of Jesus inscribed on each; upon his instructions, she dipped the pieces of host in a bit of wine and swallowed them on three occasions, thereby easing her labor pains. In fact, the majority of miracles attributed to the two friars had to do with the healing of ailments. The testimonies, moreover, were all local. Sanctity of the two friars radiated out from the sites of their monasteries and most of the first witnesses had personal contact with the saints. In selecting witnesses, the Church privileged the elites, for the testimonies came from "people of discretion, honor, and integrity," but above all from "the noble, literate, and men of prudence." In fact, the nobility constituted one-quarter of all testimonies in the investigation of Bonaventura, both in 1727 and in 1737–40, but they were absent in the case for

Domenico. The different social profiles of the witnesses suggests an elite clientele for Bonaventura who appropriated the friar's sanctity for their class. After the death of Bonaventura, the nobility with drawn swords guarded his body in the sacristy of the church in Potenza to discourage relic-seekers from the common crowd. In both sets of testimonies, rural folk were almost completely absent; the social scale of witnesses seldom descended below that of the master-artisans. Many of the witnesses were related and each family group shared and defended its stories of supernatural wonder and holy fame. Bearing in mind the different social groups that constituted the clienteles of the two friars, they constituted together the upper echelons of urban society: the nobility, patriciate, merchants, and liberal professions. The preponderance of the nobility for Bonaventura swayed the case in his favor: he, not his teacher Domenico, was ultimately blessed by the Church.

For the laity sanctity was first and foremost the ability to work wonders. When questioned about the heroic virtues of the friars, all professed ignorance of this theological idea. The heroic Counter-Reformation saint canonized in the early seventeenth century, the model of theological virtue for the official Church, seemed an alien figure for the laity of later generations. Theirs were healing saints, who eased the pain of childbirth, cured dysentery, dropsy, fevers, and the many aches and pains that afflicted the men and women of early modern Europe.

Hero and healer – two contrasting roles, two visions of sainthood, one privileged by the ecclesiastical hierarchy, the other embraced by the laity: in the two centuries of Catholic renewal, the first model of the heroic saint, fashioned by clerics for clerics during the militant decades of the Counter-Reformation, seemed to yield gradually to the healing saint of the eighteenth century, so close to the heart of the laity. Let us examine in greater detail this shift in sanctity.

While the seventeenth-century supplied the Church with only fourteen early modern saints, the seventy years from 1700 to 1770 yielded nineteen canonizations and five beatifications. The decades 1721–30 and 1761–70 were particularly rich in their saintly harvests. Three distinct periods are discernible in the history of canonization: from 1610 to 1622, an initial period of hesitation gave way to the canonizations of five model heroic saints of the Counter-Reformation; from 1658 to 1690, nine "secondary" Counter-Reformation saints were recognized by Rome; after a hiatus of twenty-two years, in 1712 the papacy quickened the making of saints, approving clusters of new saints in 1726 (five canonizations), 1745–46 (four), and 1767 (five).

The five saints canonized between 1610 and 1622 were heroes of the

Table 8.1. *Canonizations and beatifications by decade 1600–1770*

	Canonizations	Beatifications
1600–1610	1	—
1611–1620	—	—
1621–1630	4	—
1631–1640	—	—
1641–1650	—	—
1651–1660	1	—
1661–1670	4	—
1671–1680	3	—
1681–1690	1	—
1691–1700	—	—
1701–1710	—	—
1711–1720	2	—
1721–1730	6	1
1731–1740	2	—
1741–1750	4	—
1751–1760	—	—
1761–1770	5	4

Counter-Reformation: Borromeo, Xavier, Ignatius, Teresa, and Neri embodied the theological virtues and clerical roles to be imitated by later generations. They served as exemplars for the second cluster of "secondary" Counter-Reformation saints canonized between 1664 and 1671 (Thomas of Villaneuva, Francisco Borgia, François de Sales, Peter of Alcantara, María Magdalena dei Pazzi, Gaetano, Louis Betrand, and Rosa of Lima). The exemplary bishop, established by the life and legends of Borromeo, was replicated in the persons of François de Sales and Thomas of Villaneuva; the first Jesuit missionary, Xavier, found his following among Thomas of Villaneuva, preacher to Spanish Moriscos, and Louis Betrand, missionary to the Indians in Spanish America; Ignatius, the erstwhile nobleman and founder-saint, inspired his fellow Jesuit general and Spanish grandee Francisco Borgia to saintly glory; the exemplary virtues of Teresa's mysticism and miracles found echoes in the lives of Magdalena dei Pazzi and Rosa of Lima; and the asceticism of Peter of Alcantara and the charity of Gaetano reflected the piety of the Oratorian Neri. If this second cluster of saints represented imitations of the first-generation heroes, eighteenth-century canonizations expressed a greater variety of sanctity, closer to the visions of the laity.

Known for his personal piety, Pope Benedict XIII (1724–30) created a

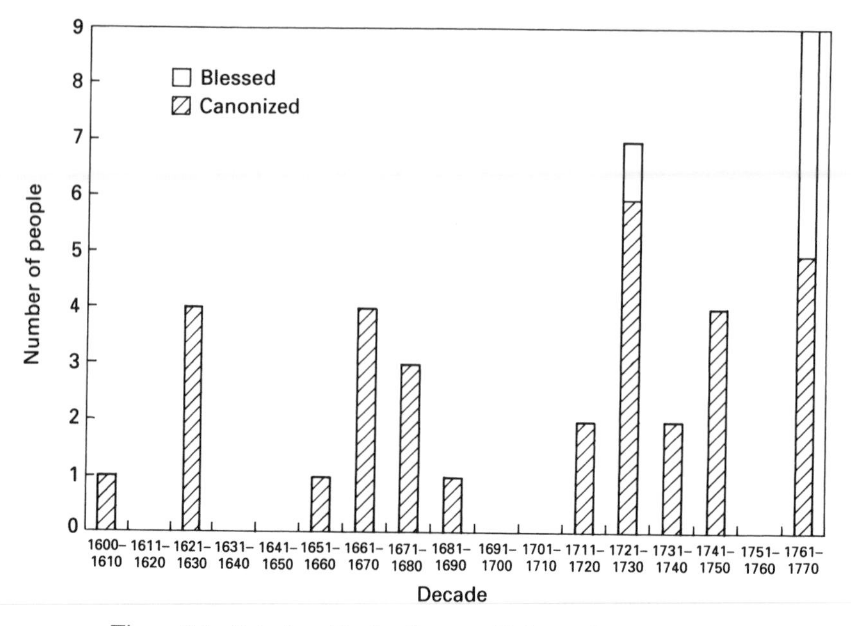

Figure 8.1. Sainthood in the Counter-Reformation

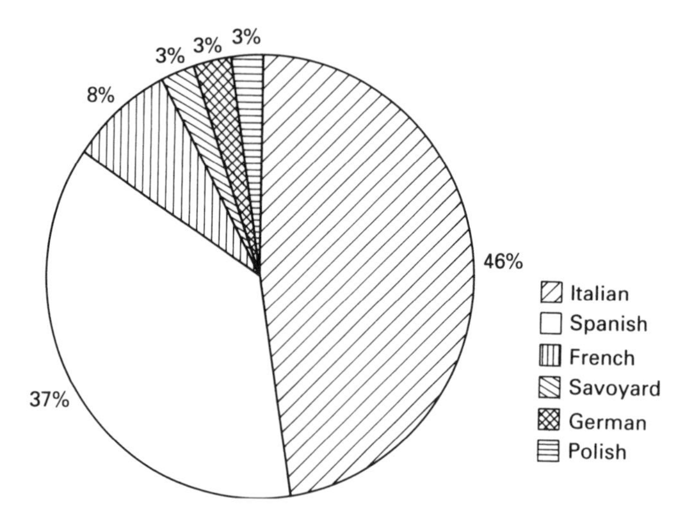

Figure 8.2. Nationalities of the Counter-Reformation saints

new cluster of saints during his reign whose virtues departed from the heroism of the Counter-Reformation: in 1724 he canonized the Capuchin laybrother Felix of Cantalice, venerated for his simplicity, poverty, and charity in caring for the sick and poor of Rome; in 1726, he declared saints Stanislas Kostka (1550–68) and Luigi Gonzaga (1568–91), two Jesuit novices who embodied youthful chastity, having joined the Society over the objection of their families, leading pious and austere lives, and crowning with exemplary deaths their sickly young lives. Preachers and ministers to the common people were also recognized: the Jesuit preacher Jean François Régis, canonized in 1737 by Clement XII (1730–40); Camillius of Lellis, the tireless priest in hospitals and Fidelis of Sigmaringen (Mark Rey), Capuchin preacher, both sainted by Benedict XIV (1740–58). The pontiff most favorable to the new saints of the people was Clement XIII (1758–69); his canonizations included those of Girolamo Emiliani, recognized for his care of orphans, Giuseppe of Cupertino, a Franciscan friar, and Seraphino, a Capuchin laybrother, both beloved by the people for their supernatural healing powers; the Theatine Giovanni Marinoni was also blessed in part for his zeal in the foundation of the *monti di pietà*.

Comparing the seventeenth and eighteenth centuries, one may speak of a shift of paradigms: from the militant, glorious sainthood of the Jesuits to a model inspired by Franciscan spirituality, characterized by simplicity, populism, and healing. In the heyday of the Counter-Reformation, those ambitious for sainthood left home and traveled far, in search of heroic deeds and perhaps martyrdom among strangers. During the eighteenth century, those reputed for holiness stayed home, their sanctity often limited to a narrow geographic radius, instructing, comforting, and healing compatriots and neighbors. Naturally, both models of holiness co-existed in early modern Catholicism. But as the prestige of the papacy declined during the Enlightenment, reaching a nadir on the eve of the French Revolution, Catholic Europe seemed to have lost its appetite for bloody martyrdom. And the order that provided so many martyrs and commemorated saintliness with so much ardor – the Society of Jesus – was itself attacked by the Catholic states and dissolved in 1773 by papal decree.

9 Holy women, beatas, demoniacs

In her autobiography, Ana de San Bartolomé (1549–1626), a Discalced Carmelite nun and one of Teresa of Avila's earliest companions in the work of convent reform, reported on approaching the saintly mother for spiritual advice. Burning with zeal to save souls, Sister Ana was told one day by her father confessor to beware of her charity, for this desire came from the devil. In the words of Ana:

> I went to our Saint [Teresa], to ask her if this were true, and I told her all that had happened. And she told me not to worry, that it was not the devil, for she had gone through that same way of prayer, with confessors who did not understand it. With that I was comforted and I believed that, just as the Saint told me, it was of God.

The prayer in question was silent or mental prayer, "recollection" in the theological terminology of the time; and the same doubt planted in Sister Ana's mind by her confessor was suggested to Teresa by several of her male confessors. Her posthumous fame was sealed by the canonization of 1622, but Teresa struggled during her lifetime to convince skeptical and hostile male clerics. Twice investigated by the Inquisition for heresy, Teresa undertook to write down her spiritual autobiography in anticipation of an inquisitorial confession. Her ultimate success was a testimony not only to her will and ability, but also to the hostility and restrictions placed on female religiosity by the Tridentine Church.

Two sets of questions are paramount: first, I will analyze the specific ways in which women in early modern Catholicism expressed their religiosity in the larger context of the structures created by male ecclesiastical authorities, a dialectic of male control, patronage, and repression and of female subversion, cooperation, and submission; second, I will examine three states of female religiosity (spiritual marriage, lay sanctity, and demonic possession) in conjunction with three estates of female life history (virginity, widowhood, and sexual hysteria). In the process, we will encounter women saints, beatas, nuns, and laywomen, who have left behind their stories in autobiographies, hagiographies, mystical writings, letters, and files of ecclesiastical and secular courts.

A greater suspicion of female religiosity in early modern Catholicism reflected both the Tridentine preoccupation with clerical celibacy and the traditional injunction against female religious leadership. In an age of Catholic revival the Church listened with ambivalent feelings to women's voices; it elicited, edited, censored, and propagated the words of religious women. Teresa of Avila was a case in point. Having struggled for more than twenty years to find her spiritual voice and inner peace, the 47-year-old Carmelite nun composed a spiritual autobiography for the examination of possible doctrinal errors. The text of the *Vida* represented a contest between Teresa's self-presentation and the dictates of her male confessors; as she herself put it:

> Since my confessors commanded me and gave me plenty of leeway to write about the favors and the kind of prayer the Lord has granted me, I wish they would also have allowed me to tell very clearly and minutely about my great sins and wretched life. This would be a consolation. But they didn't want me to. In fact I was very much restricted in those matters.

Restrictions aside, Teresa wrote a subtle portrait of her spiritual ascent, ignoring her *converso* ancestry in the description of childhood, while placing the blame of her faults with both herself and her confessors and attributing her spiritual growth to direct divine inspiration. One of the confessors who commanded her to write was the Dominican Domingo Báñez. In 1575 he summarized Teresa's *Vida* for the Inquisition, finding no "bad doctrine" in it and praising her visions as godly. Nevertheless, he opposed the duplication of Teresa's testimony because, in his words, "it is not fitting that writings by women be made public."

Upon Báñez's recommendation, the Inquisition impounded Teresa's *Vida* and held it until 1586, four years after her death when her saintly reputation had spread throughout Spain. The reception of Teresa's autobiography – it was printed, translated, and used in the canonization process – belied the danger at the moment of its creation. Teresa's attempt to justify and defend her visions and meditations against the charge of illuminism before the Inquisition succeeded beyond all expectations: the *Vida* became the single most important work of mysticism in early modern Catholicism and served as the exemplum for the shaping and writing of the religious life of women.

None of the other four women saints of the Counter-Reformation attained the same degree of authority and authorship as Teresa of Avila: Caterina dei Ricci (1522–90), a Dominican nun in Prato, Florence, left behind numerous letters, but her fame was spread by her anonymously published biography by Tommaso Neri, a Dominican confessor at her convent, who wrote on her at the request of Filippo Neri; María Magdalena dei Pazzi (1566–1607), a Carmelite nun in Florence, owed her mystical fame to two confessors, Fathers Puccini and Cepari, who composed biographies of her; Jeanne Françoise de Chantal (1572–1641), founder of the Visitation Order and spiritual daughter of François de Sales, left behind a voluminous correspondence but few substantial spiritual works; and the life of Rosa of Lima (1586–1617), beata, Dominican tertiary, and saint, is known to posterity only through the lengthy testimony of her patron, the accountant Gonzalo de la Maza.

Below the level of sanctity, the religious experience of many women is recorded in their own writings or by dictation; the majority of these texts remained in manuscripts, buried in convent archives until their discovery centuries later. The exceptions to the rule, such as the spiritual and epistolary writings of Marie Guyart (1599–1672), better known under her religious name of Marie de L'Incarnation (not to be confused with Madame Acarie who took a similar name as a lay Carmelite sister), Ursuline missionary to Quebec, also emerged under male editorship; her writings and letters from New France were posthumously published by her son, a Benedictine monk. Or in the case of María Agreda (1602–65), female authorship faced outright rejection: her immensely successful book, a purported biography of the Virgin Mary revealed in visions, *The Mystical City of God*, published after her death in 1670, was denigrated by theologians at the Sorbonne as a deluded work promoting the suspicious doctrine of the Immaculate Conception. Still other women left opaque records of their religious experiences, whether through the dossiers of the Spanish Inquisition or the histrionic accounts of demonic possession. Although Teresa's autobiography inspired many generations of pious women to emulate her spiritual path, none attained her success in combining the roles of mystic and religious founder in one. For the women of Catholic Europe, their heroic struggle took place not at the pulpit and in the market square preaching sermons, nor in the torture chamber and execution grounds undergoing martyrdom, but in the enclosed confines of the convents and in the boundless imagination of the mind.

In comparing three religious roles ascribed to the women of early modern Catholicism – nun, beata, and demoniac – we can explore in greater detail the struggle between male control and female autonomy within the ecclesiastical hierarchy and examine the dynamics between religious values (sanctity/evil) and secular factors (class/sexuality).

As the institutionalization of female Christian virtues, convent life epitomized the triumph of celestial marriage over human sexuality. Four of the five Counter-Reformation women saints were nuns; the fifth, Rosa of Lima, was a Dominican tertiary and beata whose family could not afford to place her in a convent. When we speak of nuns we speak of numerous individuals and the most diverse personalities, but the structure of convent life and the style of female sanctity created strong molds of conformity. With its members drawn by and large from the upper echelons of Catholic society, the convent provided limited upward social mobility: Ana de San Bartolomé was of peasant stock and had served for many years as a laysister and Teresa's personal assistant before being elected abbess; and the Spanish mystic Isabel de Jesús (1586–1648), who came from a family of shepherds, gained entrance to the Augustinian convent at Villa de Arenao only as a servant. With the exception of the Discalced Carmelites in Spain, the religious movement of women in early modern Catholic Europe followed established social channels. Whereas Teresa and her companions founded new convents, establishing piety and devotion as the criteria for entry, overlooking Jewish ancestry or poverty, other female religious foundations quickly adjusted to existing social landscapes. The Ursulines began as a socially mixed community attracting working women in northern Italian cities, but it soon became the favored institution of the elites in France, attracting women from the nobility and the urban elites. The Visitation nuns, founded by Jeanne Françoise de Chantal, born into the *noblesse de robe* and married into the *noblesse d'épée*, favored by Anne of Austria, queen of France, attracted daughters from the best families.

The spiritual achievements of religious women, in particular mysticism, must be seen against this social reality. While female mystical experiences followed an established speech-act – the wordless ecstasies, the interior voices, the images of Christ, and the divine-erotic union – their reception by the patriarchal ecclesiastical hierarchy depended on class and family. What mattered was control. All female mystical experiences sanctioned by the Tridentine Church occurred in the setting of the convent, usually in the chapel, often during mass, where the ecstasies were witnessed, at first by members of the religious community and later, as the reputation of the nun spread, to the external world. Teresa wrote of the many involuntary ecstasies experienced in public, for which she felt great shame (although they greatly enhanced her saintly reputation); Caterina dei Ricci caused a great sensation by her extraordinary ecstasies that began in February 1542 that were repeated every week for the next twelve years, during which she beheld and enacted the scenes preceding the crucifixion; María Agreda's first rapture, witnessed by her fellow nuns, became a spectacle when her superior allowed laypeople to come and gaze until she begged to be left alone. All three women counted on powerful protectors and patrons: Caterina had her uncle Tommaso, a Dominican friar and confessor at her convent and a wide circle of correspondents, including the saintly Neri in Rome; Teresa relied on her *hidalgo* father, on her relatives in the convent, on the powerful noblewoman Luisa de la Cerda, and on her ability to win supportive confessors against doubtful ones and maneuvering Jesuits against Dominicans; and María Agreda won the admiration and friendship of King Philip IV, who relied on her for political and spiritual advice. The significance of patronage in the career of a nun-mystic is further illustrated by the example of Isabel de Jesús: the peasant lay nun encountered a hostile confessor who dismissed her visions as demonic for fifteen years and only found a hearing when she dictated her life-story and visions to a sympathetic choir nun Inés del Santísimo in 1645, thus providing the stuff of simple sanctity to make Inés's career (she was elected abbess later) and a model for the propagation of peasant simplicity by the Church (it endorsed and published the writing in 1675).

Mysticism provided an alternative source of authority for religious women. The fourteenth-century mystic St. Catherine of Siena (1347–80) inspired several women of the Counter-Reformation: Teresa read her life and visions; Rosa of Lima modeled herself on the saint; and María Magdalena dei Pazzi was baptized in honor of her. In time, Teresa herself also served as a model: Ana de San Bartolomé's autobiography, *Defense of the Teresian Legacy*, invoked the memory and visions of the saint and was itself enormously successful, being translated into Flemish, French, German, and Italian; Maria de San Alberto (1568–1640) and Cecilia del Nacimiento (1570–1646), both daughters of the humanist Cecilia Morillas and Discalced Carmelites in Valladolid, vigorously promoted the cause of Teresa's canonization, praising her as "a mistress of masters [*la maestra de maestros*]" and "more learned than the learned men [*doctora que a los doctores*]," and calling her "a captain of pious squadrons of men and virgins"; Marcela de San Félix (1605–87), an illegitimate daughter of the playwright Lope de Vega and a Trinitarian nun in Madrid, used Teresa's treatise on mysticism *Interior Castle* as inspiration for her own literary composition; Marie de L'Incarnation read Teresa before leaving her infant son for the convent; Rosa of Lima was fired by her readings of St. Teresa; and in Agreda, as Sister María's mystical reputation soared, it was repeated that Teresa had prophesied the town would produce a most flagrant flower for the garden of the Lord.

The images and language of mysticism also allowed religious women to circumvent the controlling authority of male clerics. When Ana de San Bartolomé went to establish a Discalced Carmelite convent in Paris, she got into a protracted struggle with her confessor and superior Pierre de Bérulle over ecclesiastical authority and the interpretation of Carmelite rules; in her frustration and suffering, Ana was comforted by mystical visions of the departed Saint Teresa. When Isabel de Jesús met with indifference and rejection in pursuing her religious vocation, Christ appeared to her in a vision and said, "I shall make of you one of the great works that I have built since my incarnation." The comforting Christ, moreover, appeared as both young lover and mother; and in her ecstasies Isabel was comforted not only by divine union with the celestial spouse but also by the nurturing milk of his breast. The most poignant examples may be the visions of Teresa, who had been gifted with the discernment of spirit, seeing piety and sin in the deepest recesses of the male clerics who tried to exercise authority over her.

The erotic language of ecstasy, well established in medieval mysticism, masked the interior sexual struggles that accompanied religious vocations and the enclosure of convents. Again, Teresa's experiences served as a paradigm. Admitting to many sins and temptations after her entrance to the convent at Avila, Teresa fell into profound melancholy that resulted in a protracted physical paralysis and ailments that afflicted the remainder of her life. The intensity of sexual temptations, and the corresponding force of mysticism, seemed to follow the life cycle of these religious women. The early years of sexual maturity proved particularly trying: Rosa of Lima spent her late teens and early twenties in a mosquito-infested hut of her own construction, taming her body with a waist chain, a hair shirt, a crown of thorns, and daily flagellation; María Agreda, who grew up in the tiny convent her mother had established, suffered terribly during the first three years after she took monastic vows, repeatedly sick and constantly fighting off sexual temptations with severe penance and self-mortifications. A religious vocation was perhaps only slightly easier for widows: Marie de L'Incarnation, widowed after a short marriage at the age of nineteen, suffered many temptations (and propositions) before she joined the Ursulines at the age of thirty-two. Her desire for union with God was so strong that she experienced this turmoil:

> One day, being with some people who spoke a little too freely and whom I could neither reprimand nor leave, I spoke of this to my divine spouse. He urged me to leave and go with him to my room. Human respect held me back but he urged me anew with a loving movement to leave with him . . . As soon as I entered my room, his spirit took possession of mine. My body unable to sustain me, I fell to the ground, so sudden and powerful was this attraction.

Even Jeanne Françoise de Chantal, happy in a nine-year marriage that bore her four grown children, had to repel repeated marriage proposals and temptations as an attractive widow at twenty-nine. When pressed to marry a widowed friend of her father, Jeanne tattooed the name of Jesus onto her breast, to the surprise and disapproval of her spiritual director, François de Sales. Only Isabel de Jesús, forcibly married off at the age of fourteen to a toothless old man, seemed to have been immune from sexual temptations. She bore her marital cross as a martyr for twenty-four years, according to the life-story she dictated, and found solace in the mystical visions of Jesus as spouse and mother.

Obsessed by celibacy, enclosed in small communities, and controlled by male clerics, religious women inscribed their psychic struggles on their own bodies: paralysis, fevers, pains, hallucinations, fainting spells, and periodic sickness reflected both physical and spiritual confinement. In an age of Catholic missions and renewal, most religious women found themselves excluded in testifying to their faith; yet they burned with missionary zeal: Teresa was grief-stricken by the loss of so many souls in the Indies and she cried to God to answer her prayers "since [she] was not able to do anything else"; as a girl, Rosa of Lima confided to her friend her desire to "run off to the provinces of the savages in order that the idolators would torture her to death for the love of Christ," a story that echoed Teresa's childhood fantasy of running off to the Moors with her brother to be martyred; María Agreda, who never left her small home town, had visions of the cosmos and the world, and saw herself transported to preach the faith to Indians in New Mexico. The spirit of missions that fired so many men in Catholic Europe burned with equal flame in many women. Marie de L'Incarnation gave the most eloquent testimony:

> Then at the age of thirty-four or thirty-five [1633–34], I entered into that state . . . This was an outpouring of apostolic spirit . . . My body was in our monastery but my spirit, united to that of Jesus, could not remain shut up there. This apostolic spirit carried me in thought to the Indies, to Japan, to America, to the East, and to the West, to parts of Canada, to the country of the Hurons – in short, to every part of the inhabited world where there were human souls who belonged by right to Jesus Christ. In spirit I roamed through the vast stretches of the Indies, of Japan and China, and kept company with those laboring to spread the Gospel there. I felt closely united to these workers because I felt that I was one with them in spirit.

Marie de L'Incarnation was one of a handful of women missionaries in the masculine missionary enterprise of early modern Europe. Sponsored by the French Jesuits, whose *Relations* from New France she had read, Marie and two Ursuline nuns landed in Quebec in 1639. Their mission to teach Christianity to daughters of Hurons and Algonquins met with little success, in large part due to the Native Americans' antipathy to the cloistered life of Catholic womanhood, but they succeeded eventually in attracting vocations from the French colonial settlements.

The heroic life of Marie de L'Incarnation was unusual; and other clerics turned out to be more hostile to women missionaries than the French Jesuits. María Agreda's vision of her transport to New Mexico got her into trouble twice with the Spanish Inquisition. María had her first vision of New Mexico as a young nun of nineteen or twenty. After she had told her confessor, the story slowly spread until it reached the ears of Alonso de Benavides, director of the Franciscan missions in New Mexico. He sought her out in 1630; in his enthusiasm to gain support and funding from the king, Benavides apparently exaggerated the story: it turned into a miracle in that María found herself carried to New Mexico through the air many times, preaching to the Indians and more than once winning the crown of martyrdom. When questioned by the Inquisition in 1635 and 1649, María equivocated, blaming Benavides for exaggeration, excusing her weak memory, and attributing the evangelization to an angel. Disclaiming the more sensational aspects of Benavides's report of her bilocation, she told the inquisitors that she was sure only that God had chosen her as a lowly servant and her vision had not come from the devil.

Spain, the land of so many women mystics, was also the land of the Inquisition. The Holy Office defended the Catholic faith not only against heretics and *conversos*, but also against eruptions of the supernatural, whose provenance could be divine or demonic. As the religious order of rational theology, the Dominicans, who staffed the Inquisition, deeply suspected the mysticism of religious women and Jesuits; and to some hostile clerics, Teresa's visions (of doubtful origins) were only one step removed from the *Spiritual Exercises* of Ignatius. Subjected to the ever-present suspicion of illuminism, female religious mystics were protected at least by their confined status; the parlatory grill, the heavy gate, and the walls of the convent conspired to contain the spirit of ecstasy. Such protection, however, did not extend to the laysisters who lived outside the convents, the beatas who shared the mystical visions of their cloistered sisters.

Drawn from families unable to afford dowries for convents, beatas were religious women in early modern Europe who enjoyed a popular reputation for sanctity. They usually selected the habit and rule of a particular religious order and continued to live at home or in a shared community with other pious women. Whereas the theater of piety for nuns was the enclosed cloister, for beatas it was the parish of their town: the parish church where they prayed, confessed, and attended mass, and the streets and homes where they visited women's prisons, counseled reformed prostitutes, and did other charitable work abandoned by the enclosed nuns. It has been argued that the more restrictive marriage and convent markets of the early seventeenth century made beatas more visible in Mediterranean Catholicism. Some became hermits, practicing severe mortification while their saintly reputation spread; others grew to become religious leaders of small congregations, teaching their followers (and sometimes their confessors) the message of their mystical visions; all were closely watched by the ecclesiastical hierarchy for fear of disorder in the disturbing combination of lay and female religiosity. Unlike the cloistered nuns, whose writings conveyed their own voices and visions, the stories of beatas have come down to us often through hostile sources. Our knowledge of their world is gleaned from records of ecclesiastical investigations; but it seemed to have been a world remarkably similar to the mystical imagination of their cloistered sisters.

Dossiers from the Spanish Inquisition illuminate the persistent hostility toward religious women and the fine line between female sanctity and female heresy. In 1575, the inquisitors in Seville attacked beatas as followers of illuminism, describing the phenomenon of autonomous female religiosity as "an invention of the *alumbrados* of this time, who thus detached daughters from service and obedience from their fathers, and wives from their husbands." Also in the same year, the same inquisition investigated Teresa and her close associates, Isabel de San Jerónimo and María de San José, leaders of the Discalced Carmelites in Seville, also on the charge of illuminism. Between 1609 and 1645, the Holy Office in Seville prosecuted twelve beatas on various charges: *alumbrado* heresy, free spirit heresy, false ecstasies, false prophecies, false revelations, false visions, and false stigmata. While the charges against four women were suspended, two were sentenced to public recantation at an *auto de fe*, and five to terms of reclusion (house arrest). Madre Barbara de Jesús was denounced in 1609, for example, for leading prayer meetings of women who went into trances; their visions of the heavenly spouse as a "handsome young man" were dismissed as demonic delusions. Madre Catalina de Jesús seemed to be the most threatening: she taught, wrote, preached, and prophesied; honored as a living saint, Catalina's followers, numbered some 700 in Seville and nearby villages, knelt to kiss her hands in the street, believed her visions, cherished bits of her clothing and hair, and prized her portraits inscribed with the title "Santa Catalina"; this "second St. Teresa," as Catalina appeared to her disciples, was particularly galling to the inquisitors for her inversion of gender hierarchy because her first disciple and lieutenant was her father confessor, the priest Juan de Villapando.

A second particularly striking example in colonial Peru again illustrates the links between female sanctity and heresy. It concerned a group of religious women in Lima from 1614 to 1625: the Spaniard Luisa Melgarejo, wife of Dr. Juan de Soto, the rector of the University of San Marcos; her niece, Inés de Ubitarte, a Dominican nun born in the colonies; María de Santo Domingo, a third-order Dominican laysister, also a Creole; Inés Velasco, wife of a merchant in Lima, born in Seville; Isabel de Jesús, an Indian born in Lima; and Ana María Pérez, a mulatta servant. These women shared two connections in the colonial capital: they all knew

Gonzalo de la Maza, an accountant for the Tribunal of the Holy Crusades, and his wife, María de Uzátequi, whose house served as a meeting place for the beatas (Ana María Pérez was their cook); and they were all devoted to the Dominican tertiary, the living saint, Rosa Flores, who would later be canonized under the name of Rosa of Lima.

Rosa's father was a former arquebusier and became a mine overseer in Quives, a small town some forty miles northeast of Lima. As a minor official in the vast Spanish colonial empire, Gaspar Flores and his family lived in an outpost of Catholic and Spanish civilization at the foothills of the Andes, supervising the forced Indian mineworkers during Rosa's teenage years (1596–1604). Rosa remembered her father's choleric temper, as Gonzalo's biography would have it, and the young girl grew up seeking consolation in her intense religious imaginations, away from a overprotective mother and a violent father. Much of Rosa's short life (thirty-one years) conformed to the model of the female mystic: intense and frequent visions, ecstasies, union with Christ, severe self-punishment, sleep and food deprivation, and hallucination of a physical battle with the devil. As Rosa's fame spread, she became the center of a group of religious women in Lima who saw in the young virgin a living saint; befriended by María de Uzátequi and Gonzalo de la Maza, Rosa accepted their patronage and went to live in their house almost as an adopted daughter. When Rosa died in 1617, her fame was such that a huge crowd mobbed the cathedral, tearing at her clothing for pieces of relic; and her funeral was attended by the viceroy, archbishop, and all the ecclesiastical and secular dignitaries of Lima.

Yet after eight years, the Inquisition cracked down. The religious women in Rosa's circle were all investigated in 1625. Luisa Melgarejo, an intimate friend of Rosa who saw the saint ascending to heaven in a vision, was protected by her elevated status. Her niece, Inés de Ubitarte, was denounced by her own brother, a Dominican; the Holy Office confiscated her notebooks of ecstasies and visions and condemned her for demonic visions. Inés Velasco had also kept notebooks of her mystical experiences; all fifty-four were confiscated and burned by the Inquisition. Isabel de Jesús was condemned for fabricating miracles and for curing the sick with amulets. The women were reconciled with the Church at an *auto de fe*, but the harshest punishment was meted out to the mulatta Ana María Pérez, found guilty of false prophecy and ecstasy, and sentenced to 200 lashes and five years of house arrest.

Unlike Rosa of Lima, most of the religious women punished in 1625 were married, although they had abstained from sexual relations with their husbands. But like Rosa, the beatas imitated St. Teresa: Rosa told her life story on Gonzalo's urging; Luisa Melgarejo wrote down her own visions also on his advice; and Inés Velasco read three or four chapters of Teresa's autobiography. Also like Rosa, these women went to the same confessors. Luisa Melgarejo confessed exclusively to four Jesuits, who used her visions to support beatification of members of their own order; and when she was denounced to the Holy Office, they defended her. Others confessed to the Dominicans, such as Isabel de Jesús, who lashed herself 5,000 times on the advice of her confessor. It seemed that Jesuit–Dominican rivalry might have played a role in the 1625 crackdown, although we have only fragmentary information. Perhaps Rosa's sanctity was affirmed by her shrewd politics, for she had no fewer than eight Dominican and four Jesuit confessors and spiritual directors. Perhaps, too, she would have been investigated and denounced in Seville. All we know for certain is that even in 1647 the Jesuit Juan Muñoz, who played a part in the 1625 denunciations, still condemned the many women who, unhindered by the Inquisition, arrogated to themselves "matters divine" and "the arts of the demon."

The charge of false prophecy and demonic possession, repeated periodically in the investigation of Spanish beatas, struck a dramatic note against the background of witchhunts that reached a crescendo from the 1580s to the 1630s. The penance imposed on the beatas by the Inquisition, however, was lenient compared to the savage executions that swept both Protestant and Catholic Europe. It has been well established that women constituted the vast majority of victims in the witchhunts; it is also a fact that the Spanish Inquisition downplayed the significance of witchcraft, especially after the 1610 investigation of witchcraft at Logroño in the Basque Country. Magic, witchcraft, and demonic possession: these were criminalized to a far greater extent in countries consumed by confessional conflicts – in France, Germany, and the Low Countries – than in the heartland of the Catholic renewal. Several notorious cases of demonic possession in convents in the early seventeenth century reached the highest secular authorities in France and the Spanish Netherlands; they provide us with still another insight into the relationship between religious women and male clerics, and the murky dynamics between sexual hysteria and mystical sublimation.

The first case began in 1609 in Marseilles. During the summer of that year, a young nun at the Ursuline convent of Aix-en-Provence was terrorized by nocturnal hallucinations. Concerned for her frail health and convinced she was assaulted by the devil, her ecclesiastical superiors subjected her to exorcism before Christmas. By next spring, the demon in possession of Sister Madeleine Demandolx de la Palud denounced the priest Louis Gaufridy, a friend and spiritual director of her family, especially of Madeleine's mother. The possession became a sensation in southern France. Two well-known exorcists – Father Sebastian Michaelis, prior of St. Maximin at Sainte-Baume and the Antwerp Dominican Domptius – took charge of Madeleine and summoned Gaufridy to answer charges; supported by his bishop, Gaufridy confronted the exorcists and regained his benefice. Michaelis, however, appealed to the secular arm, the Parlement of Aix, and the accused cleric was arrested, examined for the mark of the devil, and confessed to a demonic pact. In exchange for his soul, Gaufridy had supposedly struck a deal with the devil thirteen or fourteen years earlier with the bargain that he could make any woman fall in love with him. Indeed, the parish priest at Marseilles turned out to be an irresistible devil, seducing many women in his spiritual charge including, apparently, both Madeleine and her mother. Convicted of witchcraft and heresy, Gaufridy died at the stake and the young Ursuline, after further exorcism, was cured of her nightmares and visions.

Scandalized by the news from Marseilles, the Bridgettine nuns at Lille in the Spanish Netherlands also succumbed to the devil. A recent religious congregation in Lille (1604), the Bridgettine convent, a place of mysticism and severe asceticism, showed early signs of trouble in 1608: shouts, noises, and specters at night were reported by the nuns. In 1612, two nuns were afflicted by contortions and "demonic speech"; the possession spread to other inmates of the cloister. Briefly imprisoned by the episcopal court in Tournai, the two sisters returned mute to the convent. The patron of the Bridgettines, Nicholas de Montmorency, director of the Conseil des finances of the archducal government, called in Domptius and Michaelis. In May, they successfully exorcised sisters Françoise Boulennoir and Catherine Fournier and the novice Péronne Imbert, but the leading demon resided in Marie de Sanis, around whom the other three nuns/demons formed a choir. Marie confessed to being the "princess of magicians" who had infiltrated the convent because the devil was enraged with the piety of the new foundation; after further confessing to the black sabbath and the usual sexual perversities, the possessed nun accused the priest Jean Leduc, canon at St. Pierre and aumoner of the convent. Believing himself also bewitched on account of his childless marriage, Montmorency had Leduc arrested in June 1613. The colleagues of the accused appealed to the papal nuncio Bentivoglio, who in turn appealed to Archduke Albert, who transferred the case to Brussels under a special commission of the leading ecclesiastics of the Spanish Netherlands. In 1614 the papal nuncio, with the concurrence of the ecclesiastical commission and the support of Rome (but bitterly opposed by Montmorency), proclaimed Leduc's innocence. Condemned to episcopal prison, Marie de Sanis died in 1630. A contemporaneous case of demonic possession in the Spanish Netherlands also reflected ecclesiastical credulity: in 1614 two young nuns at the Cistercian convent of Verger were convicted of sorcery and burned; the father confessor and several nuns were accused of raping a young nun; and the scandal again reached the archducal court in Brussels and the Holy Office in Rome. The madness subsided by 1617 and all the imprisoned nuns were released; in 1619 the two nuns burned at the stake were posthumously rehabilitated.

Publicized by the writings of the exorcists and magistrates, the Marseilles affair proved to be a trial run for subsequent dramas. Whereas the furor of possessed women seemed contained in the Habsburg Netherlands, in Bourbon France it created the most spectacular demonic possession in Loudun. Like in Marseilles, the afflicted were Ursuline nuns. The first reports of nocturnal demonic apparitions circulated in September 1632; after the abbess Jeanne des Anges (1603–65) had fallen into periods of trances and contortions, demonic possession spread like a contagious disease and eventually seventeen sisters of the newly established Ursuline convent were afflicted. Under exorcism, Jeanne denounced the priest Urbain Grandier as the author of the possession and as the dark specter that had terrorized the nuns at night. Some of the younger nuns screamed out lasciviously at the mention of his name under exorcism; and when the sisters ripped their clothing, threw themselves on the ground, and cursed the sacraments and ecclesiastics, it seemed that a legion of demons had invaded the holy sanctuary.

A Huguenot stronghold in Poitou, where Calvinists had risen in rebellion against their king, Loudun was the target of a fervent Counter-Reformation campaign during the 1620s, directed from the top by Cardinal Richelieu and his confessor, the Capuchin friar, Father Joseph. The Ursulines, established in 1627 in Loudun and directed by the ambitious 25-year-old abbess, Jeanne des Anges, formed one of the bridgeheads of this Counter-Reformation offensive and included two relatives of the second most powerful man in France, Cardinal Richelieu. Grandier, a brilliant student at the Jesuit College at Bordeaux, obtained a benefice in Loudun in 1617. In spite of his intelligence and eloquence, his extreme self-confidence, exacerbated by his arrogance and pugnacity, created widespread resentment; and when Grandier set out to seduce the women of the town, including daughters and wives of acquaintances, he made deadly enemies. When Jeanne des Anges (or the demon) denounced him in 1633, many were eager to believe the worst. The story of Loudun is well known: found guilty by a judge appointed by Richelieu to root out sorcery, Grandier died at the stake in 1634; public opinion, bitterly divided at the time of his condemnation, eventually swung around in his favor when the Parisian elite found skepticism more fashionable than the pious credulity of the provincials.

The story of Jeanne des Anges, however, was not over. Still possessed by a small host of demons, the Ursuline abbess at Loudun was fast becoming a national celebrity, attracting dignitaries from the royal court. In the Ursuline convent at Tours, not far from Loudun, Marie de L'Incarnation heard of the possession and began hearing noises and seeing dark figures at night. To combat heresy and the devil, Cardinal Richelieu called in a new exorcist, the famous Jesuit mystic Jean-Joseph Surin (1600–65), who made slow and painful progress with Jeanne over three years: in May 1635, he expelled the demon Asmodée; in November, he further expelled Leviathan and Balaam; in January 1636, he expelled Isacaaron; but the last demon, Behemoth, resisted repeated exorcisms. Two developments seemed to have conspired to heal Jeanne. Her spiritual health grew as the relationship with Surin deepened, to the point where a transference of manic-depression occurred between the Ursuline nun and the Jesuit exorcist, resulting in Surin's occasional collapses, his momentary transfer away from Loudun, and his own struggles against demonic possession for the rest of his life. The other cure was Jeanne's growing fame. The first demon Asmodée was expelled during the visit of Gaston, the brother of Louis XIII, duke of Orléans, who witnessed and testified with his signature to the miracle. And just before her final cure, in February 1637, she saw a most beautiful angel who resembled a distinguished visitor at the exorcisms: the eighteen-year-old François de Vendôme, duke of Beaufort, son of Gabrielle d'Estrées, the mistress of the king, celebrated for his duels and seductions. In any event, the last demon Behemoth negotiated the terms of his exit: he promised to leave Jeanne if she went on pilgrimage to the tomb of François de Sales in Annecy and, when denied, compromised and agreed to depart if such a journey could be arranged *post exito*. On February 7, 1637, Jeanne was cured by St. Joseph. Her pilgrimage to Annecy, accompanied by Surin, was arranged by the highest authorities. Entering Paris in triumph, she paid visits to the queen and the cardinal, showing them the miraculous signs of her deliverance: the scented shirt touched by St. Joseph; and the names of Joseph, Mary, and Jesus in red on the back of her left hand. After her return to Loudun, Jeanne settled down to a long life of piety and devotion. Sought out as a mystic, Jeanne wrote her autobiography in later life, never again afflicted by the demons of her youth.

10 Art and architecture

Attacks on Michelangelo's *The Last Judgment* – the fresco painting behind the altar of the Sistine Chapel executed between 1534 and 1541 – reached a crescendo in 1564, the year when the great Renaissance artist died. In his polemic, *Dialogo degli errori de' pittori* (Dialogue of errors of painters), Giovanni Andrea Gilio criticized Michaelangelo for giving precedence not to the requirements of sacred art but instead to his own stylistic conceits; in particular, Gilio deplored the nudity and the mixture of Christian truth and the fabulous in *The Last Judgment*. Indeed, the Council of Trent signaled a turn in artistic creation: Session XXV of the Council in 1563 proscribed any images that would inspire false doctrine, admonished artists to avoid all impurities, and exhorted the new art to delight, teach, and move the faithful to piety through a simple, straightforward, and accurate representation of Christian doctrine and Church history. The glorification of the human body in Renaissance art evoked widespread disapproval from Italian churchmen imbued with the spirit of Trent: nudity was decried by Cardinal Paleotti, archbishop of Bologna, by the Dominican Borghini, and by Federico Borromeo, a cousin of Carlo and his successor as archbishop of Milan. In churches and convents, the genitals of the infant Jesus and the Virgin's naked succoring breasts were discreetly painted over. Jacques Boonen, bishop of Ghent and later archbishop of Mechelen, the highest ecclesiastic authority in the Spanish Netherlands, even destroyed all paintings and statues he considered indecent. The painters themselves faced censorship: in 1573, Paolo Veronese was summoned before the Inquisition in Venice to explain why extraneous, non-historical figures had appeared in his painting of the Last Supper; Caravaggio found that several of his paintings of the Virgin were rejected by his clerical patrons because they found insufficient nobility in his representations.

In the meantime, the artists themselves fell in step with the guidelines of the Counter-Reformation and, gradually, like their co-religionists in the clergy, internalized the spirit of Catholic reform. In 1577, Pope Gregory XIII founded the Accademia di San Luca in Rome to make art

Plate 10.1. *The Last Judgment*, 1536–41, by Michelangelo.

useful for the propagation of Christianity. The new spirit of religious asceticism and Catholic orthodoxy was reflected, for example, in the person of the Florentine sculptor, Bartolomeo Ammanati, a devoted follower of the Jesuits who designed their church in Florence, bequeathed his estate to their college, and who wrote in 1582 to the Accademia del Disegno in Florence to repudiate his own earlier nude sculptures. By the early seventeenth century, the tension between Counter-Reformation censorship and Renaissance styles had been replaced by a new period of creativity in the visual arts and architecture, in which the spirit of Catholic renewal served as the wellspring of imagination. The two greatest artists of the Baroque, the Italian Gianlorenzo Bernini (1598–1680) and the Fleming Peter Paul Rubens (1577–1640), identified deeply with Catholic orthodoxy: Bernini counted among his close friends Giovanni Paolo Oliva, general of the Jesuits, and undertook regular *Spiritual Exercises* under Jesuit guidance; besides executing many commissions for the Society of Jesus, Rubens was on intimate terms with the Jesuits in Antwerp and lent his talents to the glorification of the Catholic and Jesuit cause. Other artists enjoyed a similar familiarity with the Jesuits: the architect Francesco Borromini (1599–1667) bequeathed 500 scudi in his will to the Gesù, the mother church of the Jesuits; and Pietro da Cortona (1596–1669) published a *Treatise on Painting and Sculpture* in 1652 in collaboration with the Jesuit Gian Domenico Ottonelli, a work that harked back to Cardinal Paleotti's *Discorso intorno alle imagini sacre e profane* (Discourse concerning sacred and profane images) (1582), which had laid out the well-known theory of Counter-Reformation art.

The collaboration between Cortona and Ottonelli signaled still another phenomenon in the artistic life of Catholic Europe: the clergy, in addition to giving the theoretical tone to the production of art, were themselves engaged in its making. With their emphasis on talent and expression, the Jesuits, not surprisingly, counted among their numbers many painters and architects: Guillaume Courtois (Cortese, 1627–79), a pupil of Cortona; the Fleming Daniel Seghers (1590–1661), a pupil of Jan Brueghel; Andrea Pozzo (1642–1709), most famous for his vault fresco in the nave of St. Ignazio in Rome; Giuseppe Castiglione (1688–1766), missionary to China and court painter to the Ch'ing emperor Qianlong; and several less famous men such as the architects G. Tristano, Orazio Grassi, Giacomo Brianto, the painters Michele Gisberti and Rutilio Clementi, and the sculptor G. B. Fiammeri.

In surveying the art of Catholic Europe, we need not concern ourselves with the definition of the Baroque – whether Baroque art was the cultural expression of the Counter-Reformation, or whether there existed a Jesuit style in art and Church design. These questions have been raised by earlier generations of art historians; the present scholarly consensus seems to argue that such larger speculations yield generalizations that are less than useful. Instead, let us focus on four sets of questions: (1) patronage, that is, who paid – the papacy, cardinals, religious orders, confraternities?; (2) what was produced – church buildings, decorations, woodcuts, engravings?; (3) where was this production distributed in Catholic Europe?; (4) and finally, what was the content of this art? In other words, this chapter will explore the iconography of the religious art of early modern Catholicism.

For religious art, the most significant patronage emanated from the papal court, the religious orders, and the nobility, in descending order of importance. As the center of the reinvigorated papacy and the expanding Catholic world, Rome became the artistic center of early modern Europe, attracting talent from all over Italy, Spain, and northern Europe. The Baroque, a style and a sensibility developed in Rome and other Italian cities, exerted an influence not only in the Catholic north, but also in Protestant Germany, Denmark, and England. Underlying this expansion of artistic patronage was the social process that created a new ruling elite through papal politics: as new popes, new men, and new families rose to prominence, they lavished their new wealth on palaces, chapels, and paintings, cementing their newly acquired prestige, and bestowing monuments celebrating their ascent. Between the pontificates of Sixtus V and Alexander VII, from the 1580s to the 1660s, Rome was a honeycomb of commissions and a beehive of artistic energy. The popes and the great cardinals spent lavishly furnishing their titular churches, building family palaces, and constructing family burial places in the older basilicas. The artists, whether maintained as clients in the palaces of prelates or working on freelance commissions, designed and executed subjects chosen by their patrons. With the exception of the top, a genius such as Bernini, the artist lost considerable autonomy in comparison with former generations, both in terms of financial self-sufficiency and in the choice of subject matter.

In this world of patronage, the popes were of course the biggest patrons: Sixtus V began the dramatic transformation of Rome, and during his reign the dome of St. Peter's begun by Michelangelo was completed and Egyptian obelisks (as emblems of Christian triumph) were erected at new city squares; under Paul V, the nave and facade of St. Peter's was completed; and the pontificate of Urban VIII was consumed by the decoration of St. Peter's (finally consecrated in 1626), including the magnificent baldacchino and papal tomb by Bernini.

The Borghese and Barberini pontiffs left many monuments to the glory of the Church and to their families, and in the process monopolized the most gifted artistic talent of their time. Bernini, whose father Pietro sculpted for the Borghese Pope Paul V, started his career with commissions for the villa of the family; after the papal election of Maffeo Barberini as Urban VIII (who as a young cardinal already had a portrait painted by Caravaggio), Bernini worked almost exclusively on religious works, creating the papal tomb, casting bronze and marble busts of the pope, designing the piazza of St. Peter's, and building the Church of S. Andrea al Quirinale. Cortona, promoted by the cardinal-nephew Francesco Borghese, painted the ceiling of the Barberini palace. Andrea Sacchi (1599–1661), best known for his paintings of *St. Gregory and the Miracle of the Corporal* and the *Vision of St. Romuald*, was the client of Cardinal Antonio Barberini, another papal nephew.

Outside Rome, Milan was another minor artistic center under the patronage of Archbishop Federico Borromeo (1595–1631). Combining a program of humanist education and Catholic indoctrination, Borromeo founded the Ambrosiana (1607–20) as an official diocesan institution, the purpose of which was to reform sacred scholarship and the figurative arts in response to the guidelines of the Council of Trent. The Ambrosiana was simultaneously a library, art museum, and art academy. In tastes more conservative, in disposition more optimistic, Borromeo's collection of art reflected traditional themes of Christian iconography: the adoration of the magi, the holy family, the infant Jesus, praying clerics, and sacred landscapes. Absent, however, was one of the main motifs of the new Counter-Reformation art – the realistic representation of bloody martyrdom. The Ambrosiana collection emphasized the devotional purposes of pictorial narration; close to half of all paintings collected represented stories of Christ and the Madonna and other scenes of pious devotion. Unlike his contemporary art patrons in Rome, such as Cardinal Francesco Maria del Monte and the Marquis Vincenzo Giustiniani who collected art from the latest fashionable artists, Borromeo subordinated art to spiritual edification. The visual images collected were intended to record the truth of the Christian faith and the historical legitimacy of Roman Catholicism. In his search for authenticity, sacred history guided art: at the core of the Ambrosiana was a collection of 306 portraits of saints, popes, and clerics, representing every century of Church history.

Glorification served as the leitmotif not only for patronage of the papal curia, but also for the new religious orders of the Counter-Reformation. Unlike the Roman court, however, the orders had fewer resources. In the beginning of their history, the Jesuits relied particularly on the generosity of powerful patrons: the Gesù was sponsored by Cardinal Farnese, who treated the project like his own family property, dictating, for example,

Plate 10.2. The exterior of the Gesù in Rome.

the designs of the high altar; the interior decorations, paid for by the Jesuits themselves, reflected an eclectic mixture of styles. Up to the middle of the seventeenth century, no Jesuit general had displayed any particular interest in art. The first to show interest was Giovanni Paolo Oliva, general from 1664 to 1681. His friend Bernini remodeled the Jesuit novitiate church S. Andrea al Quirinale without pay; and under him, the rather austere Gesù was transformed into a magnificent Baroque church.

Churches for the new religious orders, in fact, accounted for a great part of artistic commissions: their construction involved architects to design the building, artists to paint the ceiling and altar pieces, sculptors to create statutes, stucco workers, and numerous workmen for the actual construction. Four major churches were erected in Counter-Reformation Rome: the Gesù, begun in 1568 and consecrated in 1584; the Chiesa Nuova, begun in 1575 for the Oratorians, consecrated in 1599, with the addition of an oratory in 1637; S. Andrea della Valle, begun in 1591 for the Theatines and consecrated in 1623; and S. Ignazio, another major church for the Jesuits, begun in 1626. In addition to these four churches, many other new medium and smaller churches also dotted the sacred urban space of Rome, such as S. Maria della Vittoria (1606), the church of the Discalced Carmelites, which housed Bernini's sculpture, *The Ecstasy of St. Teresa* (1645–52).

In Catholic Europe north of the Alps, religious orders and the aristocracy played the most important role in the patronage of religious art. Clerical patronage was apparently more significant in the Spanish Netherlands. Antwerp shone as a center of artistic creativity: the Jesuit church, St. Charles Borromeo, designed by the Jesuit architect Pieter Huyssens (1577–1637), incorporated elements of the Italian Baroque, and its ceiling was graced by thirty-nine paintings by Rubens; its Gothic cathedral reflected the new glories of the Counter-Reformation in two gigantic altar pieces by Rubens, *The Miracles of St. Francis Xavier* and *The Miracles of St. Ignatius*, painted in anticipation of their canonization (today in Vienna).

In the patronage of arts, the Catholic aristocracy in central Europe played a role parallel to that of the papal curia; prominent in this regard were the prince-bishops of the Holy Roman Empire and the great aristocratic Benedictine abbeys in Bavaria and Austria, whose considerable resources went into ecclesiastic architecture and decorations after recovering from the devastations of the Thirty Years War. The period of artistic creation in central Europe thus coincided with the decline in papal patronage after 1660. While ruined papal finance and the end of nepotism in Rome drove artists to seek employment elsewhere, the new wealth of northern Europe drew talent from Italy. A great deal of patronage in France sponsored secular art – Nicolas Poussin, the best talent under Louis XIV, painted as many secular as religious themes – but religious art flourished in Catholic Germany and Austria. A wave of artistic creativity began in the 1670s and lasted until the 1750s, cresting perhaps in the first quarter of the eighteenth century. This movement was much stronger in architecture than in the visual arts; its most talented representatives were Balthasar Neumann (1687–1753), who designed the Residenz and Schönborn Chapel at Würzburg and the pilgrimage church Vierzehnheiligen, and Johann Bernhard Fischer von Erlach (1696–1723), architect of the Karlskirche and the Schönbrunn Palace in Vienna. Italy exerted considerable stylistic influence, both through the apprenticeship of northern artists in Italy and the actual presence of Italian artists and workmen in the north. The first decades of the eighteenth century bestowed upon central Europe its own particular sacred architecture: the great Benedictine abbeys at Melk, begun in 1702, Ettal, 1709, and Altenburg, 1730; the churches of Catholic triumph, St. Mikulás Malá Strana in Prague (1703–11) and St. Johannes Nepomuk in Munich (1733–46).

The magnificence of great art and architecture, sponsored by the ruling elites of Catholic Europe, may obscure humbler forms of patronage: the innumerable altar pieces, votive pictures, statutes, engravings, woodcuts, and other religious objects commissioned by local elites, confraternities, and the devout masses of a renewed Catholicism. In pilgrimage sites, such as Altötting in Bavaria or in the Provence, hundreds of crudely painted votive pictures represented the ailments and bodily members cured by divine miracles. With little claim to beauty or stylistic innovation, these pictures of the common people nevertheless spoke the same language as the great paintings of Caravaggio, Cortona, or Rubens: they represented in vivid colors and realistic details the ineffable experience of the miraculous and the supernatural, using the idioms of naturalism to convey a sense of the hyper-reality of the suffering and redemption of human flesh.

Sharing a similar theological grammar, even if they differed in the rhetoric of eloquence, high art and popular art were connected by numerous ties. Nowhere was this relationship between "high" and "low" more evident than in Antwerp, the center of Catholic art in northern Europe and the printing capital of the Counter-Reformation. Artistic production constituted, in fact, the major growth sector in seventeenth-century Antwerp: from 1601 to 1625, the guild of painters enrolled 368 masters; between 1626 and 1650, another 378 new masters enrolled. Seventeenth-century Antwerp could boast of thirty-two churches, twenty-four chapels, twenty-six cloisters, and two colleges. Devotional prints constituted a considerable portion of the output of Antwerp printers: they comprised almost one-quarter of the production of Hieronimus Cock, the most important printer in the middle of the sixteenth century; between 1586 and 1650, the height of Catholic renewal, close to half of all masters enrolled in the St. Lucas guild of artists were producing religious engravings. As woodcut prints gave way to copper engravings during the second half of the century, the more exact technique permitted a higher degree of artistic sophistication and more detailed representation. Rubens and his workshop produced many such engravings, among them the cycle illustrating the life of Ignatius commissioned by the Society of Jesus to promote the sainthood of their founder. Once drawn and engraved on the copper plate, the image could be reproduced cheaply, making available large numbers of prints and Counter-Reformation themes to the devout masses.

Devotional prints combined images and text: centered around one or several visual images (the Virgin, a saint, a pious scene), the print provides for itself its own framing in the form of prayers, a narrative, and captions. Intended to entertain, instruct, and inspire, devotional prints represented artistic products consumed by the new social institutions of Catholic renewal. The three major forms of devotional prints were the *suffragia*, produced for the Jesuit Marian sodalities and confraternities in honor of their particular patrons and used for monthly devotional exercises, prints for the thousands of children enrolled in catechism classes organized by the Jesuits and the archducal government, and votive prints for pilgrims to commemorate their trips. Since the sodalities were firmly governed by the clergy, the iconography and text reflected Counter-Reformation Catholicism, and the prints served as objects in the propagation of Tridentine values to the laity. In 1594, for example, the Jesuit Melchior van Woonsel, prefect of the first Marian sodality in Antwerp, commissioned two engravings for a *suffragium*, copies of which were distributed to every member of the sodality. As Jesuit influence grew and Marian sodalities multiplied, the production of devotional prints also soared: since each member of the sodality received twelve separate monthly *suffragia*, the production of prints increased from 18,000 in 1614 for the 1,500 members to over 45,000 copies for the 3,800 sodality members half a century later. Moreover, Antwerp engravers produced not only for the local market: in 1681 they supplied nearly one-quarter of a million devotional prints for the hundreds of Marian sodalities in all of the Spanish Netherlands; their prints were sold in Cologne and Frankfurt, capturing a portion of the market for the pilgrimage to Walldürn, the most popular shrine of Catholic Germany; their market extended even to Spain and Spanish overseas possessions, where Belgian missionaries also labored in the harvest of souls. Those prints destined for overseas markets sometimes contained images specific for local tastes, such as a print representing the Virgin Mary of Lima, Peru.

The presence of the Bollandists in Antwerp gave still another impetus to the growth of devotional prints; each canonization of new saints, especially Jesuit saints, produced another crop of devotional prints. During the 1660s, for example, the Jesuits in Mechelen alone distributed more than 30,000 prints of St. Francis Xavier. Sometimes sold and sometimes given away free, devotional prints shaped popular piety during the seventeenth and most of the eighteenth centuries. But with the slackening of Catholic vigor and the decline of the Jesuits after the first decades of the eighteenth century, devotional prints underwent a prolonged slump. They would, however, serve once more as visual aid to a revived popular Catholicism in the nineteenth century.

A close relationship between function and form in the cultural production of the Counter-Reformation, so evident in the devotional prints, was also evident in Baroque architectural and dramatic representations. The Gesù, the Roman church of the new Jesuit order, may serve as a paradigm. Beginning with the 1530s Catholic reform began focused on liturgy and sacraments. The growing popularity of sermons, in large part a response to Protestant preaching, and the promotion of eucharistic devotion necessitated stylistic innovations in ecclesiastical architecture that would influence the design of the Gesù. New liturgical and sacramental needs required churches to have innovative features: a more spacious, hall-like, and uninterrupted nave to accommodate larger crowds to hear sermons; flat or wooden roofs for better acoustics; a large chancel for dispensing communion; shortened transept-arms to emphasize the centrality of space; more windows for light; and side altars for the simultaneous celebration of chantry masses. Although not the first church to incorporate these architectural innovations, the Gesù represented an unity of design that would serve as the model for many Baroque churches, including Jesuit churches as far away as China and Peru.

In contrast to the Gothic cathedral, with its cross-like plan, its parallel rows of columns, and its separation of the choir, the Baroque church, as exemplified by the Gesù, focused space and light in a central realm where sermons were preached, mass celebrated, and communion dispensed. Capping this central space and stressing its dominance was a soaring dome, which both allowed in natural light and focused attention on the painted representations of paradise and divinity through the use of ceiling frescos. The combined effect of lighting and decoration seemed to highlight the theatricality of Catholic sacraments: what was the Catholic Church if not the theater of salvation, as suggested by numerous devotional and theological treatises of Catholic reform bearing titles such as "Theatrum vitae humanae" or "Theatrum sacrum"? And was Ignatius's casting out of demons – dressed in surplice, backed by a row of Jesuits, illuminated by divine and natural light streaming into the church – so magnificently depicted by the brush of Rubens – anything less than dramatic? Indeed, Jesuit theater itself suggested a continuity between mundane and divine matters, the natural and the miraculous; and the artifice of Jesuit theater design was meant to create an illusion, directing the devout's view away from the materiality of the mundane world out toward the imagined hyper-reality of divine mysteries.

The Collegium Romanum of the Jesuits served as the center of this new Jesuit dramaturgy, with elaborate stage settings to produce the desired effect of optical illusion. In the 1650 staging of the forty-hour devotion, a practice promoted by the Jesuits at Lent to honor the eucharist, the scenic architecture was placed in the choir of the church without a proscenium, with the result that the "false stage" continued into the "real nave," giving the audience not a sense of separation between life and stage, but a continuous spatial and visual experience between individual devotion and a representation of sacrality.

This representation of the sacred gave unity to the iconography of religious art in Catholic Europe, in spite of the natural differences in styles among artists and nations. As we have mentioned, many artists of the seventeenth century identified with the spirit of Catholic renewal; some demonstrated exemplary devotion: Rubens attended mass every morning; Filippo Baldinucci took communion twice a week; Anthony van Dyck was a member of the Marian sodality in Antwerp; and Murillo belonged to a confraternity in Seville. Exercising detailed theological supervision of painters, the clergy assigned subjects and themes to counter Protestant teachings and glorify Catholic doctrines and institutions. As we shall see in the following discussion, a close connection between text and visual representation characterized the art of Tridentine Catholicism.

Protestant iconoclasm was the common enemy. The Catholic restoration in Antwerp, won by Spanish arms in 1585, created numerous opportunities for artists to restore and replace the destruction wrought by the iconoclastic fury of Calvinists. Iconoclasts, past and present, were decried in art. In the chapel built by Paul V at S. Maria Maggiore, the Virgin Mary was honored by her victory over heretics and iconoclasts: she was represented by a Byzantine icon, reputedly an authentic portrait painted by St. Luke; two frescos by Giovanni Baglione depicted the deaths of Emperors Constantine Copronyme and Leon the Armenian, two Byzantine iconoclasts; and a series of other frescos, on narratives chosen by oratorian theologians from Cardinal Baronius's *Ecclesiastical Annals*, and executed by artists at the command of the pope, depicted the Virgin's triumph over heresy. At another Roman church, S. Maria Vittoria, erected also by Paul V in 1621 to commemorate the Battle of White Mountain, at which the forces of the Catholic League defeated the Calvinist King Frederick of the Palatinate and thus won Bohemia to the Catholic cause, the Virgin Mary was depicted crushing the serpent of heresy.

Conceived as a rejoinder to *Magdeburg Centuries*, the monument of Lutheran Church history compiled by Flaccius Illyricus and other Protestant divines, Baronius's *Ecclesiastical Annals* defended the historical legitimacy of the papacy. Much of the papal patronage of art, in fact, was in answer to the Protestant challenge. The pope's own basilica, St. Peter's, represented in the totality of its artistic glory a counterargument to Protestant critique of Roman Catholicism. In addition to Bernini's baldacchino, the reputed Chair of St. Peter (dug out of a chapel by Alexander VII), and the tombs of pontiffs, St. Peter's was also the repose of monarchs faithful to Rome: the Last Stuarts, defenders of a lost cause against a new Protestant dynasty in Britain, and Christina of Sweden, daughter of Gustavus Adolph, king of Sweden and savior of Protestant

Germany in the Thirty Years War, who chose to abdicate her throne and convert to Catholicism.

Catholic sacraments and doctrines denied by Protestants provided another cluster of themes for Counter-Reformation iconography. The Jesuits promoted the cult of the fourteenth-century Bohemian martyr John Nepomuk to exalt the sacrament of confession; and a painting by Giuseppe Maria Crespi (1743) depicted him sitting in a confessional hearing the sins of the queen of Bohemia. The eucharist, under attack by Protestants as well, supplied the theme of many representations, such as one showing the Jesuit novice saint Stanislas Kostka receiving communion from the hands of angels in the Jesuit noviciate church in Rome, or St. Teresa receiving the eucharist from Christ himself at St. Aegidio's in Rome, or Rubens's sketches, "The Triumph of the Eucharist," for St. Charles Borromeo's in Antwerp. The doctrine of purgatory was defended in the painting by Guercino, *St. Gregory and the Souls of Purgatory*; and the virtue of charity or good works, anathema to Lutheranism, was asserted in a series of paintings depicting the charitable work of Carlo Borromeo (1602), commissioned for the cathedral of Milan, and in Murillo's painting of still another bishop-saint, Thomas of Villaneuva, giving alms to the poor.

A special place in Counter-Reformation iconography was reserved for saints and martyrs. Portraits of Thomas More and Edmund Campion adorned the English College in Rome; and the walls of the Jesuit church for novices in Rome, S. Andrea al Quirinale, was almost exclusively decorated by scenes of martyrdom and torture instruments: the 1570 drowning of forty young Jesuit missionaries by Calvinist pirates in the Bay of Biscay, the 1597 crucifixions of Catholic martyrs in Nagasaki, and the death of Rodolfo Acquaviva, nephew of the general of the Society and missionary to India. A strong attraction for suffering seemed to have characterized Jesuit taste in art until the middle of the seventeenth century: at the Gesù, the late sixteenth-century chapel of four martyrs depicted the tortures of St. Etienne, St. Lawrence, St. Catherine, and St. Agnes; and perhaps the most horrifying representation of all, *The Martyrdom of St. Liévin* by Rubens, depicting the bishop's tongue torn out and given to a dog, was a painting commissioned by the Jesuits at Ghent. By the middle of the seventeenth century, under the generalship of Oliva, a gentler taste turned iconography from bloody torture to triumphant glory. Pozzo's vault frescos of the new Jesuit church, S. Ignazio, showing the glory of Jesuit missions in four corners of the world, were a far cry from the austere and somber iconography of earlier decades.

While visual images reflected and even exceeded the horrors of torture described in the many books of martyrdom, the experience of mystical union, a central theme in Counter-Reformation sainthood, eloquently described in the words of Catholic saints, represented a far greater challenge to artists. Both painting and sculpture tried to capture the inner ecstasy and the divine illumination of Tridentine saints: Ignatius in ecstasy stood as a statue in the altar above his tomb at the Gesù and also in a painting of the Gesù Nuovo in Naples; the visionary Neri was depicted in a painting by Guido Reni and in a statue by Alessandro Algardi in the Chiesa Nuova; and Teresa's ecstasy, described vividly in her own words, inspired Bernini's sculpture in S. Maria della Vittoria.

New saints and new themes aside, the art of Catholic Europe continued to depict traditional iconography: the annunciation, the nativity, the adoration of the magi, the flight from Egypt, the Holy Family, the baptism of Jesus, Christ's passion and crucifixion, his resurrection and apparition, all stories from Scripture; the medieval legends of the Virgin and the Holy Family; and stories of apostles and medieval saints. The frescoes, altar pieces, paintings, and statues created a new iconography of Catholic renewal while forging continuity with traditional devotion; they would grace a landscape dotted with the Baroque churches and the palaces of princes and prelates in a triumphant Catholic world.

11 The Iberian Church and empires

In the *Historia ecclesiástica indiana*, the Franciscan Gerónimo de Mendieta (1525–1604), who labored as a missionary in Mexico from 1554 until his death, wrote of the religious mission of the universal Spanish monarchy:

> I am firmly convinced that as those Catholic Monarchs [Ferdinand and Isabella] were granted the mission of beginning to extirpate those three diabolical squadrons "perfidious" Judaism, "false" Mohammedianism and "blind" idolatry along with the fourth squadron of the heretics whose remedy and medicine is the Holy Inquisition, in like manner the business of completing this task has been reserved for their royal successors; so that as Ferdinand and Isabella cleansed Spain of these wicked sects, in like manner their royal descendants will accomplish the universal destruction of these sects throughout the whole world and the final conversion of all the peoples of the earth to the bosom of the Church.

Franciscan friars accompanied the first conquistadores. In the wake of Hernando Cortès's campaign in central Mexico, Aztec temples were destroyed, Aztec priests massacred, and crucifixes marked the territorial expansion of Catholic civilization. Under the aegis of the Iberian empires, missionaries carried the Catholic faith to the Americas, Africa, India, and the Philippines. Unlike the missions in China and Japan, evangelization and military conquest in the Iberian colonies went hand in hand. Catholicism came in the wake of priests and friars, but also in the persons of the royal official, soldier, and colonial settler. As European officials resettled the indigenous populations to exert taxation and forced labor, and as colonial settlers constructed towns based on Iberian models, the Catholic clergy built churches and missions for the numerous indigenous peoples compelled to enter the bosom of the Church.

This story of evangelization, so well documented by European sources and often told in the heroic mode, has been challenged by studies that show widespread resistance to Christianization, based on the study of sources written in indigenous languages or on the archives of the Inquisition. Christianization, therefore, represented a complex process and a wide spectrum of responses, ranging from sincere conversion, through misunderstood appropriation and outward conformity, to outright rejection. Christian rituals and symbols, sometimes juxtaposed with indigenous cults, reflected the intricate ethnic mixture of the Iberian empires and the difficulties of enforcing colonial rule. From the high plateau of central Mexico to the inaccessible Andean mountains and jungles of the Amazon, the empire of Catholicism evoked great millenarian hopes and bitter disappointments among the harvesters of souls.

The first Franciscan friars to the New World thought of Spanish conquest and Christian conversion as the harbinger of the millennium. Castigating the colonizers for their brutality and greed, the friars saw the Indians as childlike and innocent and sought to protect their wards against the worst depredations of conquest. Armed with episcopal jurisdiction granted by the papacy, the friars were elated by the massive baptisms among the conquered populations. For Mendieta, the Indian Church was similar to the primitive apostolic Church and a City of God, to be built by Franciscans and Indians, so Mendieta thought, stood to oppose the City of Man peopled by rapacious colonizers. But the inhabitants of the City of God were dying off in droves. European diseases and Spanish exploitation decimated the Indians; the indigenous population in the central Mexican plateau fell from six million in 1548 to one million in 1605. As Spanish settlers streamed into Mexico and as an indigenous Spanish population (the Creoles) filled out the corners of the new colonial society, the City of Man emerged triumphant.

The millennial hopes of the first Franciscans gave way to a new ecclesio-political reality. With the consolidation of royal authority, Spanish ecclesiastical institutions were duplicated in the overseas empire: the arrival of bishops, secular priests, and the Inquisition undermined the extensive authority of the friars and shifted the focus of Catholicism from evangelizing the Indians to serving the needs of the ever-expanding colonial population. The Mexican Church councils of 1555, 1565, and 1585 repeatedly affirmed episcopal authority and the significance of the parish. While continuing to champion the cause of the Indians, the friars themselves, numbering 380 in the 1550s, were split on the issue of indigenous evangelization. The pro-Indian party included friars sympathetic to indigenous traditions; Bernardino de Sahagún, the great Nahuatl linguist and ethnographer, exemplified the best tradition in Franciscan missionary work. While Sahagún, Mendieta, and other friars praised the childlike innocence of the Indians – they were meek, gentle, simple, humble, obedient, patient, and poor – other Franciscans saw them as timid, opportunistic, and hypocritical. As "children," Mendieta argued, Indians could not be enslaved, but they were also unable to attain the same status as Europeans: "I mean that they are made to be pupils, not teachers; parishioners, not priests; and for this they are the best in the world." Believing that Christianity should be superimposed upon traditional social structures, all of which ought to be carefully preserved provided they did not clash directly with the new religion, the friars resisted the 1550 royal decree to teach Spanish to Indians. To the new Mexican Church, however, where Creoles played an ever-important role, Christianization implied the acceptance of Spanish ways. The only true converts were the Hispanized Indians. But this option was open only to a small Indian and mestizo elite, who learned Spanish, adopted Spanish dress, sent their sons to Christian schools, married their daughters to Spaniards, and moved to urban centers designed in the image of Spanish cities. On the broken formation of a nominally Christian Indian population, the Church carved a new landscape shaped by the familiar contours of Spain. The missionary realm, meanwhile, extended to the dense jungles of the Yucatan in the south.

Conquered in 1544 from Mexico, the Mayans of Yucatan rose in rebellion two years later against Spanish rule. Protected by Franciscan missionaries from savage reprisals after the suppression of the uprising, the Mayans seemed eager to embrace Christianity. The handful of Franciscan missionaries, conversant in Mayan, traveled and preached to the villagers, who flocked to the Christian sacraments in great numbers. Again, the Franciscans played out their role as guardians of an exploited, childlike people. Their vision was shattered in 1562 when a young Mayan convert discovered idols and human skulls hidden in a cave. Diego de Landa, the provincial of the Franciscans, suspected his flock of practicing the traditional religious rite of human sacrifice in secret. In his rage, Landa invoked the full rigor of colonial repression: more than 4,500 Indians were interrogated under torture, of whom 158 died; and hundreds were flogged, fined, and pressed into forced labor. Returning to Spain after his service as bishop of Yucatan (1571–79), Diego de Landa waxed nostalgic over his missionary work and remembered the Indians' "betrayal" with a bitterness tempered somewhat by time. For the Mayans, the year 1562 marked a catastrophic turn: the Spanish presence, which they saw as temporary, and the Christian religion, with its interesting novelties, had become the harsh rule of the "Lord Dios." But even as evangelization made its slow progress in the Yucatan, resentment against colonial rule persisted. The *Book of Chilam Balam of Chumayel*, an eighteenth-century Mayan codice, accepted Christian teachings and hailed the return of Christ in Last Judgment, at which time Christ would expel all Spaniards and restore the land to the Mayans.

In the Andean highlands, the other center of Spanish colonial rule administered by the viceroyalty of Lima, Christian evangelization encountered enduring resistance in the inaccessible mountains throughout the colonial period. Unlike Hernando Cortès, who welcomed Franciscan missionaries, the conqueror of Peru, Francisco Pizarro, resented the presence of the friars. The distance from Spain, the difficulties of the terrain, and the scale of indigenous resistance all limited the extent of evangelization. Whereas 800–900 missionaries labored in mid-century Mexico (380 Franciscans, 212 Augustinians, 210 Dominicans, and others), only 350 priests served Peru in 1563. Although the number of clergy had increased tenfold by 1620, the even-sharper color lines in the Andean region retarded evangelization. The first generation of mestizos (children of conquistadores and women from the Indian nobility) was quickly absorbed into the Creole elites by the end of the sixteenth century. Spanish and Christian civilization concentrated along the coastal strip, based on the capital city of Lima, and in large cities in the inland plateau, such as the ancient Inca capital of Cuzco, tucked away amidst undisturbed Indian settlements in the higher altitudes, where Spanish presence was extremely thin. Similar to the process in Mexico, Spanish conquest initially destroyed the imperial cults – the religions of the Aztec and Inca empires. But a complex religious tradition in the Andes, lumped together as "idolatry" by Christian clerics, survived and adapted to the new hegemonic religion of Catholicism.

Traditional Andean religion, as it has been reconstructed by historians and ethnographers, consisted of ancestral and totemic cults centered on devotional rituals to mummified ancestors and sacred natural formations such as rock outcroppings, trees, and mountains. The locality of the sacred in nature and in the *huacas* (ancestors and mythical figures turned to stone and immortalized for eternity) combined family and kinship rituals with divine rites. Fragmented by high mountain valleys and the multiplicity of clans, traditional Andean religion represented the bedrock underlying the Inca imperial cult, which, in turn, signified not so much the hegemony of a conquerors' religion, but the political domination of the Incas and the juxtaposition of local and imperial cults. When the Spaniards toppled the Inca Sun God and his dominion, they merely replaced the veneer of Inca imperial hegemony with their own.

Resistance to Spanish rule, in any event, was strong and persistent. The 1565 Taki Onqoy movement among the Incas envisioned a return of the Inca gods and the restoration of Inca rule; the rebellion of the Tupa Amaru (1571) embodied a more overt resort to arms. After the establishment of royal authority in 1570 over both Spanish and Indian subjects, the crown embarked upon a twin program of pacification and Christianization. The resettlement program, undertaken by Viceroy Francisco de Toledo, was not always successful. Protected by their chiefs,

Indian communities often escaped the vigilance and control of colonial authority as long as they accepted the outward forms of Christianity and provided the requisite corvée and tax assignments. Alongside established Indian settlements, renamed *pueblos viejos* in the administrative language of the viceroyal regime, new grid-based Spanish towns were established (sometimes next to older settlements), with squares, streets, palaces, and churches. There Catholicism flourished among the Spanish-speakers: the *peninsulares*, the Creoles, and a small mestizo population, from whose ranks would come the first Spanish-American saint (Rosa of Lima). The geography of early Christianity replicated itself in the Andes: in Lima a Dominican college (later university) was established in 1548; the Jesuit College of San Pablo followed in 1568; the cathedral, churches, and convents replicated European civilization, while the indigenous tradition was analyzed, studied, and recorded in the Spanish–Quechuan dictionaries, manuals, and catechisms produced by missionaries.

In spite of the evangelical enthusiasm of many missionaries, the majority of clerics were not sanguine. Severely understaffed, inadequately trained in indigenous languages, and distrustful of mestizo and indigenous converts, the clergy could not simply ignore the persistence of traditional beliefs and rituals. In 1640, Pedro de Villagómez, archbishop of Lima (1641–71), launched a series of idolatry inspections (*visitas de idolatría*) to combat the vestiges of "indigenous superstitions." Carried out sporadically until 1750, the idolatry inspectors (usually the local Creole secular clerics for whom this appointment meant an advancement) traveled to different Indian villages, inviting denunciations of idolatry. What idolatry represented to the clergy became clear in the practices they condemned: in addition to toppling *huacas*, suppressing ancestral cults, and erecting crucifixes, the inspectors denounced banquets, feasting, fornication, and drinking, collapsing charges of idolatry and immorality. The *chicha*, an indigenous drink made primarily for ritual use but increasingly consumed outside the ritual context and condemned in these visitations, was a case in point. Backed by secular coercion, the inspectors inspired fear in the communities, especially since the occasional abuses of power received only minor reprimands at worst. Quite often, the inspectors targeted Indian notables, using the language of heresy to describe prohibited adherence to tradition. As protectors of their communities, Indian notables competed directly with parish priests for the resources of the communities: some encouraged Indians to withhold the tithe; others led their communities in protest against the *mita* (rotational forced labor); still others competed with priests in the wine and textile trades. Such overt material considerations were at work, for example, in San Juan de Machaca in 1657, when the inspector and his agents confiscated the

Indians' llamas on the pretext that the animals were used in ancestor worship. What the anti-idolatry campaign succeeded in doing, beyond driving Andean religion into more remote recesses and from the surveillance of the Church, was to deepen disrespect for the practitioners of Christian discipline. Catholic evangelization in the Iberian empires was implicated in numerous ways by the colonial regime that supported it.

Nothing spoke more eloquently of the colonial regime of Catholicism in the Spanish Americas than the policy toward an indigenous clergy. Racial prejudice governed ecclesiastical policy as much as it shaped colonial society. The Inquisition, established in 1570 in Mexico City and Lima, targeted *conversos* even in these new shores of the Spanish empire. Although excluded from the jurisdiction of the Holy Office, Indians, regarded as deficient in reason, were classified together with Moors and Jews, peoples marginalized in the Christian community. The first two Mexican provincial Church councils (1555, 1565) prohibited Indians, mestizos, and mulattos, together with descendants of Moors, Jews, and others sentenced by the Holy Office, from entering the clergy. This measure of exclusion, somewhat relaxed in the third Mexican council (1585), allowed for the ordination of clergy of mixed blood (mestizos and mulattos), although in practice very few were actually ordained. In Peru, the first generation of Spanish settlers clamored against the exclusion of their mestizo offspring and in 1588 succeeded in having the crown accept legitimate mestizos for ordination. Again, in practice, the first mestizos (children of Spanish fathers and Indian noble women) were soon reclassified as Creoles in subsequent generations, as the Creole–mestizo elites quickly reshaped their marriage strategies to embrace new peninsular immigrants. The Spanish Jesuit, José de Acosta (1540–1600), provincial in Peru where he worked for more than a decade, wrote against indigenous ordination in his 1577 work, *De procuranda Indorum salute* (On procuring the salvation of Indians); for him, mestizos were inherently suspect because they were succored by the milk of their Indian mothers. Small wonder that the few prominent converts chafed at their treatment. Felipe Guaman Poma de Ayala (1526–1615), of Inca nobility and a sincere Christian who recorded the traditional religion of the Andes, chastised the Spaniards for leading Indians into sin.

Even with relaxed legislation, few Indians and mestizos were ordained. In 1650, Juan Palafox y Mendoza, archbishop of Puebla de Los Angeles, reported that he knew only one good full-blooded Indian Catholic priest in Mexico City, a son and grandson of chiefs. To be sure, some churchmen spoke out in dissent. Alonso de la Peña, archbishop of Quito (1596–1687), argued for ordaining blacks and mestizos, but his was a lonely voice that found no echo. Acosta aside, the Jesuits in Peru tried to overcome the color barrier, but in 1618 the viceroy closed the college to Indians. Bending to the prejudice of Spanish elites, in 1648 Lupercio Zurbano, provincial of Peru, warned the rector of the Jesuit college to admit no mestizos or mulattos. The College of San Pablo, in fact, was very much integrated into colonial society. The college educated the sons of the Spanish elites; it was one of the largest slave-holders in the entire viceroyalty, owning 1,550 slaves in 1764; and the thirteen sodalities at the college were organized along class and color lines, divided into those for clerics, Spanish gentlemen, Spanish merchants, university students, humanities students, "ladino" Indians, Peruvian Indians, Chilean Indians, *criollo* negroes (born in America), mulattos, *bozales* negroes (born in Africa), Spanish children, and Negro children. After its initial elan, the missionary Church was quickly domesticated by the interest of Spanish settlers. Isolated voices and sporadic attempts at preaching the Gospel to all notwithstanding, Catholicism left an ambivalent heritage in the Iberian empires. Only in 1769 did the Spanish monarchy order all prelates in their overseas dominions to establish quotas in seminaries for indigenous peoples, where they would occupy one-quarter to one-third of all places.

In one instance, however, the millenarian vision of the first Franciscan friars came into being in Spanish America. The scene was the Río de la Plata, far from the centers of colonial power; the actors were Jesuits, relative latecomers to the mission fields, arriving only after 1570; and the chorus consisted of Guaraní Indians living in tribal villages. The first Spanish settlers at Asunción took Guaraní wives; their grandchildren, classified as Spaniards, provided many Jesuit recruits. To these Creole priests were added many European Jesuits during the seventeenth and eighteenth centuries – Belgians, Germans, and Italians – making the Jesuit mission more international in scope and less beholden to the interest of Spanish colonial society. Lured to baptism and Christian settlements by music and Christian rituals, the Guaraní converted in whole tribes under the authority of their chiefs. The first Indian Christian settlement, the *reducción*, was established in 1610 in Guairá when the Indians fled to escape exploitation by the colonists. A Guaraní language school was established by the Creole Jesuit Roque Gonzalez in the early seventeenth century and, by mid-century, the Guaraní mission had attracted the strong support of Claudio Acquaviva, general of the Society in Rome, who directed surplus Jesuits from Belgium to Paraguay. Over the next century, a steady supply of German, Austrian, and Bohemian Jesuits added to the strength of the Jesuit mission.

The turning point in the mission came in the 1630s. Attacked by bands of slave-hunters out of São Paulo, many Indians fled the *reducciónes*, abandoning Christianity and settled agriculture for nomadism and shamanism. In 1631, Jesuit missionaries evacuated more than 12,000 Indians up the Guairá to establish new *reducciónes*; they also persuaded the Spanish viceroy in Lima to provide firearms to the Indians for self-defense. In 1641, the army of the *reducciónes*, under the leadership of their own chiefs and the Jesuits, defeated the forces of the slave-hunters and their Indian allies. In this frontier region, the Christianized Indians of the *reducciónes* served to secure territorial control for the Spanish crown against unpacified and unchristianized Indian tribes in exchange for tax exemptions. More than pastors and chaplains, the Jesuits in the *reducciónes* served as physicians and middlemen between the indigenous tribal society practicing communal property and the larger colonial society that could both guarantee and threaten the Indians' autonomy. This mediating role was particularly well played out in the 1690s, when Jesuit missionaries converted the Chiquitos, forest nomads who inhabited the eastern foothills of the Andes in Brazil and Paraguay, who accepted Christianity to sue for peace with the Spanish viceroyalty. By protecting the Indians from Spanish exploitation, the Jesuits displaced the traditional tribal shamans by exercising even greater magical powers and offering their services for free.

Christianity, as it was adapted for the rituals of the *reducciónes*, represented a successful syncretic blend of indigenous rituals and Christian signs. Conducted in indigenous languages, Christian sacraments existed alongside the music, processions, and dances central to traditional Indian rituals. This paradise of Indian Christians, protected for 150 years, was destroyed in the 1750s. A territorial treaty between Spain and Portugal dictated the evacuation of the *reducciónes* on the banks of the Uruguay; the Jesuits, loyal to their flock, joined the Guaraní in a futile resistance, which was finally crushed in 1754 by a joint Spanish–Portuguese army. Thirteen years later, in 1767, the Indians demonstrated their own loyalty to the Jesuits, rising in revolt in Potosí when royal troops came to arrest the fathers in the aftermath of the Bourbon suppression.

The history of the Guaraní Indians represented a successful encounter with Christianity, at least during the period of Jesuit *reducciónes*. But it may be legitimate to ask how much they had really understood Catholicism. Between the extremes of outright rejection and complete conversion there existed a broad spectrum of responses: close to the spectral end of conversion one may classify Indian responses as syncretism (the blending of indigenous and Christian religions), nepantilism (from a Nahua word denoting the middle), or external conformity; closer to the rejection end, one may classify the responses as dissimulation, passive resistance, and rebellion. The simple concept of Christianization, in fact, belies the complexity of responses and religious encounters that were shaped by class, ethnicity, geography, and individuality. The records of the Inquisition and the Idolatry Inspection reveal the intricate texture of religious life that eludes the most subtle schemes of theological classification. There was, for example, Magdalena Callao, a famous healer from Cañete, who consulted a rock formation and employed Andean medicine and massage in her healing arts; when questioned by the idolatry inspector in 1661, she admitted that she also invoked the name of God and the Virgin Mary when she performed her rites. Or take the example of Domingo García of Arahuay in Canta, imprisoned for idolatry in the 1740s, accused among other things of planning to smear llama's blood on the foundation walls of the local church to strengthen it, a custom he had learned from ancestors.

More poignant still were the handful of "man-gods" in colonial Mexico, religious leaders who combined the traditional role of shaman with that of the Christian messiah. These recurrent man-gods, apparently converted to Catholicism, resorted to a far older traditional conception of religious power – of prophecy, of divine archetypes, of cycles of time – in order to counter the hegemonic message of Christianity. In addition to these man-gods investigated and disciplined by the Holy Office – Gregorio Juan in 1659, Juan Coatl in 1665, and Antonio Pérez in 1761 – there were certainly others who had escaped the surveillance of Spanish Catholicism. On a larger scale, the Marian cults of colonial Mexico had a similarly ambivalent character. Cults to the Virgin sprang up everywhere, in Mexico City, at Guadalupe, Los Remedios, Puebla, and Ocotlan. According to tradition, Our Lady of Ocotlan near Tlaxcala appeared in 1541 to an Indian in the very spot where a sanctuary dedicated to the goddess Xochiquetzal had stood. For Gregorio Juan, the man-god and shaman dedicated to the cult of the goddess Soapile, the Virgin of the Indians, it was an act of devotion to the anti-Virgin of the Christians.

If these examples of syncretism argued against a simple model of Christianization (they represented, if anything, examples of counter-acculturation in which Christian signs and rituals were used for anti-Christian and anti-Spanish purposes), the heady mix of Christianity and indigenous religions could also undermine orthodoxy among the ranks of the Spanish clergy. In 1578, the Dominican Francisco de la Cruz was burned by the Inquisition in Lima. The friar, a pupil of the great defender of Indian rights, Bartolomé de Las Casas in Valladolid, had fathered a child by his mistress. A self-proclaimed prophet after his arrival in Peru, Fray Francisco revealed several apocalyptic visions: "the Spanish

Babylon" would be destroyed by God for its destruction of the Indians, who were descendants of the ten lost tribes of Israel; in this aftermath, only a few Christians would escape to the Americas, the site of the millenarian kingdom; and in the new earthly paradise, the Christian-settlers would live on *encomiendas*; the clergy would marry; and the Creole colonialists would live happily in polygamy. Uniting this fantasy of sexual plenty on the part of a Spanish friar and the vestiges of ancestral religion practiced in Mexico and the Andes was the vision of a time of apocalypse that had torn asunder the fabric of indigenous civilizations and the hope of an eternal return that would heal the brutality and injustice of that apocalypse.

Politics, race, and syncretism – three themes central to Catholic evangelization in the Spanish Americas – were equally significant for the history of Christianity in the Portuguese seaborne empire, established long before the Council of Trent. In the late fifteenth century, a small number of Africans from Congo and Angola had been brought back to Lisbon under royal patronage for theological education. Aside from the islands of São Tomé and Cape Verde, populated mostly by mulattos in the sixteenth century, the major object of Portuguese interest was the Kingdom of the Congo. Dom Henrique, a son of King Alfonso I of Congo (1506–43), the first Christian king, was consecrated titular bishop in Portugal in 1518. Our knowledge of the Catholic enterprise in West Africa comes only from Portuguese sources; the massive baptisms and sporadic missionary activities indicated only a slight acquaintance with Christianity. That initial encounter, however superficial, shipwrecked on the reef of the slave trade. By the second half of the sixteenth century, the Congo mission had failed; and the small Portuguese enclaves of São Tomé and Cape Verde off the mainland coast sheltered few unacclimatized European priests, who suffered high mortality rates, and depended on trade routes for their existence. The other Portuguese enclaves – in the Indian Ocean (Mozambique, Goa, Sri Lanka) and in East Asia (Macao, Nagasaki) – were also established along the maritime and commercial routes of Portuguese fleets. Little more than frontier outposts, even in Goa and Macao, these Portuguese fortifications and settlements reinforced the colonial character of Catholicism, as officials, soldiers, merchants, sailors, and clerics affirmed their religious and ethnic superiority amidst a sea of non-Christians.

The debate over the ordination of non-European clergy in Portuguese dominions mirrored the discussion in the Spanish Americas. A minority, fair-minded and often outspoken, advocated the training of African and Asian priests; the majority of colonists and clerics adamantly opposed racial equality; and the Portuguese crown showed little will to enforce any policy at all until the enlightened reforms of the marquis de Pombal in the 1750s. In São Tomé a seminary for training the local mulatto inhabitants opened in 1571, but it was closed down by Bishop Martinho de Ulhoa (1578–91) who favored sending students to Coimbra. For Ulhoa, ethnicity and orthodoxy went hand in hand; distrustful of the innate character of mulattos, he advocated sending European clerics to São Tomé. Very few Portuguese priests, however, were willing to serve in the tropics. The seminary was reopened in 1595, where it trained a mediocre secular clergy for local service. The distinction between a superior European clergy and an inferior African clergy was maintained in the Portuguese empire. The Jesuits in Angola trained Africans and mulattos only for the secular priesthood and did not admit any into their own ranks. Likewise, the Jesuit college in Goa, India, established in 1541, trained many Indians as auxiliaries to European priests. In addition to racial prejudice, the general feeling among missionaries concluded that sound theological (and Latin) education was only to be had in Europe. But even where the non-European clergy succeeded in getting their training in Europe, the color barrier still obstructed fair treatment. Such was the case of Mattheus de Castro, a Goan Christian from the brahmin caste. After he was refused ordination by the archbishop of Goa, he went to Rome in 1625, received his ordination, and after being consecrated bishop of Chrysopolis was appointed vicar-apostolic in Bijapur by the enthusiastic cardinals of the Congregation for the Propagation of Faith. But when he returned to India, Portuguese civil and ecclesiastical authorities refused to recognize his credentials; one Jesuit even called him "a bare-bottomed Nigger."

It was evident that the African slave trade determined racial prejudice in Portuguese Catholicism. The overseas Church was a major slaveholder; and its expenditure in Angola drew heavily on profits from the slave trade. The major Jesuit college for the education of African clergy, in Luanda, was founded by a notorious slave-trader who became a lay-brother of the Society. From time to time, European churchmen condemned African slavery: the Portuguese Dominican Fernando Oliveira (1555), Archbishop Alonso de Montufar of Mexico (1560), the Spanish Dominicans Tomás de Mercado (1569) and Bartolomé de Albornoz (1573), and the Jesuit Alonso de Sandoval (1627) all denounced the brutality and inhumanity of the slave trade between Africa and the Americas. Yet theirs remained lonely voices of dissent. Even the great court preacher, the Portuguese Jesuit Antonío Vieira (1608–97), a champion of the rights of Indians, supported African slavery because it would alleviate the lot of the Indians in Brazil.

Given this pervasive attitude of European superiority, few missionaries took seriously the indigenous cultures they encountered beyond learning the vernaculars in order to evangelize. A notable exception was the Italian Jesuit Roberto de' Nobili (1577–1656), who immersed himself in the study of Sanskrit and brahminic texts, hoping thus to unlock the secrets of Hinduism that would open the way to the concordance of faiths and the conversions of the upper castes. His effort was bitterly opposed; and the attempt to find cultural concordances between Christianity and the native religion never achieved the same success as in China (see chap. 12).

Overworked missionaries and massive baptisms represented two symptoms in the problem of evangelization. Two bright spots in this otherwise imperfect picture were the Philippines and Goa. In the Philippines Spanish missionaries had made more than half a million converts by 1650; and Goa, ecclesiastical capital for the Portuguese seaborne empire in Africa and Asia, was the site of the archbishopric and the Inquisition. A congregation of indigenous Goan priests, established in 1691, prevented the collapse of Catholicism when the Dutch wrestled Sri Lanka from Portuguese hands. The loyalty of the Goan clergy and the Filipino population aside, Catholic rituals existed alongside traditional feasts and rites that excited little comment from missionaries, except perhaps for recent arrivals from Europe. In Africa, where the missionary effort was but a thin veneer, the Catholic coat of rituals barely concealed the traditional body of beliefs and practices. Polygamy persisted in Congo, Angola, and Mozambique, even among baptized Africans. For the African ruling elites, Catholic rituals provided another language for the legitimation of their own power, one bolstered by alliance with the Portuguese. King Alfonso I of Congo was consecrated by Portuguese missionaries during the performance of the traditional ceremony of kingship; and the "emperor" of Monomotapa on the east African coast accepted Christianity in 1629 to elaborate yet another set of royal symbols to consolidate his leadership in the Karanga tribal confederation.

While Christian symbols reinforced the power of some indigenous rulers, they could also undermine European colonialism. In the depth of the slave trade, Christian symbols and messages nourished an African Christianity of resistance. A young woman from the Congolese aristocracy, Kimpa Vita, dreamed of St. Anthony. The movement she founded, with herself in the role of prophet and rituals incorporating Catholic hymns and prayers, proclaimed Congo the Holy Land, Christ the son of a black Virgin born in Mbanza Kongo, and her own age the time for the restoration of Congolese greatness. Alarmed by her large following,

Italian Capuchin missionaries persuaded the Congo king, Pedro IV, to have her arrested and executed in 1706.

The Catholic faith, however, triumphed elsewhere by means other than fire and force, as missionaries traveled beyond the Indian Ocean to the further shores of Asia.

12 The Catholic missions in Asia

In the midst of savage persecutions against Christian missionaries and native converts in early seventeenth-century Japan, a bitter polemic was published in 1620. Entitled *Ha Daiusu* (Deus destroyed), the treatise, written by Fabian Fucan, described the antagonism between Japanese civilization and Christianity:

> Japan is the land of the gods . . . The Three Divine Regalia became the protectors of the empire, so that among all the customs of our land there is not one which depends not on the Way of the gods . . . And the divine Prince Shokoku, being a Buddha manifest in human form . . . made Buddha's Law flourish. From that time on our land also became the land of the Buddhas. And this, this the adherents of Deus plan to subvert! . . . The adherents of Deus have no recourse but to subvert the Royal Sway, overthrow the Buddhas and the gods, eliminate the customs of Japan, and then to import the customs of their own countries; thus only will advance the plot they have concocted to usurp the country themselves.

Fabian Fucan, this fierce foe of Christians, used to be a Jesuit. He joined the Society in 1586 at the age of nineteen; after twenty-two years as a laybrother (he was never ordained) he left the Society and Christianity in bitter disillusionment. In *Deus Destroyed*, Fucan cites as further evidence of Christianity's perniciousness the Spanish conquest of Luzon and Mexico. Indeed, after 1582, rumors of a planned invasion of Japan by Spanish troops from the Philippines began to circulate in Japan, leading to the first edict prohibiting Christianity and the repression ordered by Toyotomi Hideyoshi, the supreme warlord who had recently unified Japan.

The Iberian pattern of conquest, settlement, and evangelization dashed on the further shores of the Pacific. In China, Japan, and, to a certain extent, the Philippines, the spread of Christianity depended on instruments other than those of colonial conquest. The existence of considerable sources written in Chinese, Japanese, and Tagalog for Christianity by converts and missionaries and polemics against it written in Chinese and Japanese allow us to reconstruct the dialogue between European Catholicism and three non-European civilizations. Comparing the attractions of Christian rituals and doctrines in the three Asian societies mentioned, this chapter will explore both the progress of Catholic evangelization from the perspective of the missionary churches and the meaning of conversion for supporters and opponents of Christianity.

The Philippines

While the Philippines formed part of the Spanish empire, the Spanish presence in the islands was limited largely to the walled city of Manila. Settled permanently in 1565, Manila served as the entrepôt linking Acapulco (and by extension Mexico and Spain) to the Chinese and Japanese trade networks, shipping silver, spices, and textiles across the Pacific. Unlike Mexico and Peru, there were no indigenous empires to defeat, temples to destroy, and "pagan" cults to eradicate in the Philippines. Largely effected by a peaceful "conquest," the Spanish presence never exceeded several hundred troops and even fewer clerics in the early modern period; and, again unlike the Americas, colonial immigration from the motherland never developed. Relying instead on the loyalty of village chiefs and the submission of perhaps half a million converts, Spanish colonial rule depended more on the persuasion of missionaries than on the muskets of soldiers. Favorably impressed by the Filipinos as friendly, sweet, and eager to accept the sacraments, the missionaries nonetheless chastised their many "pagan superstitions," contrasting the civility of "Christians" to the crudeness of the "ethnos." How then does one interpret the massive acceptance of Christianity? Not only was the knowledge of Spanish limited, but the Spanish clergy, steadfastly refusing to admit native clergy until the middle of the eighteenth century, were spread thin in the field of missions; in 1700, 150 years after the initial evangelization, there were only 400 Spanish priests among 600,000 indigenous Catholics. What then was the allure of Christianity?

An answer is provided by the Christian Tagalog printer, Tomás Pinpin, who worked for the Dominicans in the early seventeenth century. In his 1610 Spanish grammar for Tagalog speakers, Pinpin enjoined his reader to learn Spanish because "[Spanish] is the source of a lot of other things and it is like the inside of things, and everything else is only its external covering." The "other things" alluded to by Pinpin were the dress, arms, and gait of the Spaniards, eagerly acquired by the village elites who served as the crucial middlemen between Spanish colonial officials and the indigenous populations. The rule of village elites, traditionally dependent on their ability to attract followers, was institutionalized by the Spanish colonial regime, replacing the fluid exercise of charismatic leadership with one defined by genealogy in an externally ordered hierarchy. Renamed *principales*, the village elites collected taxes and tributes for Manila, in exchange for tax exemption and the material signs of Spanish authority (clothes, coins, swords, titles, etc.). By entering into an exchange with the colonial authorities (understood as submission by the Spaniards), village elites, in fact, vastly expanded their network of exchange, further strengthening the indebtedness of commoners and slaves on their ability to bestow gifts and favors. Very often members of confraternities in their communities, the village elites were seen as pillars of the Catholic mission by Spanish clerics.

Interpreted as divine intervention by the missionaries, the success of evangelization was in fact the integration of the Spanish presence into an indigenous economy of exchange, marked by the giving of gifts and the ritual recognition of indebtedness. Spanish words and Christian sacraments became objects of circulation, creating a bond of mutual obligation between the Spanish clergy and the converts. The vastly different understanding of evangelization was manifest in the sacrament of confession: whereas the missionaries demanded the conformity of individual conscience to a prescribed theological understanding, Tagalog confessants often discoursed endlessly on various themes to the annoyance of the fathers. Vicente Rafael has interpreted both conversion and colonial rule as debt transactions, in which the Spaniards and their God, speaking an alien and threatening language, were placated by periodic token payments of debt, whether in the form of tribute payments or sacramental conformity. The understanding of Christianity was shaped by traditional beliefs in spirits, both ancestral and evil, that crossed the boundary between the living and the dead, unknowable forces in a fluid universe that required periodic debt offerings. By promising a new universe of salvation, Christianity provided a language to transcend death; and, by subordinating it to an ultimate authority, death could be anticipated and the world of spirits tamed and placated. This was the "sweet death" described by the Tagalog printer Gaspar Aquino de Belen, who published the first Tagalog poem on the Passion of Christ in 1703. Slowly, Tagalog society acquired the language and mentality of Spanish Catholicism. In 1750, indigenous priests served in 142 of the 564 parishes and the Philippines would become one of the lasting achievements of the Catholic missions.

Japan

The first Portuguese traders arrived in Japan in 1543. Six years later, Francisco Xavier came. The Jesuit saint had heard of the Land of the

Rising Sun from a Japanese fugitive in Malacca, a Christian convert who acted as Xavier's first guide. In 1559 a Jesuit mission was established in Kyoto, the imperial capital. For almost a century, the Catholic enterprise in Japan seemed to flourish (claiming an estimated 150,000 Japanese Christians in 1582 and 222,000 in 1609); temporary setbacks in 1587 led to sporadic persecutions until the final repression of 1614 that would last more than two decades. Both the spectacular success initially and the brutal suppression thereafter depended on two sets of factors: the Portuguese trade that linked Macao with Japan and the internal politics of a war-torn Japan that would achieve unity in 1591.

The island of Kyushu in western Japan became a bastion of Catholicism. Destination for the China–Macao trade, the feudal lords (*daimyo*) who controlled the Kyushuan ports welcomed the first Jesuit missionaries to strengthen their overseas commercial ties. Omura Sumitada, baptized Dom Bartolomeu in 1563, was the first of a series of Christian *daimyo* in Japan of the Warring States. Through their intervention, the Jesuits succeeded also in establishing themselves in the political center of the country (Kyoto–Osaka), where their fortunes rose in the wake of Oda Nobunaga, the most powerful warlord whose ruthlessness, intelligence, and curiosity for things foreign seemed to bode well for Christianity. Determined to crush the powerful Buddhist True Pure Land Sect, a sectarian movement and religious monarchy that had established extensive territorial control, Nobunaga welcomed Portuguese military technology and Catholicism as counterweights in his campaign to unify the country and to establish himself as the *shogun*, the supreme general and power behind the powerless emperor.

The 1580s represented a turning point. In 1580, Omura Sumitada ceded Nagasaki to the Jesuits; the former fishing village of 1,500 grew into the entrepôt for the Portuguese–China trade and became a bastion for Catholicism. Two years later, Nobunaga was assassinated, but his successor, Toyotomi Hideyoshi, continued to protect Christians. Jesuit missionary policy also changed drastically in these years. The Jesuit *visitador* Alessandro Valignano reversed the policy of discrimination against an indigenous clergy, instituted by Francisco Cabral, the first mission superior, who had spent ten years in Japan learning little of its language and holding the natives in contempt. In a series of meetings with his fellow fathers (1580–81), Valignano stressed that "above all, we must accommodate." Summing up from reports and experience in the mission field, Valignano drew up guidelines for future evangelization: the Jesuits had to live immaculately, maintain politeness, give attention to rank, dress, and courtesies; they were to eat Japanese food, keep no pigs or goats, and slaughter no cows (the Japanese were scandalized by the unhygienic habits of European food customs); and churches were to be in Japanese styles. Perhaps the most important departure was the decision to train a full-fledged Japanese clergy. At the time of Valignano's visitation, only fifty-five Jesuits (including twenty-three European priests) ministered to 150,000 Japanese Christians. Relying heavily on Japanese brothers to interpret and preach, the mission had maintained a two-tier system, barring Japanese Jesuits from ordination. With the change in policy, two seminaries were established in 1580 for the education of both European and Japanese students; a college, St. Paul's, opened in the same year; and a novitiate admitted six Europeans and six Japanese in 1583.

This policy shift came too late. Renewed warfare after Nobunaga's demise damaged the foundations of missionary work; and the first Japanese priests – the Jesuits Sebastião Kimura and Luis Niabara – were not ordained until 1601. When full-scale repression commenced in 1614, the Japan mission had ordained merely fifteen indigenous priests (eight Jesuits and seven seculars).

The generation after 1580 represented both the apogee of the Japan mission and the beginning of its end. Valignano's catechism, written in Latin and translated into Japanese, was the first vernacular Christian text (1580). With the importation of a moveable printing press in 1590, the Jesuits published a steady stream of Japanese books, whether it be the translation of Luis de Granada (1599) or the anti-Buddhist polemic of Fabian Fucan (1605), one of their Japanese brothers. Christianity was the mode among the ruling elite: two *daimyo* clans in Kyushu (the Omura and the Otomo) competed for the Portuguese ships, granting privileges to the Jesuits and destroying Buddhist temples; many prominent generals and noblewomen in the entourage of Hideyoshi in central Japan were fervent Christians; and Christian samurai armies went into battle accompanied by flags of the cross and Jesuit chaplains. Attacking Buddhism as the invention of the Devil, just like Protestantism, Jesuit missionaries appealed to the military code of the samurai. In *Fides no doxi* (Guide to the faith), published in 1592, conversion to Christianity was infused with military metaphor:

> It is of absolute necessity that a general who has received a castle to keep for his lord be determined rather to cast away his life than capitulate immediately when the enemy comes to lay siege to the place. In the same manner, it is of absolute necessity that a Christian rather cast away his life than worship Buddhas or gods.

Buddhism, thus, represented the main enemy. Paradoxically, several Japanese Jesuits and many of the four hundred *Dojuku* (laybrothers) in 1582 were former Buddhist monks; the Japanese called Christianity the "religion of the Southern Barbarians," confusing the Catholic faith with that of another alien religion, Buddhism, that had long been integrated into Japanese culture. It was characteristic that the enemies of Otomo Sorin Yoshishige (1530–87), the Christian *daimyo* of Bungo in Kyushu, scorned his allegiance to "an Indian sect."

The parallels between Buddhism and Christianity proved the mission's undoing. After succeeding to the mantle of Nobunaga, Hideyoshi continued the work of unification as the mightiest warlord of Japan. On the eve of his expedition to Kyushu in 1586, Hideyoshi received in audience at Osaka the Jesuit provincial Gaspar Coelho, who pompously promised to deliver Japanese Christian help in Hideyoshi's conquest of Kyushu and Portuguese military aid later in a planned invasion of China. Coelho, in the words of George Elison, belonged to "the military adventurist faction" of the Jesuits. Inspired by the union of the Iberian crowns in 1580, fantastic schemes were concocted in Manila and Macao to send Spanish troops to help Japanese Christians and conquer China. The bellicose pomposity of the Jesuit provincial and rumors of Spanish military intervention deepened the distrust of Hideyoshi, who had fought for his master Nobunaga in crushing armed Buddhist monks and their followers. After the rapid submission of Kyushu, Hideyoshi published edicts in 1587 restricting the practice of Christianity and expelling all missionaries. Comparing Christians to the True Pure Land sectarians, Hideyoshi's edict decried the departure from traditional ways and likened Nagasaki to Mount Hiei, the temple-fortress of the Buddhist sectarians crushed in 1571 after a long siege. At issue was the establishment of central authority in a reunified country, and the coexistence of different religions under a common allegiance to secular authorities. Christianity, intolerant of Buddhism and swearing allegiance to a foreign king and an alien God, threatened to challenge the order of things in the Japanese polity.

Although a few churches were destroyed, Hideyoshi, preoccupied by the invasion of Korea, refrained from carrying out the full provisions of his edicts. In 1590, Valignano returned to Japan with four young Japanese samurai who had gone to Europe in 1584 as emissaries of a Christian *daimyo* (they were received with great curiosity and pomp in Italy), and immediately overruled Coelho's plan for armed resistance. The respite granted the mission lasted until 1597, its expiration was triggered more by the quarrel amongst Catholics than by government repression. In spite of vehement Jesuit opposition, Spanish Franciscans from Manila reached Japan in 1593, breaking the missionary monopoly of the Jesuits and threatening the commercial monopoly of Portuguese Macao. The acrimonious exchange between the fathers and the friars, between Portuguese and Spaniards, set the stage for the first bloody martyrdoms.

In 1596, the Spanish galleon *San Felipe* was shipwrecked on Shikoku en route to Mexico. The local *daimyo* reported to the central government that the heavily armed ship carried a rich cargo and many friars. While negotiating for their release, the Spanish pilot of the *San Felipe* reportedly tried to impress the Japanese officials with a world map that showed the extent of Spanish conquest, embellishing further on the role of the friars in expanding the dominion of the Catholic king. Informed of this incident, Hideyoshi ordered the cargo seized, the ship released, and the arrest of all missionaries in the vicinity of the imperial capital. A group of twenty-four were sent to Nagasaki (six European Franciscans, ten Japanese Franciscan laybrothers, three Japanese Jesuit brothers, and five Japanese laity), where two more Japanese Christians joined their ranks: all twenty-six were crucified in 1597 in the first of the many bloody theaters of martyrdom in the history of Japanese Catholicism.

After Hideyoshi's death in 1599, Christianity was given a reprieve for fifteen years. Although the new hegemon Ieyasu Tokugawa seemed to tolerate Christianity, the Portuguese no longer enjoyed a commercial monopoly; their competitors, the Dutch and the English, spared no opportunity to paint the blackest picture of Catholicism, repeating the anti-Jesuit litany current in Protestant Europe. Under the Tokugawa regime, the different Buddhist sects were grouped under the authority of a government ministry and all Japanese subjects organized into Buddhist parishes in order to strengthen government control. The Christians stood out. Sporadic local persecutions, especially by an anti-Christian *daimyo* in Arima in Kyushu, brought out massive demonstrations of faith and the willingness to suffer martyrdom by Japanese Christians. Impressed by their organization and alarmed at their independence, Ieyasu Tokugawa issued an edict in 1614 expelling all foreign missionaries. Gathered in Nagasaki in November 1614, some eighty-five Jesuits, eight friars, two secular priests, and a large number of Japanese clerics, laybrothers, and leading Catholics set sail from Japan. Another eighteen Jesuits, fifteen friars, and an unknown number of Japanese brothers and laybrothers stayed behind illegally. For two years, Catholicism still flourished: except at Arima, there were no executions, and the atmosphere of martyrdom even strengthened the appeal of Christianity, which spread to northern and western Honshu, areas hitherto unexplored by missionaries. Operating clandestinely, sheltered by Japanese Christians, and tolerated by many *daimyo*, European and Japanese clerics continued to minister to the faithful. But when Hidetada succeeded Ieyasu in 1616, the new *shogun*, hostile to Christianity and foreign contact in general, initiated organized persecutions. Two European priests executed in 1617 heralded a long line of martyrs. In spite of Hidetada's policy of "closed country," missionaries still smuggled into Japan from Macao and Manila. The discovery of such a group in 1622 infuriated Hidetada: fifty-five Christians (including nine European priests) were executed in Nagasaki; and the *shogun* demanded massive repression from all his *daimyo* as a demonstration of their loyalty. Not only were missionaries targeted, but all Japanese Christians who refused to renounce their faith and all who sheltered Christians were punishable by death. A total of 2,126 Christians were executed, mostly between 1614 and 1639.

A new policy was instituted to break the spirit of martyrdom: instead of outright executions, elaborate and excruciating tortures were devised to elicit recantations. The Portuguese Jesuit Christovão Ferreira (1580–1650) was its most prominent victim. Sent to Japan in 1610, Ferreira was vice-provincial of the Society in Japan when he was captured in 1633. Broken under torture, Ferreira renounced his faith and became a Zen Buddhist, took the name Sawano Chuan and, to the shock of his fellow fratres, published a virulent anti-Christian polemic in Japanese, *Deceit Disclosed* (1636). Several attempts to contact Ferreira ended in disaster: Japanese authorities captured a group of Jesuits in 1642 and executed them; a second group sent in 1643 was also captured and, under torture, all ten Jesuits apostatized. These setbacks for Jesuit arms and the Catholic cause, unparalleled elsewhere, paled in significance to the massive martyrdoms suffered by the Japanese Church. Among the Japanese Jesuits interrogated by the apostate Ferreira was Casui Kibe, ordained in Rome after being refused the sacerdotal dignity by his fellow European Jesuits in Macao; he returned to Japan in 1630 to meet his martyrdom.

The denouement came in 1638. Oppressed by excessive exactions and brutal injustice, the Christian peasants of Shimabara (near Nagasaki) rose in rebellion. Joined by Christian *ronin* (lordless samurai), the rebels defeated and resisted government troops until overwhelmed by sheer numbers. More than 37,000 men, women, and children perished. After 1638, Japanese authorities tightened their search for Christians even more, while promoting anti-Christian polemics. In addition to the tracts by Fucan and Ferreira that refuted Christianity with a combination of Buddhist and Confucian arguments, an anonymous chapbook, *Kirishitan Monogatari* (1639), illustrated with woodcuts, depicted Christianity as the subversion of Japanese ways by barbaric and monstrous European clerics, represented with exaggerated racist features. At least 113 such anti-Christian chapbooks circulated in the seventeenth and eighteenth centuries, propagating a nativist and xenophobic rejection of Christianity. The intensity of anti-Christian repression notwithstanding, the authorities discovered 608 Japanese Christians in Omura in 1657, of whom 411 refused to recant and died for their faith. The last European missionary to enter Japan was the Italian Jesuit Giovanni Battista Sidotti: captured in 1708, he was imprisoned until 1714; when he tried to proselytize his jailers, he was put to death by starvation.

Japanese Christianity outlived European missionaries and the Tokugawa regime. A small group of clandestine Japanese Christians survived in remote villages of northwestern Kyushu and the offshore islands. Farmers and fisherfolk, these hidden Christians conformed outwardly to Buddhism while hiding Christian cult objects in secret cabinets. Designated religious servers and baptizers transmitted Christian prayers and rituals by oral tradition; these positions of leadership, inherited within families, held Christianity together through tight-knit household and community solidarity, and by the practice of endogamy. They constituted the remnants of a promising mission that ended in bloody martyrdom, discovered by European missionaries only after 1868 with the opening of Japan to the West.

China

The progress of Catholicism in early modern China was altogether more peaceful. Xavier, the apostle to India and Japan, died in the Portuguese enclave of Macao in 1552 awaiting permission to enter China. That permission was granted by the provincial governor of Kuangdong and Kuangsi in 1580 to the Italian Jesuit Michele Ruggieri, who, alone among his fratres in Macao, had taken the pains to learn the Chinese language and rituals. Ruggieri was joined by Matteo Ricci, but the initial Jesuit presence in China was very modest in scope: shaved and dressed like Buddhist monks, the two Jesuits were viewed as such by the Chinese, and they made some converts among the common people, some of whom probably accepted Christianity as a variant of Buddhism and Taoism, all three religions promising health, wealth, and longevity.

Unlike in Japan, the Chinese mission made slow progress and the breakthrough was due to the accomplishment of a single exceptional man: the Jesuit Matteo Ricci (1552–1610). The young missionary arrived in China with shaved head, dressed as a Buddhist monk, residing in a humble house in a provincial town; by the time he died in Beijing, Ricci had long discarded monkish garb for the robes of a revered Confucian scholar, and the tomb of the deceased sage was honored by an imperial tablet and visited by the leading officials and scholars of the capital.

Adhering to Valignano's policy of "sweet conversion" (*il modo soave* in contrast to the uncompromising Spanish way), Ricci established the basic principles of the China mission that would endure until the early eighteenth century. Valignano's 1579 *Instruction* to the China–Japan missionaries is eloquent on the need for adaptation:

> Do not attempt in any way to persuade these people to change their customs, their habits, and their behavior, as long as they are not evidently contrary to religion and morality. What could be more absurd, indeed, than to transport France, Italy, or some other European country to the Chinese? Do not bring them our countries but the faith, which does not reject or harm the customs and habits of any people, so long as they are not perverse; but, on the contrary, wishes to see them preserved in their entirety.

Ricci understood these directives well. To win converts, therefore, European missionaries had to adapt to Chinese ways and Christianity had to become a part of Chinese culture; above all, the Confucian scholars and officials, who constituted the intellectual and ruling elites of the country, had to be won over by the demonstration of the concordance between Confucianism and Christianity. The conviction of that concordance came to Ricci through his long years of immersion in the Chinese classics. A superb linguist, Ricci spent the first ten years of his mission mastering the Confucian texts and the subtleties of scholarly culture. His first literary endeavor was not a translation of Christian catechism into Chinese, but a rendering of the *Four Books* (the basic canon of Confucianism) into Latin. "Li Madou," as Ricci was known to his scholarly friends and acquaintances, achieved fame when a world map he had annotated in Chinese was published by an acquaintance. Consolidating his scholarly reputation by publications in elegant classical Chinese and by numerous meetings with Chinese scholars during which he demonstrated his own prodigious memory and mnemonic skills, Ricci and the other Jesuits were accepted as "western scholars" who had learned the Chinese way. Integrated into the network of scholars – forged by common experience of academy, civil service examination, and imperial bureaucratic office – Ricci gained residence in the imperial capital Beijing. Through Ricci's literary reputation, the ensemble of European civilization (astronomy, mathematics, music, and religion) became attractive to the Confucian elites: many flocked to converse with him; some studied European science; and a few converted to Christianity.

The missionary effort in these early years represented Christianity as a system of social ethics and individual morality profoundly consonant with Confucianism; Christianity, in fact, would perfect the original Confucianism of ancient China, by removing the encrustations of Song dynasty metaphysics and Buddhist corruption, and by restoring the pristine monotheism of Chinese philosophy. The very words used to represent their missionary enterprise suggested this compatibility: Christianity aimed to supplement Confucianism and replace Buddhism (*bu Ru yi Fo*);

and Jesuits were called Confucians from western countries (*Xiguo Ru*) or western scholars (*Xi shi*). While they also preached to the common people, the Jesuits concentrated on the literati elites; they spoke of ethics rather than original sin, and rarely mentioned or displayed the crucifix for fear of creating a negative impression of their religion. Different signs for different people, the Jesuits represented esoteric Taoist alchemists for some, hoping for the elixir of immortality, while their philosophy of social ethics appealed strongly to the reformist Confucian scholar-officials, who saw their own socio-political order in the midst of a grave crisis.

Practically all converts and sympathizers of Catholicism among the Confucian literati–official elites belonged to the Tunglin movement, an opposition group named after the famous Tunglin Academy that opposed the regimes of powerful eunuchs and conservative officials. To these Confucian scholars, Christianity promised to offer personal and collective regeneration, and a restoration of cosmic and social order. Three prominent officials came to be called "the pillars of the Church" in Jesuit letters: Xu Guangqi (1562–1633) baptized in 1601, Li Zhizao (1557–1630), baptized in 1610, and Yang Tingyun (1557–1627), baptized in 1611. Offering patronage, protection, and friendship, the "three pillars" gave invaluable aid to the Jesuit enterprise by lending it immense prestige. Xu was at one time grand secretary; his ancestral home near Shanghai served as one of the centers of Chinese Catholicism into the twentieth century. Li collaborated with Ricci on various publications, including the definitive edition of the European world map and translations from European astronomy and geometry; refusing to renounce his concubines, Li finally accepted baptism from Ricci one year before the Jesuit's death. Yang, dedicated in his youth to finding a synthesis between Confucianism and Buddhism, eventually found the balance between his public role as a scholar-official and his private faith as a Christian; he defended the Christian Church with vigor during the 1616 persecutions in Nanjing.

Although established as official missionary policy, Ricci's accommodationist approach was privately criticized by other Jesuits. Niccolò Longobardo, for example, questioned Ricci's choice of terms to signify the Christian God; instead of *Tian* (Heaven) or *Shangde* (God on High), terms from ancient Chinese texts appropriated to signify the Christian deity, he advocated the transliteration of Latin words. Others went much further than Ricci's restraint and private conversions: in 1611 Alfonso Vagnoni (1566–1640) opened the first public Catholic Church in Canton, accompanied by public street processions. Transferred to Nanjing, the southern capital of the Ming dynasty, Vagnoni continued his more flamboyant style, organizing charity within the Chinese Christian community and publicly attacking Buddhism for corrupting Chinese morals. In 1615, Shen Que, vice-minister of the Nanjing Board of Rites, submitted two memorials to the imperial court, asking for the expulsion of European missionaries who were undermining the traditional ways of China. Shen's memorials, countered by the public defense of Christianity published by Xu and Yang, elicited no response from the court. Acting on his own, the minister of the Board of Rites in Beijing endorsed Shen's memorial and issued an edict to expel all foreign missionaries. Protected by their extensive network of friendship with the literati elites, the Jesuits suffered few practical setbacks, except in Nanjing, where fathers Vagnoni and Alonso de Semedo were arrested, flogged, and expelled to Macao. Two other Jesuits were also expelled from Beijing. In 1616 there were only fourteen Jesuits left in China (eight European priests and six Chinese brothers). The storm soon blew over; the Catholic mission survived a far greater crisis in mid-century when the political order of the Ming dynasty disintegrated amidst peasant uprisings and the invasion of the Manchu.

Catholicism seemed to enjoy a secure foundation during the last two decades of the Ming dynasty. A new reign in 1627 swept the eunuchs from power and brought in reformist mandarins, including Xu and others sympathetic to the Jesuits. Earlier, in 1621, the Belgian Jesuit Nicholas Trigault had returned from a highly successful journey to Europe with fresh funding and new recruits for the China mission. Above all, he achieved two things: permission from Pope Paul V for the celebration of mass in Chinese and other adaptations to Confucian rituals; and publicity for the mission through the publication of Ricci's *Journal*. From the 1620s until the suppression of the Society of Jesus, the China mission, in spite of the long and harsh journey (one-third of Jesuits from Lisbon to Macao died en route) attracted dedicated missionaries from Europe to supplement the clergy recruited from the Portuguese, Eurasians, and Chinese in Macao: they came from Italy, Portugal, France, Belgium, Germany, Austria, and Poland, making China the most international of the mission fields of early modern Catholicism. During the 1620s and 1630s, Catholicism made progress in many parts of China; aside from the established centers in Beijing, Nanjing, Hangzhou, and Canton, new communities developed in the interior provinces of Shaanxi and Shanxi, and the southeastern coastal province of Fujian. In 1625, a tenth-century Nestorian tablet was discovered in Xian, confirming the antiquity of Christianity in China to the jubilation of Jesuits and Chinese Catholics. In 1630, two Jesuits were appointed to assist in the emendation of the Imperial Calendar, one of whom, the German Johann Adam Schall von Bell (1591–1666) would achieve great fame.

Having survived the carnage of civil war and Manchu conquest, the Catholic mission during the early Ch'ing dynasty shifted its focus, in part, from Confucian literati and concordance with Confucianism to the Manchu aristocracy and service to the imperial court. Rewarded for his astronomical achievements, Schall was appointed mandarin in the Bureau of Astronomy by the Shunzhi emperor. Reluctantly accepting the rank for the good of the Church, Schall developed warm relations with Shunzhi and helped to preserve a footing for Catholicism in the new dynastic order. Its fortunes closely tied to the court, the Church suffered a second setback in 1664, when the death of Shunzhi unleashed a bitter denunciation by the anti-Christian mandarin, Yang Guangxian. Charging Schall with selecting an inauspicious day in 1658 for the burial of the empress's son, an event that supposedly led to her death and the demise of the emperor, Yang's accusation used crucifixion scenes to represent Schall and the Jesuits as evil magicians, playing to the fears of the shamanist Manchu court. Schall and other Jesuits in Beijing were arrested; his Christian Chinese assistants at the Bureau of Astronomy executed, and all European missionaries rounded up and imprisoned in Canton. On the day of Schall's execution, an earthquake shook Beijing. Convinced of the innocence of the Jesuits, the court released the westerners. Schall died in 1666. For two years, the Catholic Church was in limbo. Yang Guangxian, appointed to succeed Schall, failed, however, to produce an accurate calendar. When the young emperor Kangxi assumed personal rule in 1668, the Catholic cause emerged triumphant when Ferdinand Verbiest, the Belgian Jesuit who was assistant to Schall, accurately predicted an eclipse while Yang failed. With Schall's name restored, Yang disgraced, and Christianity officially recognized in 1692, the Catholic cause would achieve its greatest success between 1670 and 1720.

Even while Catholicism took native roots in China, sharp disagreements between the missionary orders cast a shadow over the future growth of Christianity. The first Chinese priest, Luo Wenzao (1617–91), baptized Gregorio Lopez by Spanish Dominicans from Manila in his native province of Fujian, shuttled between Luzon and China, his travels facilitated by the China–Philippines trade and the migration from Fujian to Luzon. Ordained in 1654 and named bishop *in partibus infidelibus* in 1673 by the Congregation for the Propagation of Faith, Luo's promotion was opposed by his own superiors in Manila. Finally consecrated in 1685 in Canton by an Italian Franciscan bishop, Bernardino della Chiesa, Luo became the first bishop of Nanjing in 1690. The opposition to his episcopal nomination in Manila stemmed from Luo's support for the Jesuit way of conversion, which was bitterly opposed by the Dominicans. The so-called Chinese Rites Controversy traced its origins to the arrival of Spanish friars from the Philippines in the 1630s. Landing without official permission in southeastern China, the Spanish friars from the Philippines braved danger and martyrdom, which existed more in their imagination than in reality, and envisioned a massive evangelization of China on the model of the Americas. Their opposition to the Valignano–Ricci missionary strategy sharpened sufficiently by 1639 so that the archbishop of Manila wrote to Rome harshly criticizing the Jesuits. A series of petitions and reports filed by both sides resulted in two rulings: the 1645 condemnation of ancestral and Confucian worship declared by the Holy Office; and the 1656 ruling by Pope Alexander VII endorsing the Jesuit position. These two contradictory rulings depended on different Latin translations of key Chinese words denoting the site and titles of the rites; the Jesuits argued for their essence as rooted in filial piety and respect, the Dominicans denouncing them as pagan worship. In addition to this central dispute, the Dominicans also opposed the use of *Tian* to denote Heaven and God in Jesuit liturgical texts; and they argued for imposing the positive precepts of the Church, such as openly displaying the crucifix, condemning Confucianism as pagan, and baptizing women in accordance with European liturgy (thus disregarding Chinese sensibilities that prohibited physical contact between unrelated men and women).

Respect for indigenous customs, to the point of accommodating and incorporating native rituals into Christian practices, also characterized the Jesuit Indian mission in a policy formulated and defended by the Italian Father Roberto de Nobili against his detractors. But similar to the situation in China, criticism was also raised in the middle of the seventeenth century at Nobili's effort to harmonize Hinduism and Christianity and for representing Jesuits as western brahmins. Unlike China, the acrimonious exchange in the India mission took place within the Jesuit order, whereas in the Middle Kingdom it pitted the Jesuits against the mendicant orders, especially the Dominicans.

This missionary rivalry, reflected in the animosity between Jesuits and Dominicans in Catholic Europe, was complicated at the turn of the century by the arrival of the French. Both the papacy and the French monarchy maneuvered to sidestep the patronage rights granted to the Iberian kings in overseas missions (the Patronato and Padroado): the Missions étrangères of secular priests was founded in Paris with the support of Louis XIV to help promote French overseas interests, and the papacy readily appointed priests from the mission as vicars apostolic to Asia in order to bypass the chain of authority linking Lisbon, Goa, and Macao. It was the rash action of such a vicar apostolic, Charles Maigrot, who banned Chinese Christians from attending ceremonies in honor of their dead and of Confucius that sparked the controversy in 1693. In his ignorance of Chinese, Maigrot condemned as contrary to Christianity both Confucianism and by extension the Chinese classics. An explosion of pamphlets in Europe attacked and defended the Jesuit position in China. When the Jesuits in China asked Emperor Kangxi to write to the pope explaining that ancestor worship was not religious in nature, their action shocked a Church that already contained many enemies of the Society.

At this crucial juncture, the Chinese Church counted between 200,000 and 500,000 converts; the mission comprised sixty Jesuit priests (including six Chinese), twenty-nine Franciscans, eight Dominicans, six Augustinians, two Lazarists, and fifteen French seculars of the Missions étrangères. Extended across the provinces of the Ch'ing Empire, the Catholic Church had nourished three generations of Christians, for whom Christianity formed an integral part of their cultural identity. Jesuit presses in Hangzhou and Beijing had published hundreds of titles in Chinese, ranging from liturgical, devotional, and doctrinal tracts to biographies of leading Chinese converts. A 1678 biography of Xu Guangqi, compiled by the Jesuit Joachim Couplet and composed by the Confucian scholar Zhang Xingyao (1633–1715), for example, upheld the model of a pious Confucian–Christian sage who saw Catholicism as the fulfillment of Confucian ethics. For Zhang, a prominent leader in the Hangzhou Catholic community, one of the largest in China, European missionaries played a supportive but secondary role in a well-organized community of believers, who had integrated Christianity into the fabric of Chinese life.

That interwoven fabric was ripped apart in the early years of the eighteenth century. In 1705 Charles Maillard de Tournon, a French secular sent as legate by Pope Clement XI, arrived in China. Bringing Maigrot with him to an imperial audience in 1706 in Beijing, the legate conveyed the papal condemnation of ancestor worship, in accordance with earlier prohibitions. Losing patience with the clerics, Emperor Kangxi ordered Maigrot expelled, and instructed all European missionaries to subscribe to "the way of Father Ricci" before they were issued a residence permit. Tournon issued a counter-order. Before the papal legate died in 1710 while being held by the Portuguese in Macao, Clement XI elevated Tournon to the purple. Five years later, Clement published a bull in support of Tournon's ruling. The second papal legate, Jean Ambrose Charles Mezzabarba, visited Beijing in 1720; this audience also ended in disaster when Kangxi castigated the westerner for his ignorance of the Confucian classics. In 1739, Benedict XIV affirmed all previous prohibitions of Chinese rites.

The Catholic Church survived in China; but it attracted few converts from the literati–official elites. Divorced from Confucian philosophy and the literati–official establishment, Christianity had become just another religion in the empire, alongside Islam, Judaism, and Buddhism, all tolerated but marginal to the central concerns of Chinese society. Banned from the celestial empire by an edict of the Emperor Yongzheng (1724), European missionaries, with the exception of the few Jesuit courtiers in Beijing, still smuggled into the inland provinces to preach, protected by leading Chinese convert families. Increasingly perceived as alien to Chinese traditions and contrary to imperial law, Christianity in China suffered several sporadic persecutions during the 1730s and 1740s. Several European missionaries were martyred at the hands of zealous provincial officials; others were expelled to Macao. Chinese Catholics – fined, caned, and exiled – also testified to the faith. Although the anti-Christian edict remained the law of the Ch'ing Empire, its enforcement was selective and sporadic, but it foreshadowed the much sharper conflict between Christianity and Chinese society that would come in the nineteenth century.

13 From triumph to crisis

Speaking to a gathering of confessors in his see of Milan, Archbishop Federico Borromeo exhorted the priests to be diligent in their examination of conscience, for they were "the fibers, arteries, and sinews of the body of the Holy Church . . . through secret channels they make it move, and if they are ill-disposed, the other members cannot function and remain languid." If Catholic society represented a body, the clergy constituted its nerves; their task was to discipline the weak flesh, prone to sin and languor, for as the German Jesuit Wilhelm Hausen wrote in his *Tägliche Hausmission* (1773), a devotional prescription for everyday Christian order for the laity, "Your [the lay reader's] body is your most dangerous enemy."

The metaphors of nerves and flesh provide us with an understanding of the relationship between Catholic renewal and society at large. Jolted by the Protestant Reformation, the ecclesiastical hierarchy mobilized the body Catholic into action: the Council of Trent represented a moment of synergy, whereby the nerve of the body religious, the clergy, set out to strengthen the "fibers, arteries, and sinews" by first defining and reforming itself. Just as the nerves mobilize the body to act in the face of danger, the language of this clerical nerve center invoked the metaphor of military mobilization. Images of combat, battle, vigilance, and victory infused the rhetoric of Catholic renewal. The theme of struggle informs the *Spiritual Exercises* of Ignatius; it describes Teresa's journey to mystical triumph. The Jesuits were commanded by generals and their first general, in the satiric verse of the Dutch poet Jacobus Revius (1586–1658), "was canonized out of the cannons of soldiers." Even the Virgin Mary, symbol of mercy and help, assumed a more militant pose, fighting with Catholic arms at Lepanto (1571) against infidels and at White Mountain (1620) against heretics. Everywhere in Catholic Europe "elite troops" were mobilized in the struggle against Satan, directed by clerical advisors, organized in congregations, and united under the central command of archsodalities in the spiritual capitals of Catholicism.

Forming elite units in the larger Catholic society, the Tridentine clergy and their lay allies moved from self-purification to the purification of others, rolling back the frontiers of heresy and superstition and sanctifying the body social. We have come to know the elites among the clergy – the Jesuits, Capuchins, Tridentine bishops, the new diocesan priests, and other Counter-Reformation religious orders; who were their lay counterparts in this campaign of sanctification?

Louis Châtellier chose the Marian sodalities for his study of the formation of a new Catholic society. "The Europe of the Devout," however, encompassed more than the hundreds of Marian sodalities and tens of thousands of members under the aegis of the Society of Jesus. Let us begin by examining one of them: the Company of the Holy Sacrament. Organized in Paris in 1629, the Company expanded rapidly due to its immense prestige, enrolling nineteen provincial congregations by 1634 and sixty-two by the time of its suppression in 1667. At its height the Company enrolled more than 4,000 members throughout France, including practically all the spiritual elites of the Gallican Church; Vincent de Paul, Bishop Bossuet, and Fenelon were confrères as were thirty-nine bishops and fifty doctors of the Sorbonne. Some 990 members are known by name: the group consisted of 501 laymen and 405 secular clerics (the regular clergy was excluded). Two social groups dominated the lay membership: the *noblesse de robe* and the commercial bourgeoisie. In addition to *parlementaires* and jurists, the Paris chapter included twenty-five courtiers in the royal household; the three most prominent – duc de Laincourt, duc de Nemours, and prince de Conti – were close to Louis XIII. Service to the French king, in fact, mirrored devotion to the king of kings. In the 1649 *Annales of the Company*, René de Voyer d'Argenson wrote that the Company had the honor "to renew the memory of the actions and sufferings of Jesus Christ, its master and model, in the various stages of his birth, his life, and his death."

Many activities sanctified the life of its members: spiritual colloquies, readings of pious texts, charitable donations, hospital and prison visits, conversion of fallen women and Protestants, supporting missions and seminaries. A constant stream of news from the wider body of the Catholic world flowed through the arteries of these elite spiritual coteries: relations, newsletters, and books informed them of the missions in Canada, the violation of the Edict of Nantes by Huguenots in different parts of France, the miseries of Catholic Ireland, and the fall of the Ming dynasty in China. Convinced they lived in "this corrupt century," as a letter from the Company at Angers exclaimed, the members of the Holy Sacrament saw themselves as elite Christians at a time when "evil is everywhere just as sin is universal." Castigating the debauchery of courtiers, the "gross stupidity" of peasants, and the corruption of the Gallican

Church, the Company confrères compared themselves to the early apostles.

Sanctification to some, sanctimony to others: the Company of the Holy Sacrament was not without enemies. Molière described the *dévot* succinctly in these sardonic lines of *Tartuffe* (Act III, Scene 2):

> Laurent, put away my hair shirt and my scourge
> and pray that Heaven will always enlighten you.
> If anyone comes to see me
> I am going to the prisoners to distribute alms.

In one aspect, at least, Molière was wrong: the Company shunned publicity. Operating in secrecy, the Holy Sacrament remained hidden in the body social just as the real substance of Christ was concealed in the form of bread and wine, thus run the self-image of the Company. Working through royal institutions, members strove to enact legislation against sins, blasphemy, and Protestants. Clerical members petitioned the king to abolish the Edict of Nantes or to apply it *à la rigueur*; *parlementaires* and magistrates tried to prosecute blasphemers and libertines. As formulated by J.-B. Nolleau in *Politica christiana*, the Company believed that "eternal salvation be the supreme law of the people [*salus aeterna populi suprema lex esto*]." While all shared in the spirituality of Christ, everyone must follow his own social condition. Divided with regard to the Jesuits and Jansenists, the Holy Sacrament brothers nonetheless were staunch monarchists, for "the Christian kings are not only the images of God . . . but they are the images of Jesus Christ, the King of kings, Lord of lords," as Antoine Godeau, member of the Académie française and the Company exulted. Royalism notwithstanding, the Paris Chapter was suppressed in 1667 together with all independent bodies within the Gallican Church although the provincial companies continued to meet after 1667.

Master of his own body, the *dévot* was one in total control, "and all that he controls is very well controlled [*et tout ce qu'il contrôle est fort bien contrôlé*]," to quote Molière again. The peasants, however, thought differently. Despised by the *dévots* of Lyons as people marked by "a gross ignorance of the principal articles of their salvation," the rural folk of Catholic Europe sought not self-discipline and the control of their bodies but rather the relief of their ills.

The peasants in the diocese of Paris turned to a host of saints and relics for the relief of pains and illness: Sts. Roch and Sebastian guarded against the plague; Christ's robe at the Benedictine Abbey of Argenteuil healed pains, paralysis, rheumatism, and fevers; the finger of St. Ouen cured the deaf; St. Prix specialized in paralysis; St. Maur treated the handicapped; Sts. Spire and Honorine were generalists in diverse infirmities; for scrofula one went to St. Cloud; for headaches St. Avertin and St. Europe; for sore throats St. Blaise; intestinal trouble St. Mammès; to cure stones one sought out Sts. Cosme and Damien; and for sick children, one went to Sts. Quintien, Leonard, and Leu. It was the same all over rural Catholic Europe. Benedictions, processions, invocation of saints, guardian angels, St. Joseph, Virgin Mary: these were the objects of popular devotion that sought sanctification not of self, but of fields, trees, animals, houses, ships, children, and adults, the material and productive world of sins decried by the *dévots*. "To reassure and protect," in Delumeau's words – that was the object of popular devotion. Tridentine injunctions notwithstanding, persistent popular demand ensured an essential continuity in liturgy and religious sentiment in many rural areas of Catholic Europe, particularly in France, Germany, and southern Italy.

Although the Tridentine Church tried to discourage popular uses of benedictions, the clergy had to compromise. There existed numerous benedictions for sanctifying newborn babies, mothers after birth, farm animals, fields, fruit trees, rooms, furniture, houses, and ships; other formulas warded off fevers, illness, storms, hails, toothaches, and pains. While the Roman Ritual of Paul V (1614) cut down substantially the number of benedictions, most French and German dioceses used their own liturgies well into the nineteenth century. Just over half (51 percent) of the formulas (benedictions, conjurations, and exorcisms) in the Roman Ritual dealt with material well-being; the rest (49 percent) concerned the benedictions of cult objects and the ordination of priests. By comparison the diocesan rituals of Alet (1677) and Toul (1760) in France contained 64 and 61 percent prophylactic formulas, while the proportion was as high as 76 percent in a collection of benedictions for the different dioceses of the Holy Roman Empire compiled in 1777.

Clearly, the Tridentine Church and the *dévots* exercised only partial control over the sacred. The differences between popular devotion and elite spirituality were particularly manifest in the devotion to saints. One example should suffice. In 1707 Bishop Gaston de Noailles, brother of Cardinal de Noailles, was visiting Notre-Dame-en-Vaulx in Châlons when he opened the reliquary in front of a multitude of worshippers. Finding the revered relics to be three small pieces of stone wrapped in red cloth, the bishop took them away. The alarmed sacristan rang the parish bell to summon resistance. Even the notables of the town joined in the petition, beseeching the bishop to return the relic "because [the townspeople] had been deprived of a 400-year-old object of veneration of their ancestors . . . which has often been the remedy of the ills that afflict them." A lawsuit ensured but the bishop refused to give in. In his zeal to combat superstition Bishop Gaston was simply acting in the Tridentine spirit, itself reflected for example in the 1619 synodal statues of Limoges that prohibited the exhibition of false relics. His actions would have been approved by members of the Holy Sacrament Company in Marseilles, who spoke of "the piteous and deplorable state of the dioceses, in which the people are so hardened in their superstitions and abominations."

What the people demanded were saints of old, proven in their ability to intercede in the court of heaven, bringing immediate relief to afflicted bodies. What would they have thought of the bishop of Angers, Jean-Baptiste Gault, a member of the Holy Sacrament Company at Angers? Praised for miracles attributed after his recent death by fellow members in these words: "It is more than a little glory that we of the Company are giving saints to the Church. Let us give thanks to divine goodness, who has inspired us with the zeal of the first Christians in this corrupt century and wishes to make us saints"; would they have prayed for his intercession?

The evidence is ambiguous. Personified by Sts. Ignatius, Xavier, and Teresa, the heroic and individualist Counter-Reformation saints seemed to have made little headway against the traditional plethora of healing saints in rural areas: their cults were absent in early modern Brittany, their popularity minimal in the diocese of Grenoble. Where they were successful, such as the cult of St. Ignatius in Alsace, Lorraine, Luxembourg, and Bavaria, the hero-saint of the Counter-Reformation was integrated into traditional healing: Ignatius-Water, blessed on his feastday (July 31) and given out to the faithful, was said to heal possession and relieve cramps for pregnant women.

Two sets of impulses were at work in the relationship between the spiritual elites and the people of Catholic Europe: to discipline, control, and enforce sacramental conformity on the one hand; to instruct, inspire, and accommodate on the other. While these impulses were not mutually exclusive, they often worked at cross-purposes; the history of confession was a case in point.

It has been argued that the confessional signified the great transformation from late medieval to early modern Catholicism: the minute examination of conscience, the interiorization of sins, and the intimacy of self-revelation changed the focus of confession from satisfaction to contrition, from social sins to hidden guilt, from family, kinship, and the community to the individual soul. There is considerable merit in this argument. In practice, however, the Tridentine Church achieved only moderate success: in towns and nearby rural parishes, annual confession and communion was near universal by the middle of the seventeenth century, but the new model of the individual Christian responsible for his own sins before God (and the confessor) rarely extended beyond coteries of spiritual elites.

To enforce confession and communion the Tridentine Church required residential stability; it thus enhanced the authority of the bishop to examine mendicant and itinerant confessors and concentrated devotional life in parish churches, at the expense of private, family, and convent chapels. The confessional, intended to prevent sexual solicitation by the clergy, was to reform the confessors who would in turn discipline the laity. But as Stephen Haliczer has shown, sexual solicitation at confession persisted throughout early modern Spanish history and incidents seemed to have risen during the eighteenth century when the authority of the Inquisition elicited less fear and respect.

Sacramental conformity was obtained through paperwork: parish registers (the *status animarum*), certificates of confession (the *Beichtzettel* in Germany; the *fede* in Italy), and lists of approved confessors and of those who neglected annual confession and communion kept account of conformity and orthodoxy. These successes of Tridentine Catholicism were achieved with numbers, not fervor. In Borromean Milan (and elsewhere) people rushed to confession before Easter Week to fulfill their sacramental obligation. Overburdened confessors spent long hours during the rush to hear penitents; in 1584 Friar Amadeo in Milan heard more than 120 confessions daily during Holy Week, devoting no more than a few minutes to each. The sheer numbers of parishioners forced a significant relaxation of the system. Very few cases of conscience were actually reserved to bishops. Among the *inconfessi*, most refrained from communion because of conflicts with neighbors and kin, revealing the continuing social character of the traditional sacrament of peace. In fact, regular confession and frequent communion were limited to a small elite. In the rural parishes surrounding Paris, although Easter Communion attracted near total compliance, those who took the eucharist at high feastdays varied between 10 and 50 percent; a small elite of confraternity members took bi-monthly communion; and bi-weekly communion was extremely rare.

Confession and communion became the dividing line between the dévot and the Catholic masses. The former, whether cleric or lay, imitated the custom of convents in their rigorous examination of self and quest for sanctification; the latter eschewed the tighter control of the ecclesiastical and secular hierarchies by conforming to outward requirements. Introduced only in 1662 to Cologne, the confessional was slowly adopted in rural parishes: in 1663 only 27.8 percent of parishes had confessionals; in 1743, they were found in 88.4 percent of parishes. While most parish churches had one confessional, the Jesuit church in Cologne had twenty.

The Jesuits, of course, were strong advocates of frequent confession and communion. They were not the only ones. Antoine Arnauld, their fierce critic and Jansenist, composed a treatise *On Frequent Communion* (1643). Divided on the rigor of an Augustinian sense of depraved human nature, the Jansenists saw the saints as a very restricted elite whereas the Jesuits held out the promise of sanctification to a greater multitude. Casuistry came to characterize Jesuit laxity, according to their Jansenist critics, forgetting perhaps that casuistry emerged from pastoral work. Discussing cases of conscience, casuistry, as Tommaso Zerola defined it in his 1619 treatise, *Practice of the Sacrament of Penance* (*Praxis sacramenti poenitentiae*), "arose from questions about mores or the questioning of mores." The accusation of Jesuit casuistry missed the essential point: cases of conscience arose precisely out of the difficulties of applying strict Tridentine standards to measure the behavior of the Catholic multitude. Jesuit laxity was no more than adaptation to popular religiosity.

In addition to discipline and surveillance, Tridentine Catholicism developed strategies to mobilize and direct popular religiosity. Rural missions, in which the Jesuits played a prominent role, were a case in point. Following the examples of late medieval popular preachers, early Jesuits adopted apostolic missions as part of their own program. In Calabria, Alfonso Bobadilla preached in the villages after the model of St. Vincent Ferrer, the fourteenth-century Dominican preacher; other Jesuit preachers also took to the countryside: Andrea de Oviedo in the vicinity of Naples; Sylvestre Landini in Modena, Capri, and Corsica; Bernard Olivier in Tournai and Cambrai. They were soon joined by Capuchins. With the victory of Catholic arms over Protestants, Jesuit and Capuchin preachers worked to recatholicize Poitou, Moravia, Bohemia, and Silesia, their missions often facilitated by coercion and economic inducements. More peaceful persuasion obtained in later missions, such as those by the Jesuit Jean-François Régis in the Cévennes. In time preaching orders were established to evangelize the Catholic peasantry as well; the Order of Missions or the Lazarists, founded by Vincent de Paul in 1625 in Paris, was one of the first. Vincent de Paul got his start as a protégé of the noble Gondi family, who sponsored the dedicated priest to instruct peasants living on the Gondi estate; the terms of his appointment specified that "thanks to the mercy of God, the cities are provided with good ministers and religious zealots, but the poor countryfolk are seemingly deprived of all spiritual succor." Noble patronage, urban bases, and rural missions: these themes underlay all preaching missions in early modern Catholic Europe.

By the seventeenth century, rural missions developed into elaborate theaters of redemption for the people of small towns and villages. Famous preachers and their devices were legend: the Capuchin Honoré de Cannes with his skulls; the Jesuit Julien Maunoir and his theatrical sermons in Brittany; the Jesuit Paolo Segneri who traversed twenty-three dioceses in 540 missions in Italy from 1665 to 1692; his nephew Paolo Segneri the Younger, also a Jesuit, who adopted a similar rhetoric of brimstone, damnation, and redemption. The pace did not slacken in the eighteenth century: the Jesuit Pedro de Calatayud (1718–60) walked all over Spain preaching to peasants; and the Segneri method was adopted in 1715 by the count Palatine, in 1718 by the duke of Bavaria, and in 1735 by the Habsburgs in Bohemia to bring Catholic fervor to their rural subjects.

Rural missions achieved three goals. For the Church, they brought the sacraments of confession and communion to rural parishes ill served by the ecclesiastical hierarchy; such was the case in the Cévennes where Protestantism had long eroded the administrative structure of the Church. For Catholic princes, they served to strengthen confessional identity and political submission in their realms, as was the example of the 1718 Bavarian missions, instituted by Maximilian-Emmanuel II to reestablish Wittelsbach authority in areas devastated by the War of Spanish Succession; for the rural folk, missionaries represented powerful intermediaries who procured the presence of the sacred, such as in 1719 in Oberessendorf near Augsburg, where the Jesuit fathers successfully prayed for rain and attributed the miracle to St. Xavier. Still others brought bread, clothing, and alms, nourishing the body while healing the soul, preaching reconciliation and mending feuds. By the second half of the eighteenth century, the theatrical missions gave way to missions of catechism that assumed a more regular and institutionalized character: the Redemptorists in Naples visited the same villages on a regular basis and established a small community of devouts; Jesuits and Capuchins also turned more to catechism in their missions to Styria, Carniola, Carinthia, Tirol, and Bavaria. Rural missions transformed the countryside into a sacred landscape, erecting crosses at fields, roads, and village commons; the missionaries also remade the social geography, establishing a network of catechism schools, confraternities, congregations, and retreats.

Not all churchmen shared the enthusiasm of missionaries. Much of the animosity was directed against the histrionics and sensuality of Jesuit missions. The Jansenist journal *Nouvelles ecclésiastiques* disapproved of the 1758 Jesuit mission at La Charité-sur-Loire for "erecting the Cross with all of the usual mummeries and with a ceremony as well ordered as that of the Indians of Paraguay." The censorious critic concluded with the words that "France was not a country to be missionized."

Jansenist disapproval notwithstanding, Tridentine Catholicism succeeded in the long term not by suppressing "superstitions," but by grafting orthodoxy onto traditional and popular spirituality. An examination of confraternities and pilgrimages is instructive. Dedicated to the cult of saints, late medieval confraternities often organized on the basis of craft membership and neighborhood. As autonomous lay religious associations, confraternities celebrated above all the sociability of the corporations themselves, seeking collective redemption in common devotional practices and secular sociability. The Council of Trent set out to redirect confraternity life: it sought to impose clerical authority over these voluntary lay associations and it tried to separate the sacred from the profane by stressing the sanctifying aspects of fellowship over sociability. Although many traditional confraternities survived in Tridentine Catholicism, three new types of associations reflected the spirit of Catholic renewal. I have already discussed the Company of the Holy Sacrament in France, a foundation characteristic of Gallican piety in the seventeenth century. A second type of confraternity originated before Trent: the Confraternities of the Rosaries sponsored by the Dominicans of northern Europe, with the first two congregations established in Douai (1470) and Cologne (1475). With the revival of Marian devotion after Trent, a cult that took on militant and triumphant traits, Rosaries confraternities became signs of the spread of Counter-Reformation vigor. Marian sodalities represented the third and most important type of Counter-Reformation confraternity. Organized initially by Jesuits for students at their colleges, Marian sodalities came to embrace large sections of the urban population in Catholic Europe who looked upon themselves as the spiritual elite in the fight for orthodoxy.

Founded in 1563 at the Roman College by Father Jean Leunis of Liège for the most pious students, the first Marian sodality imposed upon its members minimum requirements of devotion: prayer meetings, frequent communion, and observation of feastdays of the Virgin. According to Louis Châtellier, Marian sodalities sprang from the same soil that had nourished the *devotio moderna* and the Confraternities of the Rosaries in the Low Countries and the Oratory of Divine Love in Rome, thus linking late medieval Catholic reform to the spirit of Tridentine Catholic renewal. From their beginning as a school congregation, Jesuit sodalities rapidly embraced the elites of Catholic Europe. Within twenty-five years of the first foundation the registers of sodalities included prominent clerical and lay elites in addition to students at the Jesuit colleges: the 1576 roll at Cologne listed distinguished monks, canons, episcopal officials, university members, and some prominent laymen; the 1584 membership list at Munich was headed by the papal legate for the clergy and the duke of Bavaria for the laity, a list that included abbots and monks of leading Bavarian abbeys and members of the Munich court.

With the rapid growth of Jesuit colleges, Marian sodalities reached across Catholic Europe and down the hierarchies of urban society, enrolling noblemen, magistrates, merchants, and artisans. A reflection of the order of society, Marian sodalities were divided according to estates: college students were segregated into congregations for liberal arts and theology; Latin-speaking sodalities organized the spiritual and ruling elites; their vernacular counterparts enrolled artisans and women. Essentially an urban phenomenon, Marian sodalities dotted the urban landscape of Catholic Europe with particular density in Belgium, the Rhineland, Bavaria, Lorraine, and central and northern Italy. The seventeenth century witnessed the greatest growth. In Antwerp, the sodality for married men included 320 men in 1612, 700 in 1637, and almost 1,000 in 1664; in Cologne, membership doubled between 1608 and 1654; in Lille the numbers increased from 93 to 964 in twenty years. In Cologne and Lille, cities with 45,000 inhabitants, total sodality membership in each city numbered 2,000 in 1650; in Antwerp, they numbered 4,000 in a population of 55,000. In smaller towns the proportion of sodality members was even higher: 2,500 in Douai, 3,000 in Ingolstadt, 2,000 in Fribourg, and 1,000 in Nancy.

Members in Marian sodalities played a highly visible role in society. Staging plays to honor the Catholic cause, students at the colleges drew in the urban population as they opened the college grounds to the city; members marched in processions at feastdays of the Virgin and in celebration of the victories of Catholic arms; they kept vigilance during the forty-hour prayer during Holy Week, a Jesuit invention to counter the mirth of carnival; they gathered in regular meetings to learn of the gains of Catholicism in their own locality and in the wider world of Catholic renewal. As membership expanded and as sodalities encompassed the lower ranks in urban society, the elites shrouded their sanctity in greater secrecy. The first secret congregations were established among sodality members in Naples (1611) and Rome (1637) to foster closer union among the secret members and to strengthen from within the spirit of the congregation. Drawing upon "the cream and quintessence of the congregation," the secret congregations represented an attempt to preserve the original elan of the Marian sodalities at a time of rapid expansion. Just as the nerves ruled the human body, the secret congregations gave direction to the sodalities at large in the effort to sanctify the body social. In towns of mixed confessions, secrecy reinforced the image of Jesuit sodalities as trojan horses: in Münster the Latin sodality, with many Catholic magistrates and judicial officials among its membership, recorded discussions of urban politics in code and enjoined members not to provoke Protestants by comparing the sodalities to companies of troops.

As Jesuit colleges dominated education in Catholic Europe, their former pupils, turned magistrates and officials, filled the ranks of the sodalities. In the towns of Catholic Germany often the entire magistracy belonged to Marian sodalities. In Munich membership in the Major sodality characterized service to the duke: in 1673 ducal officials and noblemen composed 71 of the 171 lay members; in 1722, more than half of all lay members consisted of officials in the service of the prince-elector. If Marian sodalities reflected the preeminence of the service class and the urban elites, this was indicative of a still larger development in Catholic society: the formation of a new elite shaped by the values of Tridentine Catholicism. Drawn primarily from the upper echelons of urban society, steeped in the values of Catholic renewal imparted at Jesuit colleges, and employed in the service of Catholic princes, this new Catholic elite was most visible in Lorraine, Belgium, and in the Germanic lands. The same families were represented in both the clerical and secular elites: in the Duchy of Luxembourg, seven men in two generations of the Wiltheim at St. Vith entered the Society of Jesus while others served on the Provincial Council; in Trier, Luxembourg, and other towns of the Mosel, the Brenners, d'Arnoulds, Bergerots, Binsfelds, and de Zorns adopted a similar family strategy in clerical and state service; in Münster the Jesuits drew their greatest support from families in the service of the territorial state, especially in the episcopal and territorial courts; in Bavaria two generations of the Wagnereckhs in the seventeenth century served the militant Catholic state as privy council chancellor and Jesuits.

Marian sodalities served as the meeting place where newly successful merchants and ambitious artisans formed ranks with the elites (albeit in different congregations), and where the values of a Catholic hierarchy of estates percolated down to its lower rungs. Their conservative nature was manifest in 1647, when the Jesuit sodalities in Naples marched to suppress the rebellion against Spanish rule.

Well adjusted to the hierarchy of power, Tridentine Catholicism reinforced the divisions in society; the noble colleges directed by the Society of Jesus were a case in point. In 1556 the first two *seminaria nobilium* run by Jesuits were established in Coimbra and Prague; by the late seventeenth century, the Society operated twenty-five noble colleges (fourteen in Italy, eight in Habsburg central Europe, and one each in Spain, Portugal, and Poland). For the four Italian noble colleges studied by Gian Paolo Brizzi, some 70–80 percent of the students came from ancient nobility. Trained in the humanities and a Catholic worldview, the alumni filled the ranks of the ruling elites. In Bologna, one of the most prominent colleges, 56 percent of all graduates became urban magistrates, 12 percent entered military service (primarily in the Papal States), 6 percent became courtiers, and 22 percent followed a clerical career (including one pope and four cardinals). Theirs was a world away from the catechism schools established in the cities of Catholic Europe, where children of artisans were instructed in the rudiments of Christian doctrine and taught respect for authority. By the early eighteenth century, when Christianization of the masses began to bear fruit, Catholic Europe was dividing into two societies with a steadily widening gulf.

At the bottom, in the rural hinterlands, the early eighteenth century represented a golden age of religious revivals: pilgrimages, confraternities, and devotion blossomed. Devout congregations, distinctive of Catholic towns in the seventeenth century, were expanding out into the countryside; by 1750, for example, it has been estimated that confraternities had been established in 70 percent of all rural parishes in Trier. A similar Catholic renewal was discernible in rural Westphalia, Speyer, Passau, Franconia, and Bavaria; the pilgrimage sites of Telgte, Walldürn, Vierzehnheiligen, Benediktbeuren, and Altötting testified to popular religious fervor in a landscape dotted with newly constructed Baroque and Rococo churches. The countryside in Provence, Naples, and Castile, to name some of the regions studied, became sacred landscape, marked by numerous holy sites that effected uncounted miracles. Still retaining the traditional character of healing, popular religiosity had been cleansed of many of the "excesses" condemned by the clergy. Wakes, carnival, dancing, drinking, and May Poles: these were some of the "superstitions" repeatedly denounced by the Tridentine clergy and their exuberant celebrations moderated and dampened, if not completely eradicated, by generations of clerical control. The parish church now emerged as the central place of worship, following the closure of rural chapels and private churches. The high altar, scene of the central sacred drama presided over by the clergy, was displacing side altars as the focus of community devotion; whereas more than 50 percent of all churches in Cologne diocese had more than three altars in 1628, by 1743 more than 82 percent of churches had only one high altar flanked by two side altars. In the definition of ritual and ecclesiastical life, the center had established its hegemony over the periphery.

With Catholic renewal, the afterlife also triumphed over this world. Images of transient life permeated the religious sentiment of the Baroque: the Vale of Tears, the skulls, hourglass, and Death. Doctrines, rituals, books, and sermons established the Church's dominion over Death; requiem masses for the faithful reflected its power of custody over purgatory. Catholic Europe resounded with the chant of "requiescat in pace." In late seventeenth-century Provence 80 percent of wills by notables and more than 50 percent by commoners demanded requiem mass; in

Table 13.1. *Requests for requiem mass in wills, Paris, 1650–1750*

	Men (%)	Women (%)
1600–1650	56	70
1650–1700	69.5	80
1700–1750	75	86.5
1750–1800	53.5	76.5

Source: Pierre Chaunu, *La mort à Paris, XVIe, XVIIe et XVIIIe siècles*, Paris, 1978.

Madrid, Cuenca, and other Spanish towns, demand for requiem mass steadily drove its price higher and higher; and in Paris the hundred years 1650–1750 represented the height of its demand (see table 13.1). In Paris alone, under Louis XIV, two million livres flowed into the coffers of the Church through endowment masses; when the provinces were added up, the total funds for requiem masses probably amounted to 10 percent of the annual royal income (between 90 and 120 million livres).

But just when "the nerves, fiber, and sinews" seemed triumphant over the body social, that cerebral center began to loose control. Gradually and unmistakably, the elites of Catholic Europe lost the militant spirit that had shaped society between 1560 and 1650. In his study of 4,016 ex-votos from Provence, Bernard Cousin concludes that the elites had lost interest in pilgrimages and ex-votos by 1730. Whereas seventeenth-century ex-votos were donated to shrines by elevated patrons (from a vice-legate in Avignon, from families of the *noblesse de robe*), after 1730 ex-votos came almost exclusively from the popular milieu, with the large majority stemming from the nineteenth century. The Counter-Reformation style went out of fashion among the elites: in France the figure of the *dévot* under Louis XIII gave way to that of the libertine under Louis XV; in Germany princes and noblemen attended operas instead of Jesuit drama; in Antwerp the eighteenth century registered only 442 names for the Marian sodalities versus 3,663 from the seventeenth. True, the decline was not universal; Spanish Catholicism retained its rigor under the Bourbon kings. But even in this heartland of Catholicism the elites lost interest in traditional religious institutions; the Holy Office was served by far fewer familiars and they were from lower social ranks in the last century of its existence.

Troubled by the relaxation in religious fervor among the elites, the

Church was also plagued by a series of disputes from within. Stemming from disagreements over theology and ecclesiology, and involving the intellectual elites alone, these disputes intensified the conflict between different segments of the Catholic elites and ultimately intensified the confrontation between Church and state. The most significant of these disputes arose over the teachings of a bishop of Ypres, Cornelius Jansen (1585–1638).

Educated at Louvain, the Flemish prelate shared St. Augustine's deep pessimism on human nature: worldly glory, concupiscence, and "reason of state" represented the values in the City of Man that undermined the City of God; only a small elite of individuals, ascetic and God-fearing, would find salvation through divine grace and predestination. Although his masterpiece *Augustinus* was not published until after his death (1640), Jansen had already gained a name by his 1635 pamphlet, *Mars gallicus*, attacking France's entry into the Thirty Years War on the side of Protestants. Such an assault on *raison d'état* did not go unanswered; and the pamphlet was roundly condemned by Cardinal Richelieu. In 1643, Urban VIII condemned in general *Augustinus*; in 1653, Innocent X condemned five propositions on grace and predestination extracted from the book. Jansen's defenders, led by Antoine Arnauld (1612–94), accepted the condemnations but denied they were to be found in Jansen's book. Amidst an uproar, Alexander VII reiterated the condemnation in 1665 and, acting in conjunction with Louis XIV, required the submission of the Gallican clergy to the condemnation of *Augustinus*. A small minority held out: the nuns at the noble abbey of Port-Royale were forcibly evicted and the abbot of St.-Cyran was briefly imprisoned at Vincennes. Made famous by Blaise Pascal, who sympathized with the Jansenists, the Flemish bishop's teachings pointed to the theological rift in Tridentine Catholicism: on one side, those who held human nature to be corrupt, divine will unknowable, and salvation restricted to a small elite; on the other side, a wide laxity regarding conscience to adapt Catholic doctrine to society, represented by Probabilism, a theory advocated by the Jesuits (that it is allowable to follow an action when in doubt if there is a solidly probable opinion, even when the case against it is more probable).

The most important consequence of the Jansenist controversy was not theological but political. To many French and Belgian bishops, and to their lay supporters, Jansenism became a symbol of opposition against excessive papal power, manifest in the papal repressions and Jesuit complicity. Pitting episcopal authority against ultramontanism, the Jansenist controversy revived the disagreement over episcopal authority that had almost wrecked the Council of Trent. Above all, the danger lay in intervention by secular rulers; although Louis XIV upheld papal authority, later Catholic princes would turn against Rome.

From the 1690s until the French Revolution, an "Enlightened Catholicism" would challenge the worldview of the Tridentine Church. Led by intellectuals, tolerated by national Churches, and supported by Catholic princes, this disagreement among the Catholic elites would undermine the spirit of Trent from within. Three intellectuals – Van Espen, Febronius, and Muratori – represented this new opening in Enlightened Catholicism.

From Louvain, a second challenge to the papacy came in the person of Zega-Bernard Van Espen (1646–1728), professor of canon law at the university. His 1700 work, *Jus ecclesiasticum universum* (Universal ecclesiastical law), defended episcopal authority and attacked ultramontanism and the Jesuits; it was condemned by the Inquisition in 1704. Van Espen's ideas were transmitted by his student, Johann Niklas von Hontheim (1701–90), a professor of law, suffragan bishop, and vice-chancellor at the University of Trier. Under the pseudonym Justinus Febronius, the Trier professor published writings that argued for the limitation of papal authority to spiritual matters. Forced to retract his ideas in 1781, Febronius nevertheless enjoyed considerable support in Germany and his criticisms of ecclesiastical authority prepared the way for the reforms by Emperor Joseph. In Italy, the *érudit* Ludovico Antonio Muratori (1672–1750), librarian of the Ambrosiana in Milan, archivist for the Este dukes in Modena, and compiler of the *Rerum italicorum scriptores*, argued for a simplified Christianity and for princely authority.

These critics of papal authority reflected the new challenge that faced the Church. By the eighteenth century, in an era of deism, philosophy, science, and sensuality, the mysteries and glory of Tridentine Catholicism were going out of fashion for the elites: sermons of hellfire and brimstone lost their power to strike fear; sensual and theatrical rituals embarrassed those who preferred a more sober and less obtrusive religion; the overweening arrogance of the Jesuits accentuated the irrelevance of papal power; and the fervor of popular religious rituals demonstrated the persistent superstitions of the common people.

The world of Catholic renewal was long over before the French Revolution. Recoiling from accommodation with Chinese civilization, the Roman Church tightened its frontiers when others crossed continental and confessional boundaries. In Catholic Europe, Portugal struck the first blow: in 1759 the Minister Pombal arrested and executed the Jesuit Gabriel Malagrida on the charge of plotting regicide; Jesuits in all Portuguese dominions were expelled; and Rome broke off diplomatic relations with Lisbon. In 1761, the Parlement of Paris investigated allegations against the Jesuits, leading to their suppression in the kingdom; in 1767, the Society was expelled from Naples and from all Spanish possessions. Responding to this concert of attacks, Pope Clement XIII declared the Society of Jesus a fit instrument in every way for the Church's mission, to be a cradle of saints, and a powerful influence for good among the laity; any attack on the Society was in error against the Church. Clement died in 1769. The new pope, Clement XIV, under intense pressure from the Catholic powers, dissolved the Jesuits in 1773.

Checked in the capitals and cities of Europe, Catholicism would soon face a far greater onslaught when France erupted in a revolutionary flood that would sweep away the boundaries of the old order.

Epilogue

The first British embassy to China in 1792, headed by George, First Earl Macartney, included Sir George Leonard Staunton and Sir George Thomas Staunton, father and son. In preparation for the trip, the senior Staunton sent his son to Naples for Chinese lessons. There the young Staunton reported to his father on negotiations with the superiors of the Chinese Seminary (the Collegio dei Cinesi founded in 1732): in exchange for Chinese instruction and interpreting, some of the four Chinese fathers there would be offered free passage to China in the British entourage.[1] Although happy with this offer, the Chinese priests were anxious at their eventual return, as news of persecutions had reached the far shores of Naples.

Gone were the days when Jesuits from Catholic Europe had anticipated glory and excitement in faraway missions. Even the oceans had deserted the Catholic cause as Dutch and English ships contested successfully the former supremacy of Portuguese and Spanish seamanship. If merchants, soldiers, and diplomats sailed from Europe in greater numbers during the late eighteenth century, the missionaries were sailing home. The suppression of the Society of Jesus by the Bourbons in the 1760s resulted in the roundup and banishment of hundreds of Jesuits from the Spanish and Portuguese domains in the Americas; the constant trickle of Jesuits in the previous centuries to the New World ended in one swift reverse flow.

Plagued by internal squabbles, attacked by Catholic monarchs, challenged by atheist and deist philosophies, the Catholic Church on the eve of the French Revolution was everywhere under siege. The rigor and purpose of Trent seemed a distant memory. Catholicism was saved from the Protestant Reformation only to fall prey, it would seem, to irreligion. The dissolution of ecclesiastical institutions by Catholic states in the two decades before 1789 and the fury of revolutionary iconoclasm and

[1] Letter dated February 21, 1792, Sir George Leonard Staunton and Sir George Thomas Staunton; Papers 1743–1801, Box XVIII-H, Duke University, Perkins Library, Special Collection.

Bonapartist hegemony over the papacy in the years that followed far surpassed the scale of secularization during the Protestant Reformation. Yet the seeds of Catholic renewal, sown during the previous centuries, would survive this harsh winter of revolutionary upheaval. After the victory over Napoleon, Catholicism would emerge in a restored world after 1815, anchored in the rural heartland and the aristocratic regime of Europe, battling the forces of revolution and change, trying to recapture the memory of bygone glory.

Bibliographical essay

1 COUNCIL OF TRENT

For the text of the canons and decrees of Trent, see Giuseppe Alberigo, et al., eds., *Conciliorum oecumenicorum decreta* (Bologna, 1973), 633–775. An English translation is available in *Canons and Decrees of the Council of Trent*, H. J. Schroder, trans. (Rockford, Ill., 1978). For the voluminous documentation that illustrated the inner workings of the Council, including correspondence, diaries, and preparatory documents of the formal decrees and canons, see *Concilium Tridentinum, diariorum, actorum, epistolarum. Tractatum nova collectio*, Societas Görresiana, ed., 13 vols. in 18 (Freiburg, 1901–61). Based primarily on this magnificent collection, Hubert Jedin wrote the standard history of the Council, *Geschichte des Konzils von Trient*, 4 vols. in 5 (Freiburg, 1950–75). Only the first two volumes have been translated into English, as *A History of the Council of Trent* (St. Louis, Mo., 1957–61), covering the years 1545–47, Sessions I–VII, from the opening of the Council to the translation to Bologna. For a short reflection on conciliar history, including the Council of Trent, see Jedin's *Ecumenical Councils of the Catholic Church: An Historical Outline*, Ernest Graf, trans. (New York, 1960).

Jedin has also written a biography of Cardinal Seripando, one of the leading figures at the Council: *Papal Legate at the Council of Trent: Cardinal Seripando* (St. Louis, Mo., 1977). Two conference collections cast interesting light on aspects of Trent, particularly on individual figures and on the interests and participation of different Catholic nations: see *Il Concilio di Trento e la riforma tridentina. Atti del Convegno storico internazionale. Trento, 2–6 settembre 1963*, 2 vols. (Freiburg, 1965), with twenty-eight contributions covering most of Catholic Europe; and *Il Concilio di Trento come crocevia della politica europea*, Hubert Jedin and Paolo Prodi, eds. (Annali dell'Istituto storico italo germanico Quaderno, 4; Bologna, 1977), with eight contributions, notably that of Jan Wladyslaw Wos on Poland and Trent. Also of interest are the heresy proceedings against Cardinal Morone and the suspicion against Cardinal Pole; see the documents published in Massimo Firpo, ed., *Il processo inquistoriale del Cardinal Giovanni Morone*, 2 vols. to date (Rome, 1981–), and his study *Inquizione Romana e Controriforma. Studi sul Cardinal Giovanni Morone e il suo processo d'eresia* (Bologna, 1992); Paolo Simoncelli, *Il caso Reginald Pole. Eresia e santità nelle polemiche religiose del cinquecento* (Rome, 1977).

2 THE NEW RELIGIOUS ORDERS

The Jesuits are the best documented of all the Catholic religious orders, thanks to meticulous archival administration and prodigious publication. See Monumenta historica Societatis Iesu, a series published by Archivum historicum Societatis Iesu. For recent studies, see John W. O'Malley, *The First Jesuits* (Cambridge, Mass., 1993). For regional studies, see Bernhard Duhr, *Geschichte der Jesuiten in den Ländern deutscher Zunge* for German-speaking central Europe, the volume on the sixteenth century published in 1907, the two volumes on the seventeenth century published in 1913, both in Freiburg; for Italy, see Pietro Tacchi Venturi and Mario Scaduto, *Storia della Compagnia di Gesù in Italia*, 5 vols. to date (Rome, 1950–); for Spain, see Antonio Astrain, *Historía de la Compañía de Jésus en la asistencia de España*, 7 vols. (Madrid, 1902–25); on Belgium, see *Les Jésuites belges, 1542–1992. 450 ans de Compagnie de Jésus dans les provinces belgiques* (Brussels, 1992).

The other religious orders have received far less scholarly attention. The book by Father Cutherbert, *The Capuchins: A Contribution to the History of the Counter-Reformation*, 2 vols. (London, 1928), is still serviceable. On Benedictine reforms, see Maarten Ultee, *The Abbey of St. Germain des Prés in the Seventeenth Century* (New Haven, Conn., 1981). On the Theatines, see Marcella Campanelli, "Note sul patrimonio dei Teatini in Italia alla vigilia dell'inchiesta innocenziana," in Giuseppe Galasso and Carla Russo, eds., *Per la storia sociale e religiosa del Mezzogiorno d'Italia*, 2 vols. (Naples, 1980), vol. I, 181–238.

More exists on women's religious orders, thanks in part to recent feminist interest in women and religion. Most of the older works are local in scope and focus on founding personalities and institutional history; among the more useful studies with social and cultural facts are: Roger Devos, *Vie religieuse féminine et société. L'origine sociale des Visitandines d'Annecy aux XVIIe et XVIIIe siècles* (Annecy, 1973), with detailed data on the social recruitment of the nuns and the internal organization of the convents; Marié-Andrée Jégou, *Les ursulines du Faubourg St.-Jacques à Paris 1607–1662* (Paris, 1981), which demonstrates the nexus between reformed convents and the devouts among the Parisian nobility; Carla Russo, *I monasteri femminili di clausura a Napoli nel secolo XVII* (Naples, 1970), based on an archiepiscopal visitation, with detailed analysis of the social profile of the convents; Gabriella Zarri, "Monasteri femminili e città (secoli XV–XVIII)," in *Storia d'Italia. Annali 9: La chiesa e il potere politico dal medioevo all'età contemporanea*, Giorgio Chittolini and Giovanni Miccoli, eds. (Turin, 1986), 359–429; for original insights into the social history of female religiosity, see P. Renée Baernstein, "The Counter-Reformation Convent: The Angelics of San Paolo in Milan, 1535–1635," Ph.D. thesis, Harvard University, 1993; Anne Conrad, *Zwischen Kloster und Welt. Ursulinen und Jesuitinnen in der katholischen Reformbewegung des 16./17. Jahrhunderts* (Mainz, 1991), a study based on a feminist perspective with original material from Cologne and useful summaries of other existing literature. For individual biographies, see T. D. Kendrick, *Mary of Agreda: The Life and Legend of a Spanish Nun* (London, 1967); and Emilio Zanette, *Suor Arcangela, monaca del seicento veneziana* (Venice, 1961), a literary but rather convoluted study of monastic feminism. A flood of literature exists on the most famous nun of early modern Catholicism, St. Teresa of Avila; one could perhaps start with her own writings: on the reform of the Discalced Carmelites, see her *Libro de los fundaciones*, in *Obras completas. Edición manual* (Madrid, 1979).

3 THE TRIUMPHANT CHURCH

On Savoy, see Achille Erba, *La Chiesa Sabauda tra cinque e seicento. Ortodossia tridentina, gallicanesimo savoiardo, e assolutismo ducale (1580–1630)* (Rome, 1979); and Angelo Torre, "Politics Cloaked in Worship: State, Church, and Local Power in Piedmont 1570–1770," *Past and Present* 134 (1992), 42–92. On Italy, the traditional scholarship on Catholic reform stressed institutional history and reform bishops, based mostly on normative sources (episcopal decrees, synodal legislations, etc.), an example being Arnaldo d'Addario, *Aspetti della Controriforma a Firenze* (Rome, 1972). More recent scholarship has diversified by using other kinds of historical documents to ask questions of lay and popular religion: see Christopher F. Black, *Italian Confraternities in the Sixteenth Century* (Cambridge, 1989). A number of regional studies are based primarily on visitation records: see Angelo Turchini, *Clero e fedeli a Rimini in età post-tridentina* (Rome, 1978); Cecilia Nubola, *Conoscere per governare. La diocesi di Trento nella visita pastorale di Ludovico Madruzzo (1579–1581)* (Bologna, 1993); and the collected articles and local studies in *Visite pastorali ed elaborazione dei dati. Esperienze e metodi*, Cecilia Nubola and Angelo Turchini, eds. (Bologna, 1993). Other works have exploited documents of the Index and the Inquisition: Paul F. Grendler, *The Roman Inquisition and the Venetian Press 1540–1605* (Princeton, 1977); Angelo Turchini, *Inquisitori e pastori. Considerazioni su popolazione romagnola, articolazione territoriale, competenza dell'Inquisizione faentina all'inizio del seicento* (Cesena, 1994).

A great deal of the research takes on regional character. Aside from the scholarship on the Papal States, which is dealt with in the bibliographical section on chapter 6 (219–20), three regions in particular have attracted attention: Milan, the center of the Borromean reform; the Mezzogiorno, the South under Spanish rule with its vastly different socio-economic and ecclesiastical structures; and the Republic of Venice, the region in Italy closest to the Protestant danger of the North. For Milan, see the two volumes of essays *Stampi, libri, e letture a Milano nell'età di Carlo Borromeo*, Nicola Raponi and Angelo Turchini, eds. (Milan, 1992), and *Ricerche sulla Chiesa di Milano nel settecento*, Antonio Acerbi and Massimo Marcocchi, eds. (Milan, 1988); see also Arnalda Dallaj, "Le processioni a Milano nella Controriforma," *Studi storici* 23 (1982), 167–83. For the South, see *Per la storia sociale e religiosa del Mezzogiorno d'Italia*, Giuseppe Galasso and Carla Russo, eds., 2 vols. (Naples, 1980), vol. I, which assembles the research (of very different quality) by many historians working on Mezzogiorno religious history; Gabriele de Rosa, *Vescovi, popolo, e magia nel Sud* (Naples, 1971), is an impassioned collection of essays which link political, social, and religious history. The latest research on Catholicism in Mezzogiorno Italy is the two-volume conference collection, *Il Concilio di Trento nella vita spirituale e culturale del Mezzogiorno tra XVI e XVII secolo*, Gabriele de Rosa and Antonio Cestaro, eds. (Potenza, 1988). See also Carla Russo, ed., *Società, Chiesa, e vita religiosa nell'Ancien Régime* (Naples, 1976), with an extensive introductory essay and readings from primarily French scholars of religion; see also Russo, ed., *Chiesa, assistenza, e società nel Mezzogiorno moderno* (Naples, 1994), and L. Osbat, *L'Inquisizione a Napoli* (Rome, 1974). Russo's own monograph, *Chiesa e comunità nella diocesi di Napoli tra cinque e settecento* (Naples, 1984), based on exhaustive use of visitation records, shows both the information and limitations contained in that genre of sources.

The symbiosis between traditional, popular Catholicism and Tridentine reform is analyzed with regard to saints' cults and healing; see two sensitive and imaginative interpretations: David Gentilcore, *From Bishop to Witch: The System of the Sacred in Early Modern Terra d'Otranto* (Manchester, 1992), and J.-M. Sallmann, "Il santo e le rappresentazioni della santità. Problemi di metodo," *Quaderni storici* 14 (1979). On Venice, in addition to the work of Grendler cited above, see the two exceptional monographs: John J. Martin, *Venice's Hidden Enemies: Italian Heretics in a Renaissance City* (Berkeley, 1993); and Brian Pullan, *Rich and Poor in Renaissance Venice: The Social Institutions of a Catholic State to 1620* (Cambridge, Mass., 1971). For a selection of articles on the social history of religion in English, see Edward Muir and Guido Ruggiero, eds., *Microhistory and the Lost Peoples of Europe* (Baltimore, 1991).

The history of Catholicism in Portugal has received relatively little attention; what scholarship there is on the social history of religion is focused on the Luso-Brazilian Inquisition. For a reference work on the Portuguese Church, see Fortunato de Almeida, *História da igreja em Portugal*, new edn., 4 vols. (Lisbon, 1968), vol. II; see also Robert Ricard, *Etudes sur l'histoire morale et religieuse du Portugal* (Paris, 1970); Samuel J. Miller, *Portugal and Rome 1748–1830* (Rome, 1978); *Inquisição*, ed. Maria Helena Carvalho Dos Santos (Lisbon, 1989–90), the three-volume proceedings of the 1987 Luso-Brazilian Congress on the Inquisition; and *Inquisição. Ensaios sobre mentalidade, heresias, e arte*, Anita Novinsky and Maria Luiza Tucci Carneiro, eds. (São Paulo, 1992), with overlapping material.

Scholarship on Spanish Catholicism is uneven: the older institutional and internal history of the Church has been replaced by a more recent socio-political interest in religion and society, particularly in the workings of the Inquisition, which tends to give an unbalanced view of the repressive side of Catholicism in early modern Spain. Among the few monographs that focus on social history of religion, the best is Sara T. Nalle, *God in La Mancha: Religious Reform and the People of Cuenca 1500–1650* (Baltimore, 1992). Carlos M. N. Eire's *From Madrid to Purgatory: The Art and Craft of Dying in Sixteenth-Century Spain* (Cambridge, 1995) represents an innovative approach to the evaluation of testaments, but is limited to the sixteenth century. Henry Kamen, *The Phoenix and the Flame: Catalonia and the Counter Reformation* (New Haven, Conn., 1993), offers a wealth of material but lacks a coherent conceptual argument. For the growing corpus of Inquisition studies, see the two-volume "state of the field" synthesis: *Historia de la Inquisición en España y America*, Joaquin Pérez Villanueva and Bartolome Escandell Bonet, eds., 2 vols. (Madrid, 1984–93). The best introduction in English is the volume of essays *The Inquisition in Early Modern Europe: Studies on Sources and Methods*, Gustav Henningsen and John Tedeschi, eds. (Dekalb, Ill., 1986), especially the article by Jaime Contreras and Gustav Henningsen offering an overview of the Spanish Inquisition. But the collection makes clear the significance of regional/national variations in the effectiveness and goals of the Inquisition.

Among the regional studies, the single best work is Jaime Contreras, *El Santo Oficio de la Inquisición de Galicia (poder, sociedad, y cultura)* (Madrid, 1982). Also useful is Jean-Pierre Dedieu, *L'administration de la foi. L'Inquisition de Tolède (XVIe–XVIIIe siècle)* (Madrid, 1989), although the Toledean sources are less extensive and Dedieu's conclusions, therefore, are less penetrating than Contreras's Galician material. For innovative attempts to use Inquisition records to reconstruct popular religion, see Sara T. Nalle, "To Sin in Thought and in Deed: Ideas and Action in Counter-Reformation Spain," forthcoming; and Jean-Pierre Dedieu, "'Christianisation' en nouvelle Castille. Catechisme, communion, messe, et confirmation dans l'Archeveche de Tolède 1540–1650," *Mélanges de la Casa de Velazquez* 15 (1979), 261–94. For the symbolism of the *auto de fe*, see Maureen Flynn, "Mimesis of the Last Judgment: The Spanish Auto de fe," *Sixteenth-Century Journal* 22 (1991), 281–97. For a historical analysis of local religion by an eminent anthropologist, see William A. Christian, *Local Religion in Sixteenth-Century Spain* (Princeton, 1981). The reflection by Julio Caro Baroja, *Las formas complejas de la vida religiosa. Religión, sociedad, y carácter en las España de los siglos XVI y XVII* (Madrid, 1978), is based on an extensive reading of early modern devotional treatises and offers many perceptive insights. Also informative is Maureen Flynn, *Sacred Charity: Confraternities and Social Welfare in Spain 1400–1700* (Ithaca, N. Y., 1989).

4 THE MILITANT CHURCH

On the Spanish Netherlands there is a small but growing literature that places greater emphasis on the socio-cultural aspects of the Catholic renewal. Three local studies are thorough: see Alfons K. L. Thijs, *Van Geuzenstadt tot Katholiek Bolwerk. Maatschappelijke Betekenis van de Kerk in Contrareformatorsch Antwerpen* (Antwerp, 1990), an extremely well-researched but densely written monograph; the stimulating work by Alain Lottin, *Lille. Citadelle de la Contre-Réforme? (1598–1668)* (Dunkirk, 1984); and *Les Jésuites dans les pays-bas et la principauté de Liège (1542–1773)*, Archives générales du Royaume, ed. (Brussels, 1991). The older synthesis by Henri Pirenne, while outdated in scholarship, still remains the best account for its insights and style and is vastly superior to the relevant articles in the *Nieuwe Algemene Geschiedenis der Nederlanden*; see his *Histoire de Belgique. IV: La révolution politique et religieuse. Le règne d'Albert et d'Isabelle. Le règne espagnol jusqu'à la paix de Munster*, 3rd rev. edn. (Brussels, 1927). Two other older works are still informative and useful: E. de Moreau, *Histoire de l'Eglise en Belgique*, 5 vols. (Brussels, 1952), vol. V, and A. Pasture, *La restauration religieuse aux Pays-Bas catholiques sous les archiducs Albert et Isabelle (1596–1633)* (Louvain, 1925). On Luxembourg, see *Piété baroque en Luxembourg*, Musée en Piconrue, ed. (Bastogne, 1995), an exhibition catalogue that includes important scholarly articles.

On Poland, the literature in western languages is limited; see Ambroise Jobert, *De Luther à Mohila. La Pologne dans la crise de la chrétienté 1517–1648* (Paris, 1974), and Bernhard Stasiewski, *Reformation und Gegenreformation in Polen. Neue Forschungsergebnisse* (Münster, 1960). For the Counter-Reformation in Bohemia, a much neglected subject, see Stephan Dolezel, "Frühe Einflüsse des Jansenismus in Böhmen," Zdenek Kalista, "Die katholische Reform von Hilarius bis zum Weissen Berg," and Josef Hemmerle, "Die Prager Universität in der neueren Zeit," all three in *Bohemia Sacra. Das Christentum in Böhmen 973–1973*, Ferdinand Seibt, ed. (Düsseldorf, 1974); see also Winfried Eberhard, "Entwicklungsphasen und Probleme der Gegenreformation und katholischen Erneuerung in Böhmen," *Römische Quartalschrift für christliche Altertumskunde und Kirchengeschichte* 84 (1989), 235–57. The richness of Czech-language material has been suggested by James D. Palmitessa, "Home, House, and Neighborhood on the Eve of White Mountain: Material Culture and Daily Life in the New City of Prague 1547–1611," Ph.D. thesis, New York University, 1995, which investigates, among other themes, the confessional conflicts in Prague on the eve of White Mountain.

There is an enormous literature on Catholicism in early modern France. I have included only those works that exemplify the leading approaches to this history. For research based primarily on visitation records, see Robert Sauzet, *Contre-Réforme et Réforme Catholique en Bas-Languedoc. Le diocèse de Nîmes au XVIIe siècle* (Paris, 1979); also by Sauzet, *Les visites pastorales dans le diocèse de Chartres pendant la première moitié du XVIIe siècle* (Rome, 1975). The geographical and sociological perspectives, so well suited to diocesan studies and initiated in method by Gabriel Le Bras, are well represented in scholarship. See Louis Châtellier, *Tradition chrétienne et renouveau catholique dans le cadre de l'ancien diocèse de Strasbourg (1650–1770)* (Paris, 1981), and the series Histoire des diocéses de France, which is very uneven in quality. The better volumes include: Jean Delumeau, ed., *Le diocèse de Rennes* (Paris, 1979); Philippe Wolff, ed., *Le diocèse de Toulouse* (Paris, 1983); and perhaps the best volume in the series, Louis Pérouas, *Le diocèse de La Rochelle de 1648 à 1724. Sociologie et pastorale* (Paris, 1964). More traditional studies have focused on institutions, diplomatic history between Paris and Rome, and episcopal reforms of pastoral care; the major works are Pierre Blet, *Le clergé de France et la monarchie. Etude sur les Assemblées Générales du Clergé de 1615 à 1666*, 2 vols. (Rome, 1959); also by Blet, *Le clergé de France, Louis XIV, et le Saint Siège de 1695 à 1715* (Vatican City, 1989); and Jeanne Ferté, *La vie religieuse dans les campagnes parisiennes (1622–1695)* (Paris, 1962). Another established theme is Jansenism; for a recent study that covers the subject in a broader historical context, see René Taveneaux, *Jansénisme et Réforme Catholique* (Nancy, 1992). New subjects of research focusing on the social history of religion have also characterized recent research; on Counter-Reformation confraternities, see Alain Tallon, *La Compagnie du Saint-Sacrament (1629–1667)* (Paris, 1990); for popular devotion to miracle-cures, see Bernard Cousin, *Le miracle et le quotidien. Les Ex-Voto provençaux. Images d'une société* (Aix-en-Provence, 1983); for the relationship between social processes and Counter-Reformation, see Keith P. Luria, *Territories of Grace: Cultural Change in the Seventeenth-Century Diocese of Grenoble* (Berkeley, 1991); Gregory Hanlon, *Confession and Community in Seventeenth-Century France: Catholic and Protestant Coexistence in Aquitaine* (Philadelphia, 1993); Philip T. Hoffman, *Church and Community in the Diocese of Lyon 1500–1789* (New Haven, Conn., 1984).

For the Duchy of Lorraine, an independent polity in the sixteenth and seventeenth centuries, whose ecclesiastical politics were more pro-papal and pro-Spanish than those of the Gallican Church, see Louis Châtellier, ed., *Les réformes en Lorraine 1520–1620* (Nancy, 1986).

There is also an immense literature on Catholicism in German-speaking central Europe. For an introductory orientation, see R. Po-chia Hsia, *Social Discipline in the Reformation: Central Europe 1550–1770* (London, 1989). Traditional historiography has focused on biographies of reform bishops and histories of diocesan reforms; they tend to adopt an institutional perspective on popular religion. See, for example, Dorothee Coenen, *Die katholische Kirche am Niederrhein von der Reformation bis zum Beginn des 18. Jahrhunderts* (Münster, 1967); Anton Brecher, *Die kirchliche Reform in Stadt und Reich. Aachen von der Mitte des 16. bis zum Anfang des 18. Jahrhunderts* (Münster, 1957); Hans Ammerich, "Formen und Wege der katholischen Reform in den Diözesen Speyer und Strassburg. Klerusreform und Seelsorge," in Volker Press, ed., *Barock am Oberrhein* (Karlsruhe, 1985), Manfred Becker-Huberti, *Die tridentinische Reform im Bistum Münster unter Fürstbischof Christoph Bernhard von Galen 1650–1678* (Münster, 1978); Edith Ennen, "Kurfürst Ferdinand von Köln (1577–1650). Ein rheinischer Kurfürst zur Zeit des Dressigjährigen Krieges," *Annalen des historischen Vereins für den Niederrhein* 163 (1961), 5–40; Hans-Joachim Köhler, *Das Ringen um die tridentinische Erneuerung im Bistum Breslau vom Abschluss des Konzils bis zur Schlacht am Weissen Berg 1564–1620* (Cologne, 1973); August Franzen, *Der Wiederaufbau des kirchlichen Lebens im Erzbistum Köln unter Ferdinand von Bayern, Erzbischof von Köln, 1612–1650* (Münster, 1941); Hansgeorg Molitor, *Kirchliche Reformversuche der Kurfürsten und Erzbischöfe vom Trier im Zeitalter der Gegenreformation* (Wiesbaden, 1967). For recent scholarship, see the special conference volume, "Katholische Reform," of the Görres-Gesellschaft and the German Historical Institute in Rome: *Römische Quartalschrift* 84 (1989), especially the articles by Heribert Raab on Trier, Franz Bosbach on Cologne, Winfried Eberhard on Bohemia, and Johannes Rainer on Inner Austria.

A growing corpus of work, however, has turned to the questions of the relationship between popular and official religion. See David Lederer, "Reforming the Spirit: Society, Madness, and Suicide in Central Europe 1517–1809," Ph.D. thesis, New York University, 1994; Wilfried Enderle, *Konfessionsbildung und Ratsregiment in der katholischen Reichsstadt Überlingen (1500–1618) im Kontext der Reformationsgeschichte der oberschwäbischen Reichsstädte* (Stuttgart, 1990); Wolfgang Zimmermann, *Rekatholisierung, Konfessionalisierung, und Ratsregiment. Der Prozess des politischen und religiösen Wandels in der österreichischen Stadt Konstanz 1548–1637* (Sigmaringen, 1994); Thomas Paul Becker, *Konfessionalisierung in Kurköln. Untersuchungen zur Durchsetzung der katholischen Reform in den Dekanaten Ahrgau und Bonn anhand von Visitationsprotokollen 1583–1761* (Bonn, 1989); Peter Thäddeus Lang, *Die Ulmer Katholiken im Zeitalter der Glaubenskämpfe. Lebensbedingungen einer konfessionellen Minderheit* (Frankfurt, 1977); R. Po-chia Hsia, *Society and Religion in Münster 1535–1618* (New Haven, Conn., 1984); Marc R. Forster, *The Counter-Reformation in the Villages: Religion and Reform in the Bishopric of Speyer* (Ithaca, N. Y., 1992); and his "The Elite and Popular Foundations of German Catholicism in the Age of Confessionalism: The *Reichskirche*," *Central European History* 26 (1994), 311–25. Cologne, in particular, has received a great deal of attention; see in particular Gérald Chaix, "De la cité chrétienne à la metropole catholique. Vie religieuse et conscience civique à Cologne au XVIe siècle," Thèse doctorat d'Etat, Université de Strasbourg, 1994, 3 vols. For two exemplary biographies that demonstrate the complexities between confessional and dynastic politics, see Robert Bireley, *Maximilian von Bayern, Adam Contzen S. J., und die Gegenreformation in Deutschland 1624–1635* (Göttingen, 1975), and Bireley, *Religion and Politics in the Age of the Counterreformation: Emperor Ferdinand II, William Lamormaini, S. J., and the Formation of Imperial Policy* (Chapel Hill, 1981).

5 THE MARTYRED CHURCH

Of the three regions discussed in this chapter the most extensive documentation and scholarship on Catholicism is that on Tudor and Stuart England. Fundamental is the splendid series of published sources by the Catholic Record Society which contains valuable information on recusancy, English seminaries on the Continent, and Jesuit activities in England. See for example *English and Welsh Jesuits 1555–1650*, Thomas M. McCoog, ed. (Catholic Record Society Publications, Records Series, 74; Southampton, 1994); the Society also publishes monographic studies, an useful example being J. C. H. Aveling, *Catholic Recusancy in the City of York 1558–1791* (Catholic Record Society Publications. Monograph Series, 2; St. Albans, 1970). The published records in this series serve as a major source for the standard work of synthesis by John Bossy, *The English Catholic Community 1570–1850* (New York, 1976). For a highly partisan and exquisitely written biography of the most famous English Jesuit martyr, see Evelyn Waugh, *Edmund Campion* (Oxford, 1935; reprint 1980).

Research on early modern Irish Catholicism is less systematic and, with exceptions, focuses on its cultural and institutional history. For an introductory survey, see Patrick J. Corish, *The Irish Catholic Experience: A Historical Survey* (Dublin, 1985), chaps. 3–5, and Corish, *A New History of Ireland*, vol. III, *Early Modern Ireland 1534–1691* (Oxford, 1976). See also the relevant chapters in "The New Gill History of Ireland": Colm Lennon, *Sixteenth-Century Ireland: The Incomplete Conquest* (Dublin, 1994), and Brendan Fitzpatrick, *Seventeenth-Century Ireland: The War of Religion* (Dublin, 1995). The more specialized studies are particularly perceptive on the Irish exile experience; see Bernadette Cunningham, "The Culture and Ideology of Irish Franciscan Historians at Louvain 1607–1650," *Historical Studies* 17 (1991), 11–30; Nicholas Canny, "The Formation of the Irish Mind: Religion, Politics, and Gaelic Irish Literature 1580–1750," *Past and Present* 95 (1982), 91–116; Gráinne Henry, *The Irish Military Community in Spanish Flanders 1586–1621* (Dublin, 1992). See also John Bossy, "The Counter-Reformation and the People of Catholic Ireland 1596–1641," *Historical Studies* 8 (1971), 155–69; and H. F. Kearney, "Ecclesiastical Politics and the Counter-Reformation in Ireland 1618–1648," *Journal of Ecclesiastical History* 11 (1960), 202–12.

Scholarship on Catholicism in the early modern Dutch Republic is strongly pro-Catholic and the two indispensable works are L. J. Rogier, *Geschiedenis van het Katholicisme in Noord-Nederland in de 16e en de 17e Eeuw*, 2 parts (Amsterdam, 1947), and P. A. Polman, *Katholiek Nederland in de 18e Eeuw*, 3 vols. (Hilversum, 1968). For a first orientation into the issues of Dutch Catholicism, see James D. Tracy, "With or Without the Counter-Reformation: The Catholic Church in the Spanish Netherlands and the Dutch Republic 1580–1650. A Review of the Literature Since 1945," *Catholic Historical Review* 71 (1985), 547–75.

6 THE PAPAL CURIA

See J. N. D. Kelly, *The Oxford Dictionary of Popes* (Oxford, 1986); Ludwig von Pastor, *History of the Popes from the Close of the Middle Ages*, 40 vols. (1891–1953). For political and institutional history of the papacy, the best research is by Paolo

Prodi; see his *Lo sviluppo dell'assolutismo nello Stato Pontificio. I: La monarchia papale e gli organi centrali di governo* (Bologna, 1968), and his *The Papal Prince: One Body and Two Souls. The Papal Monarchy in Early Modern Europe* (Cambridge, 1987). The many studies of Wolfgang Reinhard provide original insight into the social and economic history of the early modern papacy; see *Papstfinanz und Nepotismus unter Paul V. (1605–1621). Studien und Quellen zur Struktur und zur quantitativen Aspekten des päpstlichen Herrschaftssystems*, 2 vols. (Päpst und Papsttum, 6; Stuttgart, 1974); Reinhard, *Freunde und Kreaturen. "Verflechtung" als Konzept zur Erforschung historischer Führungsgruppen römische Oligarchie um 1600* (Munich, 1979); Reinhard, "Herkunft und Karriere der Päpste 1417–1963. Beiträge zu einer historischen Soziologie der römischen Kurie," *Mededelingen van het Nederlands Instituut te Rome* 38 (1976), 87–108; Reinhard, "Nepotismus. Der Funktionswandel einer papstgeschichtlichen Konstanten," *Zeitschrift für Kirchengeschichte* 86 (1975), 145–85; and Reinhard, "Ämterlaufbahn und Familienstatus. Der Aufstieg des Hauses Borghese 1537–1621," *Quellen und Forschungen aus italienischen Archiven und Bibliotheken* 54 (1974), 328–427.

On the leading cardinal households, see Markus Volkel, *Römische Kardinalshaushalte des 17. Jahrhunderts. Borghese, Barberini, Chigi* (Tübingen, 1993); on one of the *papabili*, see Hubert Jedin, *Die Autobiographie des Kardinals Giulio Antonio Santorio (+1602)* (Akademie der Wissenschaft und Literatur in Mainz. Abhandlungen der Geites- u. sozialwissenschaftlichen Klasse, 2; Wiesbaden, 1969). For the economic and social history of Rome and the Papal States, see the works of Jean Delumeau, *Vie économique et sociale de Rome dans la seconde moitié du XVIe siècle*, 2 vols. (Paris, 1957–59); and Delumeau, *L'Alun de Rome XVe–XIXe siècle* (Paris, 1962). For a study in historical geography, see Roberto Volpi, *Le regioni introvabili. Centralizzazione e regionalizzazione dello stato pontificio* (Bologna, 1983).

7 BISHOPS AND PRIESTS

There is a reasonably large hagiography on the model Counter-Reformation bishop Carlo Borromeo; two of the earliest – the 1585 *laudatio funebris* by Giovanni Pietro Bimio and the 1589 epic encomium, "Borromeis," by Giovanni Francesco Bonomi, bishop of Vercelli – are available in *San Carlo Borromeo. Due biografie del cinquecento poco conosciute*, E. Cattaneo and M. Navoni, eds. (Milan, 1984); the fourth centennial of his death has given rise to a new batch of publications, some hagiographic, such as Hedwig Bach, *Karl Borromäus. Leitbild für die Reform der Kirche nach dem Konzil von Trient* (Cologne, 1984), and others more scholarly, such as the conference volume, *San Carlo Borromeo: Catholic Reform and Ecclesiastical Politics in the Second Half of the Sixteenth Century*, John M. Headley and John B. Tomaro, eds. (Cranbury, N. J., 1988). For monographs based on visitation records, see Cecilia Nubola, *Conoscere per governare. La diocesi di Trento nella visita pastorale di Ludovico Madruzzo (1579–1581)* (Bologna, 1993); Michel Cloet, *Het Kerkelijk Leven in een landelijke Dekenij van Vlaanderen tijdens de XVIIe Eeuw. Tielt van 1609 tot 1700* (Louvain, 1968), a study of a deanery in the diocese of Ghent; the two studies by Robert Sauzet: *Les visites pastorales dans le diocèse de Chartres pendant la première moitié du XVIIe siècle* (Rome, 1975), and *Contre-Réforme et Réforme Catholique en Bas-Languedoc. Le diocèse de Nîmes au XVIIe siècle*

(Paris, 1979); Angelo Turchini, *Clero e fedeli a Rimini in età post-tridentina* (Rome, 1978).

For studies on the clergy, see Hans Ammerich, "Formen und Wege der katholischen Reform in den Diözesen Speyer und Strassburg. Klerusreform und Seelsorge," in *Barock am Oberrhein* (Karlsruhe, 1985), Volker Press, ed., Joseph Janssen, "Die Herkunft des früheren Kölner Weltklerus," *Historisches Archiv des Erzbistums Köln* 1 (1928), 59–65. For biographies on individual reform bishops, see Manfred Becker-Huberti, *Die tridentinische Reform im Bistum Münster unter Fürstbischof Christoph Bernhard von Galen 1650–1678* (Münster, 1978); Edith Ennen, "Kurfürst Ferdinand von Köln (1577–1650). Ein rheinischer Kurfürst zur Zeit des Dreissigjährigen Krieges," *Annalen des historischen Vereins für den Niederrhein* 163 (1961), 5–40; for the French clergy, see the two monographs by Pierre Blet: *Le clergé de France et la monarchie. Etude sur les Assemblés Générales du Clergé de 1615 à 1666*, 2 vols. (Rome, 1959), and *Le clergé de France, Louis XIV, et le Saint Siège de 1695 à 1715* (Vatican City, 1989), which emphasize the diplomatic history of Gallicanism. For a thorough analysis of the German College, see Peter Schmidt, *Das Collegium Germanicum in Rom und die Germaniker. Zur Funktion eines römischen Ausländerseminars (1552–1914)* (Tübingen, 1984). Many local and regional studies contain information on the clergy; among the most useful monographs are David Gentilcore, *From Bishop to Witch: The System of the Sacred in Early Modern Terra d'Otranto* (Manchester, 1992); Marc Vernard, *Réforme Protestante, Réforme Catholique dans la province d'Avignon XVIe siècle* (Paris, 1993); Sara T. Nalle, *God in La Mancha: Religious Reform and the People of Cuenca 1500–1650* (Baltimore, 1992); and in the series Histoire des diocèses de France, I have used the following volumes: Jean Delumeau, ed., *Le diocèse de Rennes* (Paris, 1979); Philippe Wolff, ed., *Le diocèse de Toulouse* (Paris, 1983); Louis Pérouas, *Le diocèse de La Rochelle de 1648 à 1724. Sociologie et pastorale* (Paris, 1964); Philip Hoffman, *Church and Community in the Diocese of Lyon 1500–1789* (New Haven, Conn., 1984); Alain Lottin, *Lille. Citadelle de la Contre-Réforme? (1598–1668)* (Dunkirk, 1984).

8 COUNTER-REFORMATION SAINTS

The fundamental source on sainthood is the monumental work by the Bollandists, *Acta sanctorum*, arranged according to feastdays. It served as the basis for the English-language *Lives of the Saints*, compiled by Alban Butler (London, 1756–59), available in a revised and enlarged four-volume version under the editorship of Herbert Thurston and Donald Attwater (New York, 1963). For an alphabetical listing, simplified from Butler, see Donald Attwater, comp., *A Dictionary of Saints: Being Also an Index to the Revised Edition of Alban Butler's "Lives of the Saints"* (London, 1938). There exist numerous biographies of individual saints, of which only several of the most prominent can be mentioned here. For a detailed study of the campaign leading to the canonization of Ignatius of Loyola, with an impressive analysis of the iconographic material, see Ursula König-Nordhoff, *Ignatius von Loyola. Studien zur Entwicklung einer neuen Heiligen-Ikonographie im Rahmen einer Kanonisations-kampagne um 1600* (Berlin, 1982). For Teresa of Avila, see Carole Slade, *St. Teresa of Avila: Author of "A Heroic Life"* (Berkeley, 1995). For Borromeo, see Giuseppe Alberigo, *Il grande Borromeo tra storia e fede* (Milan 1984); and the collection of essays, *San Carlo Borromeo: Catholic Reform and Ecclesiastical Politics in the Second Half of the Sixteenth Century*, John M. Headley and John B. Tomaro, eds. (Cranbury, N. J., 1988). A beautiful example of modern hagiography of the English Jesuit martyr (who is not canonized) is Evelyn Waugh's *Edmund Campion* (Oxford, 1935; reprint 1980).

For an analysis of the process of canonization in two healing saints in southern Italy that reveals popular attitude toward sainthood, see Jean-Michel Sallmann, "Image et fonction du saint dans la région de Naples à la fin du XVIIe et au début du XVIIIe siècle," *Mélanges de l'école française de Rome. Moyen âge. Temps modernes* 91 (1979), 827–73. For a stimulating though brief essay on early modern sainthood, see Peter Burke, "How to Be a Counter-Reformation Saint," in Burke, *The Historical Anthropology of Early Modern Italy* (Cambridge, 1987). A journal published by the Bollandists, *Analecta Bolandiana* (1882–), serves as the major vehicle of scholarly communication on hagiography; on the history of the Bollandists themselves, see Paul Peeters, *L'oeuvre des Bollandistes* (Académie Royale de Belgique, classe des lettres et des sciences morales et politiques, 54; Brussels, 1961).

9 HOLY WOMEN, BEATAS, DEMONIACS

In addition to the writings of Teresa of Avila, the best documented of all early modern religious woman – available in the complete Spanish edition by Alberto Barrientos, et al. (Madrid, 1984) and an English translation by E. Allison Peers, ed., *The Complete Works of Teresa of Avila*, 3 vols. (London, 1944–46) – see also the insightful feminist interpretation by Carole Slade, *St. Teresa of Avila: Author of "A Heroic Life"* (Berkeley, 1995). For the larger context of women in Spanish Catholicism, see José Luis Sanchez Lora, *Mujeres, conventos, y formas de la Religiosidad Barroca* (Madrid, 1988). For a selection of writings by nuns in Spain and its colonies, which both amplify and exceed the Teresian themes, see Electa Arena and Stacey Schlau, eds., *Untold Sisters: Hispanic Nuns in Their Own Works* (Albuquerque, N. M., 1989). For studies and writings on individual Spanish nuns and beatas, see Sor Juana Inés de la Cruz, *The Answer/La Respuesta*, Electa Arenal and Amanda Powell, eds. (New York, 1994); T. D. Kendrick, *Mary of Agreda: The Life and Legend of a Spanish Nun* (London, 1967); Clark Colahan, *The Visions of Sor María de Agreda: Writing Knowledge and Power* (Tucson, Ariz., 1994). For Italian women, we can start with the two female saints: Caterina dei Ricci and María Magdalena dei Pazzi, both Florentines. St. Caterina has received much more attention in scholarship, including a critical edition of sources and bibliography in the series Collectana Ricciana: under the editorship of Domenico Guglielmo M. di Agresti, five volumes of her letters (Florence, 1973–75) and other sources have been published; particularly relevant for her formative years is *S. Caterina dei Ricci. Testimonianze sull'età giovanile* (Florence, 1963). For Rosa of Lima, the first saint outside Europe, I have used the popular hagiography by Leopoldo Marechal, *Vida de Santa Rosa de Lima* (Buenos Aires, 1943), which relies on the authoritative hagiography by Leonardo Hansen, *Vita mirabilis et mors pretiosa venerabilis sororis Rosae de Sa. Marie Limensis* (1664; translated into Spanish in 1895); an excellent study in historical-anthropology that includes the first life of Rosa by her patron is the work of Luis Millones and Fernando Iwasaki

Cauti in Luis Millones, *Una partecita del cielo. La vida de Santa Rosa de Lima narrada por don Gonzalo de la Maza* (Lima, 1993).

For French religious women, see André Ravier, *Saint Jeanne de Chantal: Noble Lady, Holy Woman*, trans. Mary E. Hamilton (San Francisco, 1989), and the edition of her letters. On Marie de L'Incarnation, see the edition of her writings by Albert Jamet, *Ecrits spirituels et historiques*, 4 vols. (Paris, 1929–39); for English translations, see Irene Mahoney, ed., *Marie of the Incarnation: Selected Writings* (Mahwah, N. Y., 1989), which contains the *Relations* of 1654 (her spiritual autobiography); for her letters, see Joyce Marshall, ed., *Word from New France: The Selected Letters of Marie de L'Incarnation* (Toronto, 1967); for a recent study, see Natalie Z. Davis, *Women on the Margins* (Cambridge, Mass., 1995). For the study of beatas, see Mary Elizabeth Perry, *Gender and Disorder in Early Modern Seville* (Princeton, 1990), and Claire Guilhem, "L'Inquisition et la dévaluation des discours féminins," in Bartolomé Bennassar, ed., *L'Inquisition espagnole XVe–XIXe siècle* (Paris, 1979), 197–240; and Edward Muir and Guido Ruggiero, eds., *Sex and Gender in Historical Perspective* (Baltimore, 1990). Stephen Haliczer is working on a prosopography of women mystics in early modern Spain. For demonic possession in convents, see the excellent reconstruction by Michel Carmona, *Les diables de Loudun. Sorcellerie et politique sous Richelieu* (Paris, 1988); the selection of sources by Michel de Certeau, *La possession de Loudun* (Paris, 1980); and the analysis of changing judicial attitude from piety to skepticism by Robert Mandrou, *Magistrats et sorciers en France au XVIIe siècle. Une analyse de psychologie historique* (Paris, 1980).

10 ART AND ARCHITECTURE

While the concept of "Baroque art" seems to have fallen out of favor with art historians, two older classics still provide a first orientation on this subject: Werner Weisbach, *Der Barock als Kunst der Gegenreformation* (Berlin, 1921), a pioneering study in iconography, is brilliant but unsystematic; the more comprehensive study by Emile Mâle, *L'art religieux après le concile de Trente. Etude sur l'iconographie de la fin du XVIe siècle, du XVIIe siècle, du XVIIIe siècle* (Paris, 1932), although still useful, is not without errors and leaves out central Europe. For a more social historical perspective, see the authoritative and meticulous monograph by Francis Haskell, *Patrons and Painters: A Study in the Relations Between Italian Art and Society in the Age of the Baroque* (London, 1963). Three volumes in the *Pelican History of Art* are indispensable: Rudolf Wittkower's *Art and Architecture in Italy 1600–1750* (Harmondsworth, 1958) remains a classic; also informative are the volumes by E. H. Ter Kuile and H. Gerson, *Art and Architecture in Belgium 1600 to 1800* (Harmondsworth, 1960), and Eberhard Hempel, *Baroque Art and Architecture in Central Europe* (Harmondsworth, 1965).

Recent scholarship tends to shy away from large concepts, the exception being Santiago Sebastián, *Contrareforma y barroco. Lecturas iconográficas e iconológicas* (Madrid, 1981), which is particularly informative on Spanish and Spanish-American examples. For an instructive attempt to clarify the relationship between concepts and actual works of art, see Rudolf Wittkower and Irma B. Jaffe, eds., *Baroque Art: The Jesuit Contribution* (New York, 1972). For thematic studies, the following works are informative: Pamela M. Jones, *Federico Borromeo and the*

Ambrosiana: Art Patronage and Reform in Seventeenth-Century Milan (New York, 1993), discusses the impact of theology on art collection; Sabine Poeschel, *Studien zur Ikonographie der Erdteile in der Kunst des 16.–18. Jahrhunderts* (Augsburg, 1985), is a limited study on an far-ranging theme; Ursula König-Nordhoff, *Ignatius von Loyola. Studien zur Entwicklung einer neuen Heiligen-Ikonographie im Rahmen einer Kanonisations-kampagne um 1600* (Berlin, 1982), is a thorough and original investigation of the uses of iconography for canonization. Steven Ostrow, *Art and Spirituality in Counter-Reformation Rome* (Cambridge, 1996), is a recent work on a crucial topic.

Unfortunately, the study of less elevated religious art works – engravings, prints, woodcuts, book illustrations, votive pictures, wooden statues, church furniture, etc. – has received little attention. To get an idea of the richness of these objects in religious life, see Alfons K. L. Thijs, *Antwerpen. Internationaal Uitgeverscentrum van Devotieprenten 17de–18de Eeuw* (Louvain, 1993); and the exhibition catalogue, *Piété baroque en Luxembourg*, Musée en Piconrue, ed. (Bastogne, 1995).

11 THE IBERIAN CHURCH AND EMPIRES

Among older works that address the question of evangelization in the Iberian empires, see John Leddy Phelan, *The Millennial Kingdom of the Franciscans in the New World*, 2nd rev. edn. (Berkeley, 1970), still useful for understanding Franciscan self-image; the pioneering work of R. E. Greenleaf, *The Mexican Inquisition of the Sixteenth Century* (Albuquerque, N. M., 1969); and Charles R. Boxer, *The Church Militant and Iberian Expansion 1440–1770* (Baltimore, 1978), for its breadth of coverage. Recent scholarship, influenced by ethnography and historical anthropology and interpreting indigenous sources, has emphasized the ambivalent character of the encounter between the colonial–Christian power and the indigenous cultures. For a first orientation, see *The Inca and Aztec States 1400–1800: Anthropology and History*, George A. Collier, Renato I. Rosaldo, and John D. Wirth, eds. (New York, 1982), especially the essay by J. Jorge Klor de Alva, "Spiritual Conflict and Accommodation in New Spain: Toward a Typology of Aztec Responses to Christianity." For Mesoamerica, the works of Inga Clendinnen and Serge Gruzinski are particularly stimulating: Inga Clendinnen, *Ambivalent Conquests: Maya and Spaniard in Yucatan 1517–1570* (Cambridge, 1987); Serge Gruzinski, *Man-Gods in the Mexican Highlands: Indian Power and Colonial Society 1520–1800* (Stanford, 1989). For the Andean encounter, see Kenneth Mills, *Idolatry and Its Enemies: Colonial Andean Religion and Extirpation 1640–1750* (Princeton, 1997); his findings are also presented in Mills, "The Limits of Religious Coercion in Mid-Colonial Peru," *Past and Present* 145 (1994), 84–121. On the Jesuit presence, see Philip Caraman, *The Lost Paradise: An Account of the Jesuits in Paraguay 1607–1768* (London, 1975), a factual and straightforward exposition; and the more limited studies by Luis Martin, *The Intellectual Conquest of Peru: The Jesuit College of San Pablo 1568–1767* (New York, 1968), and Nicholas P. Cushner, *Farm and Factory: The Jesuits and the Development of Agrarian Capitalism in Colonial Quito 1600–1767* (Albany, 1982). A number of studies explored religious writings in indigenous languages to reconstruct the native adaptation of Christianity; see Louise M. Burkhart, *The Slippery Earth:*

Nahua–Christian Moral Dialogue in Sixteenth-Century Mexico (Tucson, Ariz., 1989); and Sabine McCormack, *Religion in the Andes: Visions and Imagination in Early Colonial Peru* (Princeton, 1991).

12 THE CATHOLIC MISSIONS IN ASIA

For the Philippines, two older works offer traditional narratives of Christianization and the establishment of Spanish rule: John Leddy Phelan, *The Hispanization of the Philippines: Spanish Aims and Filipino Responses 1565–1700* (Madison, Wisc., 1959); and Horacio de la Costa, *The Jesuits in the Philippines 1581–1768* (Cambridge, Mass., 1961). A more recent and stimulating interpretation, based on linguistic theories, is offered by Vincente L. Rafael, *Contracting Colonialism: Translation and Christian Conversion in Tagalog Society Under Early Spanish Rule* (Ithaca, N. Y., 1988). On Japan, the standard account is provided by C. R. Boxer, *The Christian Century in Japan 1549–1650* (Berkeley, 1967).

A more recent introductory survey that is generally reliable takes a comparative perspective to both China and Japan: Andrew C. Ross, *A Vision Betrayed: The Jesuits in Japan and China 1542–1742* (Maryknoll, N. Y., 1994). For the 1584 Japanese "embassy" to Europe, see Judith C. Brown, "Courtiers and Christians: The First Japanese Emissaries to Europe," *Renaissance Quarterly* 47:4 (1994), 872–906. George Elison, *Deus Destroyed: The Image of Christianity in Early Modern Japan* (Cambridge, Mass., 1973), with translations of the major anti-Christian tracts, represents a major analysis. For the survival of Japanese Christianity after the Tokugawa suppression, see Ann M. Harrington, *Japan's Hidden Christians* (Chicago, 1993).

For some recent research on Catholicism in China, see Charles E. Ronan and Bonnie B. C. Oh, eds., *East Meets West: The Jesuits in China 1582–1773* (Chicago, 1988); the contribution by Willard J. Peterson on reasons for Chinese conversions among the literati is particularly useful. Of the voluminous literature on Chinese Catholicism, I have included only the standard classics and the more recent research. Joseph Dehergne, *Répertoire des Jésuites de Chine, de 1552 à 1800* (Paris and Rome, 1973), Louis Pfister, *Notices biographiques et bibliographiques sur les Jésuites de l'Ancienne Mission de Chine (1552–1773)*, 2 vols. (Shanghai, 1932–34), and Fang Hao, *Chung-kuo T'ien-chu-chiao shih jen-wu chuan*, 3 vols. (A history and biography of Chinese Catholicism) (Hong Kong, 1970–73), are three fundamental works. A brilliant interpretation that argues for the basic incompatibility between the Chinese and Christian civilizations is presented by Jacques Gernet, *Chine et christianisme. La première confrontation* (Paris, 1990), a revised edition of his 1982 classic that includes a new preface (in answer to his critics) and an updated discussion of sources. The original 1982 edition is available in English translation as *China and the Christian Impact* (Cambridge, 1985). The most recent research has focused on three themes: anti-Christian polemics, indigenous Chinese Catholicism, and the impact of China on Europe. See Edward T. Kelly, "The Anti-Christian Persecution of 1616–1617 in Nanking," Ph.D. thesis, Columbia University, 1971 (Ann Arbor University Microfilms, 1976); Iso Kern, *Buddhistische Kritik am Christentum im China des 17. Jahrhunderts* (Bern, 1992); Nicolaes Standaert, *Yang Tingyun, Confucian and Christian in Late Ming China: His Life and Thought* (Leiden, 1988); D. E. Mungello, *The Forgotten Christians of*

Hangzhou (Honolulu, 1994); Mungello, *Curious Land: Jesuit Accommodation and the Origins of Sinology* (Stuttgart, 1985). An imaginative narrative on the best known Jesuit missionary in China is offered by Jonathan D. Spence, *The Memory Palace of Matteo Ricci* (New York, 1984).

For India, see Stephen Neill, *A History of Christianity in India* (Cambridge, 1985), and the stimulating essays by Iñes G. Zupanov, "Aristocratic Analogies and Demotic Descriptions in the Seventeenth-Century Madurai Mission," *Representations* 41 (1993), 123–48; and Zupanov, "Le repli du religieux. Les missionaires jésuites du 17e siècle entre la théologie chrétienne et une éthique païenne," *Annales HSS* (1996), no. 6, 1201–23.

13 FROM TRIUMPH TO CRISIS

Two books by Louis Châtellier laid the groundwork: *The Europe of the Devout: The Catholic Reformation and the Formation of a New Society* (Cambridge, 1987), and *La Religion des Pauvres. Les missions rurales en Europe et la formation du catholicisme moderne XVIe–XIXe siècle* (Paris, 1993). On the theory and practice of confession in Borromean Milan, see Wietse de Boer, "Sinews of Discipline: The Uses of Confession in Counter-Reformation Milan," Proefschrift, Erasmus Universiteit Rotterdam, 1995; for an examination of sexual solicitation by confessors, based on the study of Inquisition records in Spain, see Stephen Haliczer, *Sexuality in the Confessional: A Sacrament Profaned* (New York, 1996). Alain Tallon, *La Compagnie du Saint-Sacrement (1629–1667)* (Paris, 1990), is a thorough study of the Company based on extensive archival research. Jean Delumeau, *Rassurer et protéger. Le sentiment de sécurité dans l'Occident d'autrefois* (Paris, 1989), assembles an enormous amount of evidence on the persistence of traditional religiosity. For Jesuit education and the Italian nobility, see Gian Paolo Brizzi, *La formazione della classe dirigente nel sei–settecento. I seminaria nobilium nell'Italia centro-settentrionale* (Bologna, 1976). Bernard Cousin, *Le miracle et le quotidien. Les Ex-Voto provençaux. Images d'une société* (Aix-en-Provence, 1983), and Werner Freitag, *Volks- und Elitenfrömmigkeit in der frühen Neuzeit. Marienwallfahrten im Fürstbistum Münster* (Paderborn, 1991), present new evidence for the persistence of traditional piety and its relationship with official religion in two regions of Europe.

Index